SEARCH FOR THE GREAT
TURTLE MOTHER

SEARCH FOR
THE GREAT

TURTLE MOTHER

JACK RUDLOE

Illustrations by
Marty Capron

PINEAPPLE PRESS, INC.
Sarasota, Florida

Inquiries should be addressed to:
PINEAPPLE PRESS, INC.
P.O. Drawer 16008
Southside Station
Sarasota, Florida 34239

LIBRARY OF CONGRESS CATALOGING IN PUBLICATION DATA
Rudloe, Jack.
    Search for the Great Turtle Mother / by Jack Rudloe —   1st ed.
    280p.   cm.
    ISBN 1-56164-072-7 (hb)
    1. Sea turtles. 2. Sea turtles—Anecdotes. 3. Wildlife conservation.   I. Title.
QL666.C5R824 1995
94-44849   597.92—dc20
                                         CIP

First Edition
10 9 8 7 6 5 4 3 2 1

Design by Carol Tornatore
Printed and bound by Edwards Brothers, Ann Arbor, Michigan

CONTENTS

DEDICATION

To my aunt and uncle, Cecil and Milton Aronson, two wonderful people who have tried to make the world a little brighter. My thanks for their years of support and unwavering encouragement.

SEARCH FOR THE GREAT TURTLE MOTHER

FLORIDA—1994

MOST MYSTERIOUS ANIMAL

IT WAS TURTLING TIME. We loaded the net into our little speedboat and set out, as we did once every week. Doug Gleeson ran the 16-foot fiberglass boat. He had been with me for years, working at my tiny marine station in Panacea, Florida, where we collected marine animals to be used in university classrooms.

The sky was gloomy and overcast, the sun just a white orb pushing up from the horizon into a bank of clouds. Then it reappeared.

As the sun rose higher over the marsh, it coalesced into a huge orange sphere that gleamed sullenly through the racing clouds down on the water. Speeding over the choppy waters of Apalachee Bay, wearing our bright yellow slickers, we seemed to be following the reflection of the long straight road of fire.

The rain began as we headed across the angry waves of the channel to Elmour's Cove to set the net. I sat on top of the net, feeling the rain beating in my face, pattering on the vinyl. It was warm, and even pleasant. When we got to the right area, we lightly bounced the anchor along the bottom, checking to see where the sandbar sloped off into the channel. When we found it, we struck the net. Doug backed the boat up, and I fed the 300-yard net out in a long straight line that crossed the channel in ten feet of water, affixing buoys, fighting a tangle or two, until it stretched out in a straight line, held in place by anchors. The tide was rising, and the buoys bobbed gently in the light chop.

"The current isn't running too bad; the net will have plenty of loose webbing to tangle a turtle," I said optimistically. "It's the right season and we're in the right place, and it's stormy. Maybe we'll catch a turtle today."

Doug grinned and shrugged. "We've caught them in storms, in calm weather, on high tide, and low tide." He looked warily at the clouds that were building high up into the heavens. Ominous heavy black clouds they were, with intense rain showers off in the distance, and thunder rolling miles away. "This weather might be more than we bargained for," he added.

We ran a distance away so the boat wouldn't frighten a turtle away from the net, dropped the anchor, and waited. And waited. We watched the big red buoys that marked the end of the net and the snap-on green-and-orange corks that held the top line afloat. For a half hour we waited and watched the buoys until it was time to check the net. The permit from the Office of Endangered Species under which we worked required that we check the net every 30 minutes to prevent one of the highly endangered Kemp's ridleys we were after from drowning. Archie Carr, the late patriarch of sea turtle biology, once called the Kemp's ridley "the most mysterious animal in North America." For years no one knew where they bred, and fishermen used to call them "bastard turtles," claiming they were hybrids between loggerheads and greens. It was discovered in the late 1940s that they bred in Mexico, but the west coast of Florida is one of the main strongholds for juveniles.

So far we had caught, tagged, and released 14 Kemp's ridley sea turtles with no problem. The purpose of our contract (from the National Oceanographic and Atmospheric Administration—NOAA) was to learn something about their movements and migrations along Florida's panhandle coast. The area was a major part of their subadult habitat, yet almost nothing was known of how they used it. There would be little hope of saving them from extinction when we knew so little about their habitat requirements. Ridleys are lovers of blue crabs, especially the small ones that live around oyster bars, creeks, and marshes.

When the 30 minutes were up, we pulled the anchor and ran over to the big red float that marked one end of the net. I grabbed the cork line, lifted it, and started pulling. Standing on the bow of our 16-foot skiff, I pulled us and the boat along the length of the anchored net hand over hand, lifting it three or four feet out of the water to see if anything was entangled in the lower part. The net was 12 feet deep from the floating corks to the lead line that sat on the bottom. Hauling it up, I hoped to feel the pulsing pull, the rhythmic beat of flippers, to see the white plastron of a turtle flashing through the murky coastal water—a wish that was almost always in vain.

After a year of sitting out there, fishing 12 hours at a stretch, week in and week out, through spring, summer, fall, and winter, we had to concur that Kemp's ridley sea turtles really were endangered, because we had caught such a small number. In 1947 there were 40,000 a day coming ashore to breed at Rancho Nuevo, in Mexico, their only breeding beach. By 1960 it was 5,000, and 30 years later, the population of breeding females had declined to less than 400. But now in 1994, an estimated 580 females nested there, hopeful signs that the population was recovering.

Because their numbers have plummeted, U.S. Coast Guard vessels roam the waters, boarding shrimpers to see that they have installed panels in their nets called TEDs, or "Turtle Excluder Devices," which are basically big holes in the net designed for throwing out turtles. The turtles are frequently trapped and drowned in the big nets that shrimpers pull along the bottom for several hours at a time. Because TEDs also exclude a goodly portion of the shrimp, the economically impoverished shrimpers call them "Trawler Elimination Devices" and have blockaded ports in near-violent protests. The need to better understand the distribution of these animals in order to produce fair regulations was serious and was a large part of why we had been funded to do our study.

When we got to the end of the net, we ran a few hundred yards away and threw the anchor. There we sat until the next check watching the long flat line of motionless buoys. It was the same routine, week after week. Between 30-minute checks, we watched the tide rise, peak, and fall. As the mud flats along shore began to emerge from the falling waters, the net became taut on the strong current of the falling tide. When the tide rose the net bowed in one direction, then became flaccid, and when the tide changed, the net and corks swung the other way between the anchors on each end. Day in and day out we watched the sea go from flat calm to light chop, from no wind and clear skies to clouds and light wind, then light wind to heavy chop.

We watched migratory birds pass on the horizons until they disappeared from sight, guided by some unseen force. As the water chilled in the fall, and the fish vanished, pelicans clamored over to our boat, hoping we'd catch fish in our net and feed them. We sat there in winter as the blistering winter winds swept down upon our cramped little boat, bundled up in heavy clothing, trying to keep warm, expecting nothing to happen; and lo and behold, nothing did. Nevertheless, every 30 minutes we checked the net and wrote down a big fat zero in the column that said "number of turtles caught."

We caught up on our reading. We spelled each other. We took turns. On some days, Anne, my wife, put in six-hour shifts, and I put in six hour shifts. Sometimes we brought in volunteers, who eventually got bored and left. Hour after hour we watched the empty net and the empty water. The weather changed, the seasons changed, the fish changed, we changed, and still we fished on.

When this NOAA contract to fish for turtles began a year ago, it wasn't so routine. We ordered the bales of webbing from the factory, found fishermen to sew it in, and tie in the cork and lead lines. We interviewed shrimpers, mullet fishermen, shark fishermen, and boaters, asking where and when they saw turtles. One doesn't just throw a net in the sea. The old turtle fishermen said there were special places that turtles frequent; that they like the "sloughs" and "guts," the depressions between sandbars where the water is deeper and the current runs strong.

But even with the best advice and with the best track record, all we had was a tiny net in a big Gulf. And there was a lot of water between turtles. Turtling had been outlawed in Florida waters for the past 30 years, and the skills involved in knowing when and where to set a net were almost gone.

The beginning of the project had been especially nerve-wracking. We fished for a month with our newly built net, getting nothing but stingrays. Maybe we were doing it all wrong. Maybe the net was shaped wrong, or maybe we were in the wrong place or there at the wrong time. We had visions of never catching the first turtle—of having to turn in thousands of dollars in expenses with zero results. The first day we tried our net out we had to untangle a nightmare of snapping, biting sharks from the net. Several were so snarled up we had no choice but to haul them into the 16-foot boat so we could get the webbing off their fins and out of their snapping jaws before turning them free. Sometimes we caught dozens of giant stingrays, or spotted eagle rays that got their long poisonous barbs snared up before we could flip them out.

The main danger was not big sharks, or getting tangled up in the net and getting snatched overboard, or getting caught in a violent thunderstorm. It was dying of boredom. To avoid that fate, I had to learn patience and the art of doing nothing, of passing the time like the turtles and fish themselves did. As we sat out there with a net, week in and week out, hoping to catch a Kemp's ridley sea turtle, we carefully examined the bay bottoms, checked out the oyster bars, talked to fishermen. All the logic and reason we possessed was brought to bear on the task of catching a turtle. But then reason stopped, and in the long hours of silent waiting, I appealed to the gods of the sea, to the Turtle Mother, the guiding spirit or magnetic forces in the form of a rock that the Miskito Indian legend said directed the turtles across the sea.

I first heard about Turtle Mother from the Miskito Indians while traveling around Central America in 1975. Then I read Dr. Bernard Neitchmann's book *Caribbean Edge*:

> The old man informed us that there used to be a rock in the shape of a turtle located in the bar mouth leading to the Sandy Bay Lagoon. This rock, called the Turtle Mother, had magical properties. According to the Miskito myth, the Turtle Mother was a benevolent spirit that acted as the intermediary between the world of animals and the world of humans. When the turtles were moving in close to the mainland to nest on the beach or to feed in the shallows, the rock would swing around and point westward. When the turtles were to move out into deeper water around the cays, the rock turned and pointed towards the east. Besides foretelling the movement of turtles so that humans could more easily catch them, the Turtle Mother also could increase success by controlling both a person's luck and the movement of the turtles. If, on the other hand, an individual or the community did not observe specific taboos and thus restrict exploitation by taking only what they needed and wasting nothing, the Turtle Mother would send the turtles far out to sea beyond the reach of the turtlemen, and also cause their luck to turn bad. The Turtle Mother then symbolically balanced relationships between humans and turtles. The belief in the Turtle Mother made the Miskito responsible for maintaining prohibitions against overkill; individual greed would bring retaliation to all through the magical remove of the turtles.
>
> The Turtle Mother story had been told to Baldwin [one of Neitchmann's old turtlemen informants] when he was young, but it was all but forgotten on the lower

coast. Here in Big Sandy Bay—which along with Old Cape was the cultural hearth of the Miskito—the story had been kept alive, yet no longer did it influence Miskito behavior.

I was continuing in the tradition of the ancient people who probably fished these very bays. And when we caught sharks and rays, we released them, and tried to do so without harming them, out of a respect for life.

Why am I attracted to sea turtles? I often asked myself that as I waited for one of these rare shelled creatures to hit the net. Why had I had spent years hiking mosquito-infested breeding beaches, watching them crawl out of the surf, resuscitating them on shrimp boats, feeding them in our aquariums, and sitting with angry shrimpers during the public TED hearings? Perhaps it had something to do with the American Indian's belief that the world rests on the back of a giant turtle, or because all of North America was known as "Turtle Island" among Native Americans.

The Mayans also believed their origins were connected with the turtle. Painted on vases in Mexico and appearing in stelae throughout Central America is the maize god, who wears an ornate headdress and is shown bursting out of the carapace of a turtle. Beside him are three stones called by archaeologists "hearth stones"; but to me they might just as well be Turtle Mother rocks. The Mayans saw our constellation Orion as a turtle. The three stars that make up his belt, Mayanologists believe, were the three stones in the glyphs.

There was also god "N," considered to be one of the founders of the Mayans, first depicted as a young man emerging from a turtle or snail shell. But later he showed up on stelae and in hieroglyphics as a cantankerous, snaggletoothed old man carrying a tortoise shell. God "N" also toted a net, said to contain the wind.

While all other Mayan gods were plump, officious-looking, or placid, god N, clutching his turtle shell, was a scrawny, bad-tempered curmudgeon who wasn't going to put up with any nonsense, and you'd better not get on his bad side! But he was also the god of writing, the scribe, and so I had a special affection for him since that's what I do for a living.

For whatever reasons, turtles are the center of my universe and have been ever since I can remember, starting with little red-eared sliders with green shells. Our family lived in New York, and even in our crowded apartment we had a large dog and aquarium filled with turtles. When I was old enough to cross the street by myself, I spent all my time hanging around the local pet shop, spending hour after hour looking at the tanks of turtles. Forty-two years later, I am still at it. And my dealings with turtles are even more obsessive than ever.

Since I started Gulf Specimen Marine Lab, shrimpers and gill netters have brought in hundreds of Kemp's ridleys, loggerheads, and greens which we tagged and released. But when the fight over trawlers, sea turtles, and the Turtle Excluder Device mushroomed, the U.S. Fish and Wildlife Service decided that we were doing all that research illegally. They said we were in violation of the U.S. Endangered Species Act. By paying the fishermen a small reward, we were trafficking in endangered species, and, even though the turtles had all been released and were swimming around in the sea, it had to stop. When it did, a lot of turtles that would have been saved ended up in the stewpot, but the spirit of the law was sustained. What happened to the spirit of the turtles that were served up with rice and gravy was a more cosmic question.

The day passed slowly. The corks sat there and did nothing. There was no apparent life except for a solitary butterfly, hovering above the sea, riding a gentle north wind that blew down upon us, bringing a hint of the cold that was to come. Nothing, nothing, nothing, and everything all at the same time.

Then all at once the waters were alive with schools of bait fish rippling the surface, and that brought life to the skies. Flocks of graceful sea birds winged their way across the horizon, flying just above the water. It was a time of eating, getting all they could to put on some fat before winter came. From the needlerush marsh the clapper rails clattered and babbled and extolled the arrival of the cooler weather to come. The sea gulls, wings apart, hovered above the water, gliding ever so steadily in the air.

Our eyes feasted upon the pelicans cruising above us, circling round and round, studying the waters and the flurry of bait fish with rapt attention, their giant wings outstretched in a glide. Then they turned obliquely and crashed down hard, the water cascading up, as if someone had just shot them. Using their great mass to their advantage, they bombed from the sky to stun and swallow fish. Swimming like giant ducks, the pelicans swallowed the silvery little bumpers, anchovies, and pilchards in their great bills, then took to the air, caught the updraft and rose up, flying in gentle sigmoidal curvatures. Ducks, mergansers, and coots swam around the net and occasionally dove through it.

Now and then a ballyhoo, an elongated six-inch fish with a red-tipped, needlelike lower beak, leapt back and forth over the cork line. The sea was full of death and life. Every second something snuffed out life with the snap of its jaws. Suddenly a tarpon, pursuing mullet, jumped high above the net, soaring through the air and landing with an explosive sparkle. We jumped up, alert, wondering what would happen if the six-foot fish with its coat of silver mail slammed into our net and tangled it.

We were halfway through the day, and the tide was falling. The wind blew hard against the boat, trying to push us away from the net. Hand over hand, I strained against the cork line, lifting the webbing about a third of its 12-foot depth out of the water, hoping to feel a fighting weight down there. But the net remained taut. We watched the float line and corks stretch out tight as a fiddle string, straining against its anchors in the swift tidal current. Walking the net became a back-breaking ordeal, pulling against the wind, the whole length and weight of the boat acting as a sail, blowing us away from it. Then the winds shifted and put us on top of the net, causing us to hang up on the corner of the bow, or the cleat. Each time it had to be to be undone because it caught on everything except a turtle.

Almost casually, a head popped up beside the net: it was the grayish white beak of a ridley, just a few feet from the boat. We could see its shell, its greenish-gray, scaly body, as it took its time swimming along the cork line, checking it out. Head high out of the water, it looked about, bewildered, trying to figure what this impediment was. It was a good-sized ridley, maybe two feet across, and not more than 20 feet from our boat.

"Hit the net, please hit the net," I said softly. Then it saw us and rocketed back down.

"He was so close that if I had a cast net I could have nailed him," Doug said, shaking his head wistfully.

For the next 15 minutes we watched the empty net, hoping to see corks snatched down, to see an entangled flipper, something—but nothing happened. It wouldn't have been so bad to see a turtle ignore the net and swim on by if we hadn't had days and days and days of waiting. At least we had a sighting to report.

Four hours later, our luck changed. We were hauling back, and about a third of the way down the net, another small Kemp's ridley popped up. Usually they do a good job of tangling themselves, but this one seemed barely ensnared. As we drew closer, the turtle went into a desperate panic. Any second it could break loose.

With all our strength, clutching the cork line and webbing, pulling with all our might, we dragged the boat and ourselves toward it, fearing it would break loose. "Doug, get the dip net ready," I cried. I stood poised on the bow, ready to dive overboard and leap onto the turtle if there was even a chance that it was going to get away.

Standing by intently, ready to spring, my helper was poised with the dip net. For a second, we saw our quarry's head looking around bewildered before it popped down beneath the green murky water. Then we saw just how flimsily it was held in the webbing, entangled by just one flipper. The ridley saw us and tried to sound, frantically beating its powerful free flipper.

Certain that it was going to escape the moment it was in range, we belly flopped on the deck, trying to grab it, to bunch some webbing around it. Doug's hand shot down and seized the ensnared foreflipper that was literally hanging by a thread. Instantly the turtle reached over and clamped its parrot beak on his thumb.

Doug let out a loud yell and jerked it into the boat, where the little turtle landed on the deck and went into an explosion of fury. It gyrated around on its back, beating its flippers, its angry mouth open, ready to latch onto anything that drew near. The jaws snapped shut on the edge of a paddle, held for a second, then opened and were ready for the next bite.

"Are you all right?" I asked Doug.

"Yeah, he didn't break the skin." He looked down at the ridley. "Turtle soup," he said to it, "that's what we ought to do with you." He sucked his finger. Later he said it throbbed all night.

But this was more than a turtle. Instantly I saw that it was wearing big blue tags on his flippers. "Hey! We've got a Texas Turtle!" I snatched the turtle up from the deck where it was madly trying to scurry over the fiberglass, having a hard time gaining traction. It hissed, its mouth opened wide, and I held it up, keeping my fingers well away from those snapping jaws that could crush through a blue crab's carapace.

Still sucking his finger, Doug looked on and we carefully examined the blue plastic tag. The numbers and return information were so overgrown with barnacles and algae that we could not make it out.

"There's no question, he's from Galveston," Doug said, pointing to one of the top scutes. "There's the carapace tag." Sure enough, there was the white spot sitting out like a lone star amid the blackness of its carapace. The turtles that were released from the hatchery at the National Marine Fisheries Service in Galveston, Texas, had a living, biological tag. When they were tiny hatchlings, barely three inches long, a patch of white belly shell was grafted onto the dark back shell. The rest of the turtle's shell grew around it as proof that this was a hatchery-reared turtle even if the plastic tags were lost.

It was the fourth "head-started" turtle we had caught since the project began. These turtles were hatched on the breeding beach of Rancho Nuevo, flown up to Galveston, Texas, and raised at the National Marine Fisheries Service hatchery. When they were nine months old, they were taken out, their flippers tagged, and several thousand a year were turned loose. A massive effort was underway to protect the nests and to put head-started hatchlings back into the sea.

The project had come under much criticism from purists. They felt that all the time, effort, and money of raising thousands of little turtles in aquariums would be better invested in patrolling nesting beaches and seeing that the eggs were protected and that the little turtles made it back unimpeded into the sea. They also were concerned that pen-reared turtles would be too weak and unable to cope in the natural environment. Many of the head-started turtles were stranded on beaches, and some came up to docks and fishing boats unafraid of people. One turned up in Venezuela nine years after it was released, quite far from their normal range.

But "Texas," like all the other head-start turtles we caught in Panacea, was full of energy. His head swung around, beak open, and he tried hard to bite me as I examined him. He definitely wasn't a specimen that lent credence to the weakened-turtle theory.

The day was at an end. We triumphantly headed back to the dock with our turtle, to scrape the tag clean, and weigh and measure the turtle before turning it loose to go on with its journey along the coast. As the boat raced back to shore, we watched the sun set in all its glow and glory. On this day, we'd had a taste of what the ancient people who lived along this coast as hunter-gatherers did thousands of years before us. Turtle Mother had been generous this day.

GUATEMALA—1979

2

MAGNETIC BELLY BUTTONS

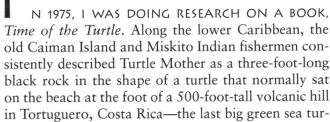

I N 1975, I WAS DOING RESEARCH ON A BOOK, *Time of the Turtle.* Along the lower Caribbean, the old Caiman Island and Miskito Indian fishermen consistently described Turtle Mother as a three-foot-long black rock in the shape of a turtle that normally sat on the beach at the foot of a 500-foot-tall volcanic hill in Tortuguero, Costa Rica—the last big green sea turtle nesting beach in the Caribbean. The rock sat facing the sea, not moving, until magically it turned. The old villagers who lived at the foot of the mountain said, "Every year when de turtle come around, dat turtle rock turn. It turn and face de land, and when de turtle is over (meaning the nesting season has finished), it turn back around to de sea."

Turtle Mother was perhaps once part of a full-blown religion, but now she was only a shadow of a myth, told by old men in villages along the Caribbean shores of Honduras, Nicaragua, Costa Rica, and Panama. The old beliefs of the past were dying out, yet somehow, the thread of the myth had survived. The tale was repeated with such consistency, almost by rote, that I didn't believe that this myth had sprung out of thin air.

My search for this magic turning stone started so innocently, so casually; it was just something I had heard about, but it stuck in my mind, and I couldn't drop it. The truth was, this thing had turned into a fetish, a quest that had just about taken over my life. All along I felt in my bones that it had some basis in fact, that it was somehow related to magnetic orientation and all the millions of submicroscopic ferromagnetic crystals that scientists had discovered in the brains of sea turtles.

When Dr. Vincent Malmstrom, a geographer from Dartmouth College, discovered in 1975 that an ancient pre-Olmec rock carving of a turtle head on the Pacific coast of Mexico had a magnetic nose, I became ecstatic. His discovery did not make the cover of *Science*, nor did it get more than a line or two in the press. But to me it was one of the most astounding findings of the century. Whoever carved the head, Dr. Malmstrom speculated in his article in *Nature*, deliberately executed it so the magnetic lines of force came to focus in the nose of the big stone turtle head.

It was bizarre and preposterous—but if true, it was the first tangible evidence of the obscure Turtle Mother myth that still scarcely survived on the Caribbean coast of Central America. There was no way the old-time turtlemen of the Miskito coast could know about biogenic magnetite, and yet, coincidentally or metaphorically, their nature spirit that manifested in the Turtle Mother rock turned like a compass needle. Dr. Malmstrom's discovery of the magnetic turtle head could indicate that the ancients knew what scientists and their advanced technology are just beginning to find out: that real flesh-and-blood sea turtles, using submicroscopic crystals of magnetite concentrated in their nose, migrate across the oceans following the earth's magnetic field.

Biogenic magnetite crystals had first been discovered in bacteria in 1973, then in the brains of homing pigeons, then yellow fin tuna, then sharks, porpoises, monarch butterflies, and sea turtles. Submicroscopic bits of lodestone seemed to occur in migratory species almost everywhere scientists looked. And there was growing speculation among scientists that these crystals helped guide sea turtles across thousands of miles of ocean in their migrations between breeding beaches and feeding grounds.

These octagonal black crystals, a millionth of an inch across, are formed inside living tissues by a process called biomineralization. The laying down of calcium in live bone tissue to create bones is a more familiar example. But in this case iron is deposited by cells to form these crystals that are living compasses deep within the animals themselves.

Dr. Kenneth Lohmann at the University of North Carolina found that hatchling loggerheads in a laboratory pool oriented to a magnetic field while swimming. In the earth's natural magnetic field they tended to swim toward the northeast, but when the magnetic field around the pool was experimentally reversed, the turtles changed their orientation and swam in nearly the opposite direction.

It was also possible that sea turtles might use magnetic fields to detect more than just direction. Because the inclination or vertical angle of the earth's field varies with latitude, and because longitudinal "stripes" of different field strengths exist in the ocean floor, turtles could use the magnetic field as a source of regional landmarks, to know where they were as well as which direction was north.

Dr. Lohmann demonstrated that hatchling loggerheads can read the inclination angles of the earth's magnetic field. The field flows from the magnetic south pole to the magnetic north pole, where the lines run perpendicular to the earth's surface and the inclination angle is said to be 90°. Near the magnetic equator where the field lines run parallel to the earth, the angle is said to be zero.

Using an elaborate magnetic coil system controlled by a computer, Dr. Lohmann tethered the hatchlings inside an upturned antenna dish and monitored their swimming behavior. When exposed to a 57° inclination, identical to that of their natal beaches on the southeast coast of Florida, they stroked due east. This direction would take them out to the Gulf Stream and carry them across the Atlantic toward the coast of Portugal.

But to his surprise, when he changed the angle to 60°, the little brown turtles abruptly changed direction and headed south. Why would just 3 degrees make such a dramatic difference? He believed this showed that the turtles have an early warning system for their survival. At 60° inclination the Gulf Stream forks; if the turtles head north they'll freeze to death in the icy waters off England. The southern fork, on the other hand, will carry them back around the Atlantic gyre where they'll grow up feeding on invertebrates in the warm Sargasso Sea.

Never mind that Vincent Malmstrom's magnetic artifact was discovered on the wrong ocean, across the isthmus of Central America and miles to the north of Tortuguero, Costa Rica, or Puerto Cabeza, Nicaragua, where a few old turtle fishermen still talked about the magic Turtle Mother rock. Myths travel the world.

"We've got to go down there and see this thing," I told Anne, my wife, after we read Malmstrom's article.

"How?" she demanded. "We're not rich. You know we can't afford to just hop on a plane and go."

"We'll find a way."

And we did. *Sports Illustrated* bought the idea. My vision of the great stone turtle on the mountain, the zoomorphic deity turning beneath the stars, drawing green turtles to the beach, convinced the editor to send us forth with plane tickets and expense money.

I called Vince Malmstrom, arranged to meet him in Guatemala on his next trip down there in a couple of months, and before I knew it we were driving up to the mountain village of Antigua near Guatemala City to meet him at a hotel for a rendezvous at noon. Malmstrom, who had been down in British Honduras measuring the astronomical alignment of pyramids, had agreed to take us to see the magnetic turtle head at Izapa, a ceremonial site on the Pacific coast of Mexico built by the Olmecs nearly 4000 years ago.

But none of us had anticipated the volcano erupting in the middle of our meeting place. The windshield wipers on our once-shiny white rental car beat back and forth, clearing off not rain but choking black dust and ash from the mountain that had blasted high into the atmosphere the night before we arrived and was now blotting out the sun, giving the Guatemalan landscape a dingy, end-of-the-world hue.

Nikkie Griffis, a longtime friend whose father had underwritten many of our expeditions for the New York Zoological Society, had met Anne and me at the airport to help with logistics and Spanish. Sitting at the wheel, the lanky young man squinted at the hazy morning sun. It was nothing but a glowing disk, rising over the mountains and giving forth an ominous haze. "It's getting so dark, I can hardly see. I hope we don't have your Turtle Mother rock crashing down on top of us."

There was a line of traffic ahead of us, creeping past the slums—crowded shacks against a backdrop of beautiful mountain forests. If this kept up we were going to be late. I hoped Dr. Malmstrom would wait for us, but the way he had stressed his schedule, I wasn't so sure. I glanced worriedly at my watch. It was now eleven o'clock. We had hit the airport in Guatemala City running, it had taken forever to rent a car, we had gotten lost in traffic, and then we managed to get stopped at a military checkpoint.

I guess we didn't have the wide-eyed, wandering-tourist look in our eyes. The soldiers went through our luggage, checked our passports to make sure we weren't revolutionaries, and then finally we headed for Antigua—only to get stuck in traffic. Nikkie anticipated my concern: "This is as fast as we can go. I'm sure after all this he'll wait for us."

Trying not to think about my appointment, I stared out of the dust-covered window. There was a shack, some naked little boys and older children playing on bare ground beneath a clothesline with a few frayed wet garments hanging out, all covered with black volcanic dust. A scrawny, almost emaciated old woman sat on the front porch, glowering down at us from her perch. The road was lower than the hilly shoulders, and I turned away, not wanting to meet her eyes. There was something malevolent about them, almost witchlike. She stared at us with recrimination, perhaps with hatred for gringos and their fancy rental cars. The car rental fee alone would buy food enough to feed her family for a year.

The disparity of wealth was enormous, evidenced by the filth-encrusted children on dirt floors, sucking sugarcane, their bellies swollen from protein deficiencies; the gaunt women, with hollow eyes, and bony features, nursing malnourished babies from their dried-up breasts. Meanwhile, our mission: chasing around Central America, staying at costly hotels, eating at good restaurants, renting cars, flying on airplanes—squandering money while abject poverty and suffering reigned all about us.

Sitting there with black snow raining down from the volcano, I felt the guilt so many gringos feel, and yet here I was, continuing my quest for a long-forgotten legend that I wasn't sure made any sense. Did I really believe deep down in a mystical turtle spirit? But if I didn't believe it, why did I keep following it?

Suddenly something thumped down on our windshield. At first I thought it was a stick or a rock, and then we saw it—a rooster's head, grotesque, open-mouthed, glazed eyes, flabby red crown, and bloody neck where it had been hacked off. The dust had blotted up the blood and turned it to mud around the wound.

"Good God, that's disgusting," declared Anne with revulsion. We had all recoiled from the windshield. "Get it off."

But there was no place to pull off, no place to stop; we had to keep pace with the traffic. As Nikkie speeded up, the decapitated head remained in place, now covered with black dust. Having fallen down at the base of the windshield, right between the two beating blades, there was no removing it. For the next five kilometers the head stayed with us.

"I think that old woman back there threw it," offered Nikkie, who often wore a serious expression. "Just as we passed, I caught some motion out of the corner of my eye. She had a nasty look about her. I think she gave us the evil eye."

It was unusual for Nikkie to say anything harsh about anyone; he always tried to find the good in people. I found myself making the sign of the "Phaig." Privately I inserted my thumb between my fore- and middle fingers and closed my hand into a fist. It was an eastern European fetish that my mother had told me about when I was a child. It was used to ward off the "evil eye," or someone's destructive envy.

"But why us? We didn't do anything" I said, slightly outraged.

"Probably she just got tired of tourists," my wife said in a worried tone. "This is the main route from Guatemala City. They must get gawked at by thousands of rich gringos. I wish that damn thing would fall off, or that we could find a place to pull over and throw it off." But that was impossible. There was no shoulder on the narrow roads, just hillsides, and a string of cars behind us.

I leaned out of the window as we moved along and reached out as far as I could to grab it, but I couldn't reach far enough. The severed head, with its mouth permanently fixed open, as if screaming recriminations, remained securely in place. I sat back down in defeat.

"I don't like this," I muttered, unable to take my gaze away from its hideous voodoo appearance. "This is a bad sign. It's a hell of a way to begin a trip."

Anne usually disagreed with my superstitions and fetishes, but this time she was silent, her jaw tight, her expression grim. A pall hung over us.

Only after the traffic sped up and we were whipping along did the rooster's head suddenly blow off, vanishing almost as abruptly as it appeared. I saw it bounce through the air, and then thankfully it was gone. Only the uneasy feeling remained behind.

The road ended in the town of Antigua, and the sky seemed even more hostile and red than it had before. The town looked different from the last time we had seen it, on our honeymoon five years before. One of the gems of Latin America, Antigua, with its old Spanish architecture, narrow streets, and marketplaces full of beautiful garments and blankets for wealthy visitors, was associated with happy times.

Today it appeared burned and sullen. The sun looked as if it were setting: a large glowing red disk that blazed through the atmospheric dust like a burning orb out of hell. We passed a house where a group of unhappy-looking Indian men stood around a small coffin or leaned grief-stricken against the unpainted wall. The white lace and flowers covering the pink plastic casket made a searing contrast to the raw poverty-stricken surroundings. It was apparent that the family had brought forth all their effort and spared no expense to say good-bye to a loved one.

At first it seemed just another tragic scene from day-to-day human suffering, of life and death. But then we happened upon another wake going on a few houses away, at another shack, another scene of grief with another lavish child-sized coffin amidst the wretched surroundings. More grief-stricken people were sitting beside the casket on the porch. The mourners stared at the stream of cars passing by with numbed anguish, and a pall of great sadness hung in the air. Was there some great natural disaster? Had the volcano exploded and killed people, or had a bus turned over?

We passed yet a third coffin, and then a fourth, growing more unnerved with each one before we turned off onto a main thoroughfare that lead to the motel where Vincent Malmstrom was staying. Maybe he could explain what we were seeing. That is, if he hadn't already left. It was 12:45.

We drove up to the motel, I knocked on the appropriate door

number, and a tall, broad-shouldered man with curly gray hair and a professorial manner appeared at the door. "Oh good, you've arrived," he said with relief, shaking my hand. "I'd invite you in, but we're just leaving." I glanced at the room: the beds were made, there was no luggage. It had the new, unused motel room look about it. A young man was sitting formally in one of the uncomfortable-looking motel chairs. Vincent Malmstrom hastily introduced him as Paul Dunn, his graduate student, who rose and shook hands with me.

"We're all checked out and ready to go," said Dr. Malmstrom hurriedly. "We've been waiting for you." He grabbed a bag and headed out the door, shook hands with Anne and Nikkie in the parking lot, and said, apologetically, "I know you're probably tired from the trip up here, but we have to keep moving. I've got a tight schedule. We've been traveling for a month now, and we only have a couple of weeks left and a lot of territory to cover."

Seeing our look of disappointment as we stood beside our dust-covered car in the parking lot, he added, "We'll stop at a restaurant down the road and relax, but we've got to put some miles behind us." He pointed toward the black, cone-shaped mountain; there was an orange glow at the apex, a black haze above it, and a fresh coat of black lava had run down the sides. "Frankly, I want to get as far away from that volcano as I can. Last night 'Fuego' was shooting out fire and hurling rocks the size of Volkswagens into the air. It was pretty frightening. It had everyone worried, but I think it has died down."

Suddenly all those coffins and grieving people came to mind, "How many people were killed?"

He shook his head. "No one. Not yet anyway. But one of the reasons I'm anxious to be off is that there could still be danger."

"But we saw a bunch of coffins, and a funeral going on just out of town," Anne persisted. "They weren't disaster victims?"

"No," he said shortly, continuing in a low voice. "They were murder victims. A bunch of peasants were machine-gunned by the police. There's a revolution going on here. I'll tell you about it later." We took off, feeling ill at ease. There were many questions I wanted answers to, but following Vincent Malmstrom's camper truck took all my attention. He was heavy on the gas, passed vehicles, and kept a relentless steady pace speeding down the road through a morbid, burned-over surrealistic landscape. All the black volcanic ash had spilled down the mountainside into the valley, paving over the landscape and smothering all that was green. Suddenly the image of that voodoo rooster head flashed into my mind. I hoped this search for Turtle Mother or whatever it was didn't take a nasty turn that we might regret. The dark mood of the mourners we had seen hung over us. No wonder someone had pelted us with the rooster head! The land and the politics had been charred. The traffic slowed to a crawl again and finally stopped where the road had been buried.

The valley below Antigua was a vast, sooty, black ash field. Along the way we were stopped at several military checkpoints and found ourselves looking down gun barrels. Nervous 16-year-olds in green khaki uniforms held automatic weapons while they riffled through our passports.

Uncountable thousands of burned black boulders had blown out of the volcano the night before. The fine dust sifted down. Even in the car it found its way into our teeth, our clothes, our mouths. Never had I viewed such a blighted landscape. Cars and trucks had backed up as crews with bulldozers cleared a pathway, groaning and straining to roll giant boulders out of the way. They were clearing a narrow pathway that wound like a river through the sea of rocks that stretched across the valley as far as the eye could see. Our car shook as the underpinning collided with one of the larger rocks protruding from the road bed. The valley looked like a scene out of a fundamentalist Christian's concept of Hell. Sitting there in that depressing alien rockscape, the biggest question of all was to myself: "What are you doing?"

The traffic started moving, Vince was getting ahead, and with my lack of Spanish, the last thing I wanted to do was get lost.

We moved out of the valley onto a modern paved highway, and 30 or 40 miles down the road, the sky became lighter, the dust thinner, and soon there was bright sunlight, green trees, and grasslands. Everyone felt better when we stopped for a much-needed lunch break. As we rested in the little cafe sipping our cold sodas, watching chickens pecking around the weeds, Vincent apologized: "Sorry for the rush, but all I could think about back there was that we had to get past the mountain before it incinerated us."

"What about the coffins?" Anne demanded. "Tell us what's going on!"

The professor glanced around nervously, worried about being overheard. In a low voice he told us about the bloody massacre that had taken place in a neighboring village. We later found out that 13 Indians (many of them children) had been gunned down over a land dispute. They had been flooded out by a wealthy landowner who opened a dam to get them to move out. In protest they burned his car. The police moved in with machine guns and mowed them down.

"I don't want to worry you," Vince cautioned grimly, "but this is a war zone. They don't usually shoot tourists; for the moment at least, both sides have an agreement not to. But just stay alert. All of Central America is blowing up: Guatemala, El Salvador, Nicaragua especially. That scene you just saw with the coffins is happening everywhere."

"But what's this fighting all about?" I persisted. "Why all the bloodshed?"

"It's about a lot of things, but mostly it's about the disparity of wealth and natural resources. A few people own everything, and they're getting even richer growing export crops—coffee, sugar, cotton, bananas, chocolate, and winter vegetables. They make a lot of money supplying you and me with luxury foods in North America."

"How does that cause a war?" Nikkie asked, joining in.

"Because they do it where poor people used to grow food for their own use," he stated emphatically. "The land owners are pushing the peasants off the land. They use them as seasonal workers and pay them next to nothing. And when people see their children starving, they fight back. Or they go into what's left of the rain forest and clear it to try and survive. But the soil's not good for agriculture there, so they have to abandon it after a few years and clear a new patch. Then the wealthy ranchers take the cleared land for cattle pasture—the rain forest beef connection."

"You mean that's why they're cutting down the rain forests—to keep from starving while we get cheap coffee and bananas?" asked Anne quietly, as we sat at the little cantina, watching the chickens scratch through the weeds.

"Exactly, and when they revolt, the Army puts it down using weapons the U.S. government gives them."

"Latin America has always been a society of a few haves and a lot of have nots," Vince continued, sipping his bottle of mineral water, "but now the population is so big that 'push is coming to shove' down here."

"So the war and the destruction of the rain forest are coming from the same source then," I concluded.

"Basically yes," Vince said tersely, cutting off the dialog. "Now let's get going. We've got to keep to the schedule if we want to get to Izapa tomorrow so you can see the turtle head."

On his map, Vince showed us our immediate destination, a tiny dot on the map called La Democracia. It was a three- or four-hour drive, en route to the Mexican border where the Izapan ceremonial site lay. So we continued our relentless pace, out of the mountains and down onto the Pacific coastal plain. The paved highway continued through scrub and agricultural lands until a small town appeared with city streets, houses, ox carts, and trucks loaded with sugarcane blocking the highway. The asphalt road was all but covered with the stripped-off leaves of cane, burned, dried, and crushed. Crushing it further beneath our wheels, we followed Malmstrom and his student in their white camper truck to the center of La Democracia and parked at a small city park next to a museum.

"This is it?" I asked, confused.

Anne shrugged, "I guess it is." She, too, sounded disappointed, "We're just along for the ride."

I guess we were expecting our first stop to be some remote archaeological site, something out of Hollywood, with ancient temples covered in vines and thick with snakes and jaguars. And this was just a grubby little sugarcane community with tractor trailers and farm trucks next to a shabby museum whose front was littered with husks and leaves.

Malmstrom got out of his vehicle, and we stood beside him and his student staring at some bizarre carved boulders evenly spaced around the square of the little plaza as decorative monuments. The professor stood there wide-eyed and moved slowly forward staring into the vacant faces of those bloated, almost grotesque creatures, obviously very much taken by something that was totally inexplicable to us. Some of them were whole-bodied figures, sitting there with their legs crossed like Buddhas and with thoughtful, almost happy looks on their faces, with fat jowls hanging down. Others were giant disembodied heads with stern and resolute expressions of great leaders bearing great responsibility. Still others appeared to be in a trance.

"Look, Paul, see how primitive they are!" Vince cried with great enthusiasm, as if he had just uncovered a chest of gold. "Nothing like the ornate carved figures on the Gulf coast. These are just boulders, barely carved, crudely rendered with no separation of head or body. Look at the ear plugs; you know how they're usually ornate in Mayan carvings. These are simply chiseled-out circles, bare representations."

There were a dozen of these statues, evenly spaced between park benches, beneath the generous shade of the ceiba trees—the ones the Maya call the "tree of life." All the statues stood about five or six feet tall—eye level—and we stared into their vacant faces. Malmstrom stepped forward and snapped a picture of one of the grotesque figures that gazed vacantly up at the sky.

Seeing our expressions of bewilderment, he stopped and explained: "This adds more credence to my theory that civilization began right here in the Pacific lowlands at Izapa (which is just up the road) and not along the Gulf of Mexico, as most archaeologists claim. You see, a civilization doesn't start out advanced and then become more primitive, and these figures are much, much cruder than the colossal Olmec heads found at La Venta."

The colossal Olmec heads he was describing were one of the greatest mysteries in all of Mesoamerican archaeology, with their thick lips, big noses, ball-player helmets and stoic, if not outright scowling, expressions.

"The earliest of these famous heads were first discovered in 1862. Someone was digging and unearthed what they thought was a pot. But when they excavated it, it turned out to be an enormous head, a helmeted ball player. It was from a civilization that predated the Mayans by a thousand years."

Vincent went on, as if he were lecturing in his Dartmouth classroom: "They found where the Olmecs had quarried the huge stones for the heads and dragged them 80 miles. But how they did that no one knows. It wasn't like bringing them over hard ground; they were brought across mud, swamp, and water. Years later, the government of Mexico dug them out and hauled them to the museum in Villa Hermosa, the state capital. It was an enormous undertaking. They broke trucks, they bent cranes. It was a national endeavor to move those things, yet the Olmecs did it without machinery."

"Perhaps they used telekinesis," I suggested humorously.

The distinguished professor shot me an irritable look, one that said I had fallen considerably in his estimation. "I don't believe that, and I don't believe Von Daniken's nonsense of little green men from outer space either." He turned away and went on with his picture taking, making me feel embarrassed at my transgression. "Let's just say there are a lot of unsolved mysteries."

Vowing to be more careful in my words, and aware of what I perceived to be his prickly nature, I followed Dr. Malmstrom and his student around the park and looked with bewilderment at these grotesque stone humans with their stern or vacant faces staring eternally up at the sky. They were called "Fat Boys" in the archaeological literature, a name that seemed meaningless. The artwork suggested a short, stocky race with thick necks, slant eyes, broad stubbed noses, thick lips, and a tendency toward obesity, who usually went around completely nude in the sweltering rain forests.

We know that in the interest of beauty the Olmecs wore elaborate feather head-dresses and hats, shaved their heads, and sharpened their teeth, filling them with metal. However, because of the mild climate and acidity of the soil where Olmec burials have been found, not one skeleton has been preserved to reveal the real physical type of the people.

We moved behind the professor and his student, watching their excitement of discovery grow, trying to see what they saw in the statues. "I'm confused," Anne said at last. "You're saying these are Olmecs. Are these the same people who carved the turtle head?"

"No, actually these are 'pre-Olmecs,'" Vince answered after snapping another picture, "a much earlier occupation. Radiocarbon dating techniques place the Monte Alto site, where they came from, at two thousand B.C." His tone changed, as if he were defending his controversial theory to an audience of skeptics. "It's my opinion that these people had their cultural hearth here on the Pacific coast, then migrated across to the Gulf coast at a later date, traveling over the centuries through the Tehuantepec Gap. They could have crossed these thorn thicket mountains, but this was the easiest way."

The great civilizations of Mesoamerica arose from agricultural village cultures that were established by about 1800 B.C. With a stable food supply based on maize, beans, and squash, populations grew and leisure time first appeared. These were the beginnings of the complex urban social patterns that were to follow with the Mayans, the Toltecs, and finally the Aztecs.

The Olmec civilization, in the second and first millennia B.C., extended from the Gulf of Mexico lowlands of Tabasco and Vera Cruz north to the valley of Mexico, across the Isthmus of Tehuantepec, and down the Pacific coast to El Salvador. By 1000 B.C., the first monumental stone sculptures of the Olmec culture were being built at urban areas such as La Venta and San Lorenzo in what is now southern Mexico. Sophisticated artists produced great stone heads and stelae and carved jade. Hieroglyphic writing and the incredibly accurate Mesoamerican system of measuring time were first invented by these Olmec people. Archaeologists generally have assumed that the culture began in the steaming swamps of the Gulf coast at La Venta where the giant Olmec heads were found, but Malmstrom didn't agree. Contrary to most archaeologists, he believed that Izapa on the Pacific Coast was the birthplace of civilization., which had then moved eastward into the Gulf of Mexico lowlands. And he had spent years and made numerous trips to Central America, studying calendars, artwork, and hieroglyphics, trying to prove his theory.

I gazed at the massive stone faces. There were two kinds of figures—either corpulent bloated bodies with deadpan or happy looks, or enormous disembodied heads with stern expressions and jowls of fat hanging down their cheeks. Unlike the Olmec heads on the Gulf of Mexico, which were impeccably carved with sharp, distinctive features, these were primitive. Although they were called "Fat Boys" in the archaeological literature, there was no sign that they were male or female, although some of the heads could have easily passed for American corporate executives.

Vincent and his student examined them carefully, and we stood by as spectators, interested but not deeply involved. It was, after all, their quest. It didn't seem to have any relationship to my search for the roots of the Turtle Mother legend except for trying to put Malmstrom's discovery of the magnetic turtle head into the broad context of pre-Columbian archaeology.

A nearby wall in the park at La Democracia had a sign about the carvings. Whoever wrote the legend depicted the Olmecs as a matriarchal society, intrigued with the amazing event of giving birth. They saw those large swollen figures outside as pregnant women, sitting in the Indian upright position of delivery. And the stern heads were those of men.

"Well, there are no turtles here," Vince said, after remembering we were still there and seeing how lost and confused I looked. "Let's go into the museum. If there are any in there we'll take a reading." He pointed to a small, shabby building at the end of the plaza.

"Why don't we see if any of these Fat Boy statues are magnetic?" I urged. "Just in case? Besides, negative readings will show how unique the turtle head at Izapa really is."

The professor shrugged dubiously. "Why not? It can't hurt anything. We're pinched on time; let's let Paul do it. It will be good practice for him." As we marched into the front door of the museum, the young man took off with compass in hand.

We were hardly in the entrance and starting to look around when Paul Dunn came running in out of breath. "I'm getting all kinds of magnetic readings on those Fat Boys. Come and see!"

Vince looked doubtful, but I was already out the door following him. I pulled my compass out and swept it up and down one of the grotesque, fat-bellied statues. It was an immense rock that stood seven feet tall, with at least a six-foot diameter of corpulent girth. Suddenly my needle jumped. I stared at it uncertainly, pulled it back, then moved it forward. It jumped again.

"Hey, the needle moved," I cried.

Paul came over, pulled out his compass and began passing it over the same statue. "See, those are magnetic too!"

Vincent Malmstrom hurried over and watched his student move his compass back and forth past the magnetic hot spot right between the fingertips of the crudely carved hands where the Fat Boy embraced the most rotund part of the belly.

"Right in the belly button," Paul announced delightedly.

"Let me see that." Vince grabbed the compass with disbelief and tried it. Again the needle deviated as he passed it across the navel. "It . . . certainly . . . did," he said, his tone puzzled, his expression one of confusion and surprise. "But it isn't a very strong field. The needle deflects only thirty degrees, not nearly as strong as the turtle head in Izapa. It's probably just a coincidence," he said uncomfortably, "but let's check the others anyhow."

The next figure also had a magnetic belly button, and Vince's befuddlement grew. Following behind him, we approached a five-foot-high rounded bald head that looked like Winston Churchill with its serious expression and heavy jowls of fat. Abruptly the needle switched from its easterly direction and pointed due north to the Fat Boy's right temple.

Then, seeing our disbelieving stares, Malmstrom laughed delightedly. "This is crazy. I bet you think I put this whole thing on—but I didn't! It's real. This head is magnetic, but only in the right temple, and so is that one over there."

"Are you sure it isn't random?" I asked suspiciously. "Maybe all the rocks are that way here."

Malmstrom didn't seem to hear. He put his compass to the temple near the ear plug of another frowning head. "This one's not magnetic at all," he said with disappointment.

"But this one sure is," cried Dr. Malmstrom's student assistant. "The north pole is his right temple, and the south pole comes out below this guy's right ear."

By this time we had attracted a swarm of small, curious children. The people sitting on the park benches beneath the towering foliage of the ceiba trees were delighted with the crazy gringos laughing and shouting over those monuments that sat in their park. They pointed their fingers and laughed at us, but Vince didn't notice as he carefully recorded his observations. Anne and Nikkie looked at me questioningly while the other two worked, and I shrugged with equal confusion.

"Can you believe this?" cried Malmstrom after we had gone around the entire perimeter of the plaza and measured all the monuments twice. He waved his notebook and summarized, "Seven out of eleven of these statues are magnetic, either in their navel or their right temple. Out of the four heads, three have a magnetic south pole below their right ears." He pointed to the head in front of the museum. "What a discovery!" he chortled.

"But it's such a small sample size, you can't tell if it's random or not," Anne said with a hint of exasperation as she sat on a park bench to reload her camera.

"In the temples? In the belly buttons?" The professor's voice rose in defense. "There's no way it could be random." His hand swept across the park, to the people who had lost interest by now and thinned out, and the rows of statues. "There's too many of them. It's just like the turtle head in Izapa; there's no way this can be simple chance. Those magnetic areas were somehow detected by these early sculptors and the statues were deliberately carved around them."

"How? How could they do that?" I cried unable to hide the suspicion growing in my mind that it was all bogus, that we had fallen in with a madman or a fraud. One minute we get off the plane, on this great expedition to behold the lone magnetic turtle head rock, and the next we're finding a plethora of Buddhas with magnetic belly buttons.

"How?" he repeated, catching my doubt. "How? I don't know how. Either the priest located these boulders up in the mountains or in a riverbed using a compass—which I doubt they had four thousand years ago—and had them carved so their navels or right temples were magnetic, or they somehow *magnetized* the rocks."

"I know you can magnetize iron with electricity," Paul Dunn offered weakly, "but can you magnetize rock?"

"It's done all the time with lightning up in the mountains," I said. "A blast of twenty-two thousand amps would align the dipoles in the iron-rich volcanic rock and produce a strong magnetic field."

"Oh good," Anne joined in sarcastically. "Maybe the priest pointed his finger at the belly buttons and commanded the heavens to strike them with lightning. Or maybe the little green men came down from outer space and zapped them!"

Vince shook his head worriedly. "Don't make it sound any more like a joke than it already does. I'm going to write this up, but no one's going to believe it. I'm glad I have witnesses. Do you realize that we've discovered the oldest magnetic artifacts in the world? They're certainly older than the magnetic bar found at San Lorenzo and they're probably older than the turtle head, which would make them a couple of thousand years older than the compasses found in China."

"But why would they magnetize the belly buttons and the temples? What purpose did it serve?" Paul puzzled.

Anne said thoughtfuly, "The navel in pre-Columbian art forms, as well as Far-Eastern religions, was of great importance." Her voice was vague at first, but grew stronger as she formulated her answer. "The Indian shamans believed that a man's life forces, his aura, emanates from his solar plexus. Its called the 'hara' in Asian cultures. And Mayans emphasized the umbilical cord as the link to life."

"That's true," added Nikkie Griffis, who studied such things. He had been silent through all the excitement and now speculated, "That's one of the chakra areas, one of the life centers they use in acupuncture."

"And magnetism in the right temples signifies thought," Paul joined in excitedly.

"If these are earth goddesses, as the sign says, then maybe the magnetic field also symbolized the life forces of the developing fetus in the womb," I speculated, feeling giddy.

Anne frowned. "This also makes them the oldest sexists in history. The women had the power in their wombs, and the men had the power in their brains. Things haven't changed much."

"I wouldn't touch that one with a ten-foot pole," Malmstrom laughed, shaking his head. "Nobody knows who they were, or what it meant. You can't really tell if these statues are male or female. Personally, I'm not going to speculate on what any of it means—I'd be a fool to. Besides, that statue over there—" he gestured to one particularly fat, bloated one that had an almost simian look "—has magnetic properties in the back of its neck. And I couldn't even find a south pole. Probably it's at the base, buried down in the earth. All I'm going to do is record the facts. Maybe it means nothing."

He shoved his notebook in his pocket. "And if it does get published in a scientific journal I hope to hell I don't get laughed out of existence. Come on, let's go into the museum and see what other wonders we can come up with." Full of doubt, we shuffled along behind him.

The museum was a sad, run-down little building. Obviously, a lot of community effort had once been put into it, but no money. Most of the really valuable archaeological pieces had long ago been sold off to collectors, and what remained in the antiquated dust-covered display cases looked like the leftovers of a pre-Columbian rummage sale.

The guard was delighted to see gringos come into his museum, pay the tiny entrance fee, and show so much interest. But when we took our compasses and started running them over every statue we came upon, he looked alarmed. When Vincent explained what we were doing and what we had just found outside, the guard became intrigued, even though his eyes registered total disbelief.

We stared at basalt carved mushrooms, some with smiling faces and some with contorted faces that grinned up at us from their stalks through yellowed glass. Some were frowning; others looked totally insane. Hallucinogenic mescaline made from mushrooms was—and still is—important in Indian culture. The guard opened the glass cases, but the carved mushrooms were negative; the compass needle didn't budge. Yet somehow they looked like they should have made it jump off the scale. The stone yokes the ball players wore around their waists as handicaps gave no reading, nor did the metates used for grinding corn.

The figures outside in the park and all the pieces in the glass cases came from a site called Monte Alto. Their history was anyone's guess, and Malmstrom was deeply disappointed that the heads had been hauled out of their natural settings back in 1966, forever destroying their true alignments that might shed light on their purpose. Now life went on around them.

A map showed that the heads and torsos, found on the Monte Alto farm, a few miles away, did not appear to have any particular order but were placed helter skelter over the countryside. Some faced small hillocks and ceremonial mounds, which was not unusual for monuments, but had they been left in place, Vincent Malmstrom might have discovered that their placement had some purpose, perhaps aligned to the summer or winter solstice or the four directions. He had made a specialty of finding repetitive celestial alignments not only in Central and South America but in Europe as well.

In the courtyard in the back of the museum were three flat round stelae, six feet long, without carving or rendition. For all practical purposes they were simply flat slabs of stone, which Malmstrom remarked, looked similar to the Mexican calendar stones. Expecting nothing, I casually ran my compass over them, just to make sure. But suddenly the needle jumped again, as the powerful attraction caused the needle to deviate sharply, a full 90 degrees. The pull was stronger than that from casually ran my compass over them, just to make sure. But suddenly the needle jumped again, as the powerful attraction caused the needle to deviate sharply, a full 90 degrees. The pull was stronger than that from any of the Fat Boys in the park out front. Why should these altars be magnetic? we wondered. The guard thought they had been used for human sacrifices. That made it even more perplexing. Were these altars really magnetized from repeated lightning strikes? Could those priests really control searing, awesome bolts from above?

We left the museum, more puzzled than when we first entered, and once again I gazed at the swollen figures. I had to agree, they looked now like earth goddesses about to give birth, with their hands clasped over their greatly distended bellies, the magnetic field between their fingertips, gazing upward with a pained or vacant expression. Their small feet were also raised up and wrapped around their abdomens.

As we climbed into the car to leave, I glanced once more at the masculine heads and recalled how little we knew about the brain, and about how we think. Although his studies were controversial, at least one scientist at Cal Tech, Dr. Joseph Kirschvin, the man who had discovered that sea turtles had ferromagnetic crystals in their brains, also had discovered traces of magnetic brain tissues in humans. What purpose it served, no one knew. We had a long journey ahead of us to see yet another magnetic statue, the turtle head at Izapa, and that, I reminded myself, was the reason we were here.

3

EL BAÚL

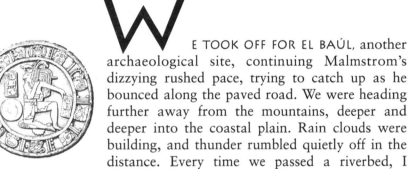

WE TOOK OFF FOR EL BAÚL, another archaeological site, continuing Malmstrom's dizzying rushed pace, trying to catch up as he bounced along the paved road. We were heading further away from the mountains, deeper and deeper into the coastal plain. Rain clouds were building, and thunder rumbled quietly off in the distance. Every time we passed a riverbed, I noticed an abundance of large round black rocks the size of the Fat Boys. I stared at them suspiciously through the car window. There were not just thousands of volcanic rocks, there were hundreds of millions. For all I knew, hundreds, maybe thousands of them had strong magnetic hot spots that would spin a compass. And the turtle's nose in Izapa and the Olmec statues with their magnetic belly buttons were merely coincidence. The more I thought about it, the more likely that seemed.

Maybe this whole trip was the biggest wild goose chase of my life. I couldn't stand it any more. When we came to the next military checkpoint, I hopped out and began hurriedly checking boulder after boulder with my compass. Once I thought the needle might have flickered a couple of degrees, but there was nothing like the pull we had just experienced, or the one that Malmstrom wrote about in *Nature* concerning the turtle head.

Certainly all the rocks possessed magnetite crystals to some degree; a sensitive magnetometer would have gone crazy among those igneous rocks formed by the cooling of volcanic lava.

"You'd better be discreet if you're going to check those rocks," Anne cautioned, watching me crouch down on my hands and knees and run the compass over the rocks. "If he gets the idea that you think he's a fraud, he may tell us to get lost, and you'll never see that turtle head. I'm warning you," Anne said in a low voice, "your skepticism was beginning to show back there, and I don't think he liked it one bit. Just cool it."

"Cool it?" I repeated with exasperation. "Cool it? We've come all the way down to Central America to see this damn magnetic turtle head. We no sooner get off the plane and the first place we stop is lousy with magnetic statues, not to mention that we've just blown fifteen hundred dollars of *Sports Illustrated*'s money to get here."

Nikkie pondered, "It does seem a bit weird." Then he offered brightly: "If everything in the country is magnetic, maybe you can make a story out of that."

The afternoon showers started. The rains splattered down on our windshield, turning the black soot into mud, and we drove on until Malmstrom mercifully stopped for a five-minute break at a little roadside shack that sold soft drinks and bottled water. We stood under the shelter watching the rain steadily pouring down, the muddy water flowing down the roadside ditch. There were rocks and boulders all over the place, popping up from the roadside weeds.

Finally I couldn't stand it. "Look, Vince, I hope you don't mind," I said, pulling out my compass, "but I want to check a few rocks. Your paper indicated that magnetic rocks were a great rarity. I'm not doubting your word, but I've really got to see for myself."

"Not a bit," he grinned magnanimously, drinking his bottled *agua*, "If I were in your shoes right now, I'd want to check too. We'll wait a few minutes for you to satisfy yourself," he added reassuringly.

The people who ran the little store watched quietly as I walked up and down the road, sweeping my compass over the rocks. Negative, always negative. The rains came again, this time blurring my vision so much that I had to give up.

Malmstrom gave me a knowing grin as I returned to shelter, soaked and covered with mud. "After I found the turtle head," he reminisced, "I must have checked every rock in the country, but I've never found any. My arm practically ended up frozen in position from pointing the compass at the rocks. By all means keep trying, but I'm afraid you'll find that lodestone is scarce as hen's teeth."

The break over, I took the wheel from Nikkie. Hell, I decided, speeding to catch up with Malmstrom's white camper truck, it would take the whole Guatemalan army armed with compasses instead of machine guns to get an idea of what percentage of those uncarved, water-worn boulders were really magnetic. As we sped past the bleak, cut-over countryside to the rhythmic beat of the windshield wipers, millions of uncheckable rocks and outcrops went by in a blur.

As our automobiles ate up the road, I did a lot of thinking about magnetism and the ancient "pre-Olmecs" who left all this stonework behind. The entire countryside was covered with volcanic rocks left over from a time when volcanoes erupted constantly and buried the land. Eighty thousand years ago the biggest blast occurred when the Volcano Agua exploded, leaving behind an enormous crater that is now Lake Atitlan.

Basaltic rocks, rich in iron, some large as trucks, others just cobbles, were strewn about and carried down the sides of the huge mountain in rushing flows of hot lava. Forests grew, and mastodons, camels, giant sloths, and other creatures roamed the land. Then early humans arrived in Central America, migrating down from the land bridge of Asia 15,000 years ago. Then agriculture flourished. People cut back the forests to plant crops and made use of this endless resource of black rock for art and tools.

But did the ancients really have knowledge of magnetism? The only proof besides Malmstrom's turtle head discovery at Izapa (and now the Fat Boys at La Democracia) was a single one-inch sliver of polished lodestone excavated from a midden at San Lorenzo. The archaeologist who unearthed it theorized that the Olmecs (who existed perhaps a thousand years after the sculptors of La Democracia) used it as a compass. It was uncovered in the jungle on the Caribbean side of Mexico and dated to about 1200 B.C. The artifact was highly polished, looked as if it had been machined, and had a groove running down its side that might have been used as a sighting device, possibly for laying out plots of land.

But that was a long way from being able to locate a boulder with a magnetic hot spot and being able to carve it so that all the lines of force were concentrated in a specific portion of the body. Geologists using magnetometers teaming up with sculptors today would have a hard time duplicating their work.

All of these possibilities we debated as we followed the geographer's camper truck to "El Baúl," which meant "belly" in spanish. It was a late pre-classic site, dated to around the time of Christ. Many pre-Columbian ball game artifacts had been found in the region and we were anxious to see more statues, to see if there was any sign of magnetism.

Before we made the trip, I had read that the Pacific coastal plain was deep rain forest. Books and papers of archaeologists who had excavated many of the famous sites described herds of wild peccaries coming by their camps, and how the screams of jaguars would be heard through the night. But that was 30 years ago, and all that had changed. There were no forests, no peccaries, not even bird life—just endless sugarcane plantations, cotton fields, and coffee and chocolate groves, all manicured and doused with

DDT. I had the feeling, when looking at pictures of those ancient, vacant stones, with their intricate carved mysteries and magnetism, that they were somehow bearing witness to it all.

The rains worsened into a torrential downpour, a solid blur of water, and Malmstrom pulled off a wrong road and got lost. We waited until the rain quit, and he asked directions from some *campesinos* at another roadside stop. This time, we turned onto a wide dirt road and drove and drove through splattering mud and sugarcane fields, until we arrived at the entrance to a *finca* or sugar plantation. We followed Dr. Malmstrom, trying not to slide through the sticky red earth and get stuck, until the road abruptly ended out in the middle of nowhere with a few thatched wooden sheds and a number of carved stones that someone had lined up beneath a long wooden shed next to a large tin barn. It was part of a large industrial mill complex where sugarcane was ground, only the mill seemed to be shut down.

"This is it—El Baúl," Dr. Malmstrom announced, after he got out and stretched. His tall figure had been cramped in the small Japanese truck. We stood there silently, again trying to make sense out of what we were seeing. Some of the carvings were Mayan, Vince told us. None of them looked even remotely like the roly-poly figures we had seen in La Democracia. The carvings appeared to be a mix of Mayan motifs and other more exotic subjects, including cross-legged men wearing turbans.

A few hundred years after the birth of Christ, the classical Mayan civilization was building enormous temples and cities throughout what is now southern Mexico, Belize, and Guatemala. Taking their cultural roots from the earlier Olmecs, and ruled by autocratic warrior kings, the Mayan city-states produced great stone pyramid temples that probably symbolized the mountain that held up the heavens in their religious system. Large populations, huge trading networks, and the wealth they generated led to the creation of altars and ball courts. They were adorned with elaborate carvings, murals, and inscriptions recording the rise and fall of the various rulers and the incessant wars between competing cities. In the 650 years from about A.D. 250 to A.D. 900, the Maya reached artistic and intellectual levels unmatched in the New World and in few places anywhere.

With population growth, warfare intensified until, by about A.D. 900, the great urban civilizations had collapsed and the cities were abandoned. Life reverted to a simpler village-based system. Experts in the field increasingly believe that the collapse was due to overpopulation and environmental destruction of the natural resource base.

It wasn't clear why these carvings we had come so far to see were even there, for we were obviously deep in the middle of someone's farm. But with public-spiritedness, someone had gone to a lot of trouble to bring them here. Here they appeared even more perplexing, sitting in a row surrounded by weeds and a corrugated iron warehouse, than if they had been in an air-conditioned museum. Far more ornate than the simple Fat Boys

we had seen earlier, these were works of art, with beautifully and intricately carved heads and distinct torsos. There were carved frogs symbolizing Chac, the rain god, and more serpents and jaguars.

"As you can see, these are much more elaborately carved than the Fat Boys in La Democracia, or even the stuff in Vera Cruz," Vincent Malmstrom lectured. "They're also much younger. We can actually date this stela to thirty-one A.D.," he said, pointing at the bar and dot calendar etched into stone. Rain began splattering down, wetting and darkening the stern gray figures of priests and animal effigies. We stepped into the palm-thatched, dark shelter that provided some protection from the rain.

When the downpour stopped momentarily, I studied the elaborately carved frog, the jaguar heads with hideous, embellished fangs, the rendition of the sun god, and a three-foot-long carved fish with human-looking eyes, all sitting here out of place, deep in an agricultural ocean of broad-leafed sugarcane that stretched on forever, without features or character. Suddenly the weirdness of this whole experience struck me: this mad driving to Antigua, the voodooish rooster head on our windshield, the coffins, Malmstrom's rushing from place to place following the path of the sun and the shadows it cast on the temple walls (which somehow reminded me of the white rabbit in *Alice*), the magnetic Fat Boys—it all seemed so alien.

What am I doing here? I worried, so far from everything I'd ever done in my life. Until now my life work had always had to do with the sea and its creatures, not ancient carved rocks. A six-foot-long surrealistic stone amphibian with bulbous eyes and a huge frog wearing an ornate collar—Chac, the rain god—grinned mockingly at me. There were monkeylike figures, wearing clothes. It all seemed so alien, but then again, was my being here really so far removed from the other things I did in life?

All these civilizations practiced zoolatry—the worship of animals. For thousands of years the Indians in Guatemala and Mexico idolized animals such as the jaguar, the serpent, the turtle, the alligator, and the feathered serpent. The Olmecs believed in deities that were part human and part animal. The well-being of humans was intimately bound up with that of the animals, so that one could not survive without the other. How big a jump was it from zoology to zoolatry?

Our culture, especially our archaeologists and psychologists, dismissed these reptilian or feline creatures as aberrations of another time. Drug-induced, to be certain. But were they? Why does a drunk experiencing delirium tremens see green snakes, pink elephants, and dragonlike creatures? Why have the Chinese, the American Indians, and the Celtic and Germanic tribes all had dragons in their myths, or dragonlike creatures such as the Loch Ness monster? Are we living in our own subconscious? Exchanging reality in the astral plane common to all mankind? I don't know.

Turtle Mother, according to the Miskito Indian belief, was part of our psyche. She was all about us, working in strict accordance with the seasons and the strengthening and weakening of the earth's magnetic field. To the ancient ones who dwelled along the seashores and coastal plains and partook of the rich estuarine and oceanic life, understanding the cycles of day and night and placating the sun became a whole way of life. They studied the movements of, and performed rituals and sacrifices to, the "father of the heavens," the parent of fires that cooked their food and kept them warm. It was all interrelated. Mankind, animals, and plants could live on Mother Earth only by retaining the good graces of Father Sun and by propitiating the gods of rains, the winds, and the seas.

The years of net fishing in the Gulf of Mexico had given me a far greater understanding. The turtles, the sharks, the alligators that we saw or caught in the nets were, according to the ancient Mayan religions, the messengers of the underworld. In Central America they decorated their pottery with motifs of these animals, or carved them in stone, imploring them in their shamanistic rituals to bring about better lives. Maybe the Fat Boys in La Democracia weren't so far afield from my search. They appeared to be in trance, in meditation, communing with the spirit world for the good of their people. The shamans studied nature and drew their power from it. These big animals were considered intermediaries between the spiritual and corporeal worlds.

Legend said these high priests or shamans could take the form of a spirit animal such as a turtle, deer, or some other creature and journey to the spirit world to petition and bargain with the "Keeper of the Animals," who protected them and controlled their movements. These men of great power went into trances, and implored the Keeper of the Animals ("Earth Owner," as the Mayans called him) to help their people; to learn when it was time to change camps, when it was time to harvest other resources, or when it was time to go from a farming life to a fishing life.

In exchange for assurances that his people would not be greedy, the Earth Owner, the "Provider," would give them enough food to eat. Earth Owner hated the squandering of life and dealt with offenders harshly. The shaman always made a promise to Earth Owner that his people would not be profligate in their reaping, and so rigid taboos were set on how much could be taken and when—a mixture of natural history and ethics.

The turtle was my personal totem. I studied turtles, tracked their movements and migrations, tagged them, and watched them nesting on the beaches. Since childhood, they had been part of my life-long quest. As a child I had hunted the woods, the streams, and the lakes for turtles and kept them in our Brooklyn apartment. When I moved to Florida as a teenager, I found bright-shelled little turtles with gray speckled skin and shells bearing totemlike geometric markings: hexagrams and pentagons with yellow centers on their bluish black shells. They were called diamondback terrapins, and commercial fishermen in the Florida panhandle swore that if you caught one and put it in your boat, the wind would blow and there would be misfortune. What a preposterous idea! However, after having boats sink beneath me, getting involved in head-on collisions while hauling terrapins in my car, and lots of other mishaps, I decided the superstition wasn't such a superstition and left them alone. Was it all a coincidence? Or was it possible that these terrapins with their grinning white jaws were really living talismans that could make the wind blow, storms brew, and arrange fate?

I looked at the darkening horizon. Although the rains had momentarily quit, great black storm clouds were creeping up on us. The sugarcane whipped back and forth in the wind as the heavy clouds came toward us ready to burst at any minute. If nothing else, the terrapins had caught my attention, starting me on the quest that led to Costa Rica were I first heard about Turtle Mother and now to Guatemala en route to Mexico to find Vincent Malmstrom's stone turtle with the magnetic nose. I looked around the ruins of the ball court; there were no turtles here. Nevertheless, I pulled out my compass and started sweeping it over the statues. Nothing happened.

Paul Dunn also walked slowly from statue to statue running his compass over each one, shaking his head. "No . . . no . . . not this one either."

I tried it too, and, like the rocks and cobbles that lay scattered around, they were all negative. By now I was becoming adept at rock measuring. When you take a reading, you have to hold the compass level and steady and get a fixed bearing on the statue. If the needle sits on 40 degrees east, you push it closer, keeping your hand level. On each and every statue there it remained, fixed in its bearing. The needle never even twitched. There was nothing magnetic or ferrous to draw it.

That is, until Paul swept his compass past a small obscure-looking stela. "Hey," he cried, "I'm getting a reading on this one. No . . . I'm getting two readings." He was checking a small stone tablet about three feet wide and 18 inches high. Etched on the stone were two faceless men sitting with their legs crossed, their arms folded across their chests, sitting in meditation in the same position that one also sees in Mesoamerican and Egyptian artwork. They looked very much like the Gemini twins of the constellations. The stela was badly worn, but the men, if they were men, were seated on a bench and had long arms and fingers. They looked almost apelike. Perhaps they were the famous Hero Twins, the children of the Maize God who, the Mayans said, died and was resurrected, bursting out of the shell of a tortoise.

"I can't believe this," Vince cried delightedly, taking the compass and checking behind his student. "You're right. I'm getting a reading on each one of these figures." His hand moved steadily, tightly gripping the instrument, and scanning down beneath their crossed legs. "They have a north pole where their arms cross, and a south pole beneath their legs. This is incredible!"

He backed up and gazed at it in disbelief. He turned to us, obviously agitated. "That means there are four separate magnetic poles in one rock—THAT'S IMPOSSIBLE!"

A strong wind gusted through the sugarcane fields, and the cloudy skies began rumbling. "Again, I don't understand," I said. "Why is that impossible?" By now I was really feeling inadequate and insecure with my lack of education in physics.

"There is no possible physical or geological reason for this that I know of. I'll have to ask some friends at the university, but every piece of magnetite has a fixed polarity. As I explained before, there's a north pole in one part of the stone and a south pole in another, usually at the bottom. Take the turtle head in Izapa: when you put the compass to its nose, it points north. But the pole runs completely through the stone. When you run it around the stone to the rear, the needle seeks the south pole. That's the way it should be. But here you have two poles in one rock, each north and south, but they're only three inches apart."

"I still don't understand," I persisted, "and I need to."

"Look, Jack. Supposing you have a bar magnet, and you break it in half. What happens? You have a two separate magnets, each with a north pole and a south pole. You can break them into a thousand magnets and they'd all have their own separate poles. You can't have more than two poles in a magnet, that's all!

"And that's what we have. There's no way such a thing could be accidental. I can't explain it. I wish we could take this stone back to M.I.T. or someplace."

There were just too many questions. These were not the pre-Olmecs, they were Mayans from the classic period, around the time of Christ. Could it be that the people in this later period possessed a secret knowledge of magnetism also? Was it carried down through the ages, represented in various occupational stages all the way up to Aztec times and Spanish contact?

Inside the little shed, where the four-poled magnetic stela was housed next to several other stones, there was a sign and a faded photograph showing an immense statue of the Earth God, a colossal rock that weighed at least 50 tons, standing high above the fields. No piece of machinery could cope with anything so immense. There it stood, looking down sternly like a leader on the croplands where farming machinery had flattened all the other pyramids and occupational middens. It looked very much like an immense Fat Boy towering above the landscape.

Malmstrom was upset. "Like the Fat Boys in La Democracia, we'll never know what their relationships to the land were. But maybe we could get permission to go in and see the if the fat god is aligned to anything."

We were wondering how much trouble it would be to get permission to test this monstrous earth god when a pickup truck came speeding up and screeched to a stop about 20 yards away. A tall, grim man stared at us through the window. Abruptly the door flew open; he jumped out and stalked over to us tensely, gripping a machine gun and extra clips of sharp, shiny bullets. It was an Israeli Uzi. Maybe we were trespassing, I thought; this did look like an awfully private place. But from his tense, aggressive expression and the way he stood poised, unmistakably ready to start shooting, it felt much more serious. That was a lot of heavy munitions to guard a few stones.

"*Buenos dias,*" said Vince to the man.

He nodded stiffly. He didn't look like a farm worker. Wearing clean khaki pants and sports shirt, he looked like a thug who put little value on human life, or perhaps an undercover policeman.

Looking us over, he asked what we were doing here. Vince nervously made small talk, telling him in his fluent Spanish that we had come a long, long way to look at their famous stones, and how glad he was that the government had preserved them. He went on to say that he was a professor, and we were students studying archaeology. The man's expression remained impassive, his eyes unconvinced.

Then suddenly five or six other men appeared out of the cane fields and stood there about 50 yards away across the old ball court plaza. Rough, angry peasant men with hard eyes, glaring at us. They looked like truculent farm workers, men who worked with their hands, and they were clutching machetes. They stood there, fingering their weapons dangerously. One slapped a bottle into his palm, over and over again, glowering at us all with hostile suspicion. Another swung his machete back and forth.

The first man, who we surmised was a *finca* boss, stepped forward to face them across the ball court plaza, spinning his Uzi around on his index finger by the trigger guard while listening to Vince's explanation. We tried to act nonchalant, going on photographing the stones and taking measurements. All of the men eyed us suspiciously as we worked.

Suddenly the overcast skies opened. We stepped back into the hut and huddled beneath the tin roof. I wondered vaguely why the men across the plaza didn't come over and get out of the rain, but they just stood there holding on to their machetes and bottles. The man in the khakis, the *finca* boss, seemed tense, but soon Vince's affable conversation put him more at ease. Vince looked and sounded like a college professor as he talked about our travels and pre-Columbian art. I think it was the camera on Anne's neck that finally convinced the boss that we were really tourists. But all the while his eyes searched the long, cobble-filled dirt roads, looking for something. Then suddenly his mood changed. He was obviously relieved that we were a bunch of *gringo* tourists and not commandos or revolutionary sympathizers.

The rain beat down harder until we could hear nothing but the torrents drumming on the thatched roof. Water leaked down, splattering over the zoomorphic rocks, darkening them and wetting us, but we hardly noticed. The man looked over Paul's shoulder as he held his compass on the Gemini twins. Finally his curiosity overcame him and he asked what he was doing.

That made us more legitimate: no one could make up a yarn like that! Relieved at the break in tensions, Vince went on to explain that we had just made a discovery in La Democracia. Even listening to the Spanish, which I barely understood, the story sounded preposterous—so preposterous that it was believable. The man told us about other archaeological sites nearby, but his attention constantly shifted between the peasants out there in the fields, now dripping wet in their soiled work clothes, and the dirt road that led through the sugarcane fields. It was obvious that the *finca* boss was waiting for someone.

"Maybe we should ask them about the big fat god and see if we can get permission to see it," I urged. "We might get the biggest magnetic reading of all."

The professor shook his head and said tersely, "No. We don't have time."

When the rain stopped, we went outside to finish taking pictures of the Mesoamerican dragons, stone frogs, and the intricately carved stelae of kings in feathered headdresses with bar and dot calendars and Mayan hieroglyphics. While scribbling my notes, I watched Vincent Malmstrom and his student having a private conference.

Moments later, Paul appeared beside us, his voice low and urgent. "Dr. Malmstrom says to pack up quick. It's getting hot here. Don't look obvious, but move fast or we'll be in the middle of a shooting war!"

We didn't know what was going on, but we didn't have to be asked twice. The man with his gun, the other guys with their hostile looks and their machetes and bottles, combined with the memories of seeing those child-sized coffins decorated with pink lace on the front porches of the shacks in Antigua filled us with dread. When we had stopped for coffee earlier that morning, Vince told us that that little piece of horror had never been reported in the newspapers. There was just a note saying the Indians had been detained. And here we were skipping around Guatemala, looking at stones as the country was exploding. Anne threw her camera into the trunk, Nikkie grabbed the wheel, and I got in the back. Following Vince, we left the men, their truck, and their guns behind.

We had driven four miles over rain-soaked, soggy dirt trails, nearly back to the main highway, when we saw a battered old yellow station wagon, full of dents and splattered with mud, speeding down the road, churning up ground. It slowed as we approached, and the occupants looked us over carefully. The wagon was packed with grim men bristling with rifles, shotguns, and machetes—ready for war.

That night at the hotel we pieced it together. Vince, tuned to the nuances of Central American politics, quickly surmised that there was a labor uprising in process and we had walked right into the middle of it. "I don't know whether the *finca* boss who was holding those other guys with the machetes at bay with his machine gun wanted us out of there or whether he was glad we were there distracting them until help showed up. You remember that other car we met on the way back? Those must have been his reinforcements."

"They looked like peasants and agricultural workers to me," I said. "Are you sure they weren't the reinforcements for the peasants?"

"I'm positive. They wouldn't have had a car and probably not the guns —although nowadays guns and revolution are everywhere. There's no telling what happened after we left. If we had stayed a few minutes longer, we might have been caught in the middle of a showdown at the O.K. Corral. The company men were headed to the end of the road, out in the middle of the sugarcane fields, to confront the rebellious farm workers and settle scores. We didn't leave a minute too soon!"

Then Vince told us that several days earlier, in the town of Retalhuleu, the boss of a government-owned *finca* and five bodyguards were machine-gunned to death. The newspapers had pictures of their bullet-ridden bodies.

"Great," Anne muttered, "and there we were, a bunch of happy turkeys, standing there in blissful ignorance, blithely taking pictures and ready for the slaughter!"

Nikkie said, "I wonder if the gross rooster head tossed on our windshield had anything to do with it? I can still see the Evil Eye that old woman gave us."

Anyway, it didn't work. Turtle Mother must have been watching out for us.

Giving us an in-depth view of Central American politics, Vince helped put the massacres, the fighting, and the murders into perspective. It wasn't just the age-old battle of the haves versus the have nots, he told us, expanding on his earlier lesson, it was a war of diminishing natural resources. As long as so much produce was exported out of the country, and fruit trees and food crops were eliminated in favor of large industrial crops like sugarcane, chocolate, and coffee, there would never be enough food to go around. One gringo like ourselves used more resources and caused more pollution than a hundred peasants who were trying to scratch out a living.

Because populations were swelling worldwide, and we no longer lived in balance with the earth, the poverty, inequity, and want were greater than ever. So it came back to Turtle Mother again: the lost ethic that said harmony can only be achieved by living in balance with the land, using resources sparingly, and being careful not to waste anything. The misery, death, and destruction resulted from not living in harmony with the earth. Maybe someday we would learn, but how much bloodshed and suffering would have to come first?

Exactly what the Fat Boys with their magnetic belly buttons or even the monolithic magnetic turtle that had brought me here in the first place had to do with the Miskito Indians' Turtle Mother legend wasn't clear. Perhaps tomorrow, after we crossed into Mexico and reached Izapa in the state of Chiapas, it would all be sorted out. All I could do was hope.

MEXICO—1979

4

THE MAGNETIC TURTLE HEAD
OF IZAPA

HERE WAS SOMETHING EERIE ABOUT IZAPA. Its large round stone balls perched on pedestals in the open fields looked like a Central American Stonehenge.

This area of the Pacific coast of Mexico and Guatemala, probably the site of several pivotal stages in the development of Central American culture, was occupied from pre-Olmec times (about 1500 B.C.) up into the Mayan era. The site had more than 80 large temple mounds and an enormous collection of richly carved gods, animal figures, and scenes of travel and warfare. Altars and elaborately carved scenes of mythological events were everywhere. Many of the figures were oceanic—one was a fish/human creature. I looked at the pyramids, the long narrow ball court, the monuments, and the altars with strange carved figures of men in boats wearing feathered headdresses riding waves filled with monstrous fishes. There were carvings of jaguar gods, serpents, and monsters with men standing in their mouths.

"This is where it all began," Vince said, his eyes glowing. "These people, whoever they were and wherever they came from, worshipped the sun. My research has shown that all the pyramids, the ball courts, and the monuments are aligned either to the mountains or to the summer or winter sunrise solstices. I'm convinced the calendar began here. And so did the Olmecs. That's what I'm mainly interested in. This magnetic turtle of yours is just a sideline for me—a digression."

"Where is the turtle?" I asked, taking in the great number of stones and stelae, anxious to finally see it.

"I'll show it to you, but before I do I want you to see something."

We followed him across the ball court to a faded, broken stela. There on the worn, etched rock was a carving of a man standing in a boat holding a cross, which some archaeologists have interpreted as a cross staff, a navigational instrument. It appeared that he had a beard, and beneath his canoe were a number of bizzare, stylized fish. Etched beneath the boat were spiraled renditions of rolling waves, and two hook-nosed deities looked on from each side. They seemed to be the wind gods blowing the current each way. "Nowhere else is the seafaring mode so prominent," said Malstrom. "I believe Izapa had early contacts with the sea. And it may have been visited early on by navigators from distant regions."

His eyes shown with excitement. "The methods used to predict solar and lunar eclipses are virtually identical for both Han dynasty Chinese astronomers and the Mesoamerican cultures. Likewise, their methods for making bark paper were also identical. They were a seafaring people; they spread their influence to the New World and traded all along this coast, all the way down to Ecuador. We can tell this based on their pottery.

"And they lived at a time when sea turtles were prevalent in all the oceans. When they made their long sea journeys, they doubtless sustained themselves on these animals. Turtles were easy to harpoon, and they could be stacked up in a boat and kept alive for weeks or months."

Then he pointed to a group of stones and stelae near the entrance of the site, which was now a park with well-trimmed grasses. "Your turtle head is over there."

We hiked over, and the tall, reserved professor suddenly grew angry at the sight of a makeshift barbed-wire fence that had been thrown up between the monuments. "This is an outrage," he cried, as if personally insulted. "Someone has turned this into a hog pen." Almost in response, several pigs got up, grunting, and moved out of our way. I wasn't interested in the hogs. Here, at last, was what I had come to see.

Compared to the other structures, the turtle head was unimpressive. It was a large black boulder about four feet long and three feet wide, sitting there among the rest of the carved stones about 60 yards south of the ceremonial ball court. Sometimes when you see a photograph you think there will be more when you actually go up and touch the object and see for yourself. But that wasn't the case. This turtle with its dark, brooding eyes and chiseled-out features was just as bizarre and enigmatic sitting there in its three-dimensional state as in the black-and-white photos I'd seen in Malmstrom's article in *Nature*. In fact, it

appeared less impressive because it was lost among all the other stones.

"Go ahead," Vince urged, "check it out. That's what you've come all this way for."

I stepped forward clutching my compass, hoping that I would get some sort of blinding revelation that this long trek would be worthwhile after all. I held the compass steady, and when the dial stopped turning and remained fixed at 110 degrees, I slowly, steadily thrust my hand and compass forward.

Suddenly the field of force gripped my compass and the needle whirled to the north, coming to rest at 60 degrees. The force was much more powerful than that of any statue we had measured so far. My hand was trembling with excitement and bewilderment, but I held it there, and when I withdrew it the dial spun back to its original position of 110 degrees. Again and again I tried it with the same results. No matter where I moved the compass around that great stony face, the needle continuously pointed to the snout until I pulled it away. Half a meter away the magnetic field faded and the turtle's nose lost its pull.

I was more bewildered than ever. The rock could speak to my compass but not to me. Somehow I hoped a lightbulb in my brain would switch on, but there was just blankness. Had I come all this way and spent other people's money just to watch a needle jump?

Then an image flooded into my mind of a real flesh-and-blood green turtle coming ashore to nest. There in the fiery surf, the great creature bends its head down and nuzzles the sand, as if smelling the ground, perhaps to see if it is in the right place before hauling its great girth up the beach. And it was in the olfactory lobes of the brain where Joseph Kirschvinc of Cal Tech first discovered the ferromagnetic crystals.

Again I took a reading, doubting what I had just seen. Vince laughed. "It's the damndest thing, isn't it? I don't know what to make out of it, all I did was describe it. As I wrote in my article in *Nature*, the sculptors may very well have associated magnetism with the migrations of sea turtles and rendered it."

Was Malmstrom right? Was this magnetic stone indeed the origin of the Turtle Mother myth? Was the legend or religion really ancient? My search to find the Turtle Mother had started so innocently, so casually, just from something I had heard, but it stuck in my mind, and I couldn't drop it. This quest had just about taken over my life.

Turtle Mother was only a shadow of a myth, told by old men in villages along the Caribbean shores of Honduras, Nicaragua, Costa Rica, and Panama. With each passing year, the old turtlemen who knew the old ways, who had lived in close relationship with the land and the sea, were dying off. And yet, somehow, the thread of the myth had survived, at least in the Caribbean. In Nicaragua and Costa Rica the tale was repeated with such consistency, almost by rote, that I couldn't believe that this myth sprang out of thin air. I felt in my bones that it had some basis in solid fact, that it was related to magnetic orientation, and while Malmstrom's magnetic turtle head didn't prove it, it added a strong piece of circumstantial evidence.

The turning of a compass needle in the legend added another. And so did all the millions of submicroscopic ferromagnetic crystals torqueing in the brains of sea turtles as they migrated across thousands of miles of ocean between breeding beaches and feeding grounds.

There was no way the old turtlemen of the Miskito coast could have known about ferromagnetic crystals. Yet they said that this magic rock in the shape of a turtle turned like a compass needle. And there was no way the pre-Olmecs, who carved the magnetic turtle head, could have known that either.

Looking at the rigid head, that chunk of magnetic stone, the first tangible piece of evidence that Turtle Mother existed, I pondered the great migrations of olive ridleys and the *Chelonia agassizi* turtles, a separate species of green turtle, that swarm the Pacific coast of Central America. Unlike the diminished Kemp's ridley in the Gulf of Mexico, which is on the verge of extinction, there are hundreds of thousands of olive ridley sea turtles. They swarm ashore on beaches from Mexico to Panama in such multitudes that they dig up each other's eggs. In spite of Mexican turtle factories up and down the coast that slaughtered them by the tens of thousands for their hides until they were banned in 1986, and in spite of the wholesale exploitation of their eggs that destroyed entire nesting colonies, olive ridleys remain the most abundant sea turtle in the world, with mass nestings in India, Africa, and Asia, as well as in Central America.

If there were such multitudes now, how many must there have been when the people who carved the stone turtle fished along the sea? Yet here was another great mystery, for nowhere in the kitchen middens (the garbage heaps of the pre-Columbian people who lived on both sides of the isthmus) has anyone ever found the first ridley bone, skull, or piece of shell. Zooarchaeologists have unearthed plenty of remains of green turtles, hawksbills, loggerheads, and even a leatherback bone or two, but not the first sign of any ridley—Kemp's or olive. Were they taboo, or was this abundance something new?

As we were discussing all this, the old caretaker, who lived in an adobe hut at the site and kept the grass cut, wandered over, collected two pesos from each of us, chatted with Vince in Spanish for a few moments, and left. "They charge according to the importance of an area," the professor explained. "Uxmal, where the big pyramids are, is a ten-peso site. Someday I hope to make Izapa equally important. Over the years I've discovered that more than forty ceremonial centers in Central America are precisely aligned to the summer or winter sunrise solstice. Izapa is the oldest and perhaps the most important of them."

The pigs that rooted around the stelae belonged to the caretaker. This irreverence irritated Vince, especially since the newly placed hog pen ran right between the turtle head stela and the upright altar behind it. "This is a disgrace! I'm going to write to the Minister of Archaeology in Mexico City when I get back," he said, snapping a picture for evidence.

I had to step over the wire fence into the soggy mire of the hog pen to scan the black snake head that stood in a direct line in front of the turtle. Even though it was only a crudely carved boulder, it caught the essence of serpents, staring ahead with its own fixed rigidity. Just as Malmstrom had reported in his paper, it was not magnetic. Once again an image flooded into my mind: a big black indigo snake that we saw recently in the Everglades lying at the edge of the water, with brilliant glossy coal black skin and scales of hexagonal and diamond shapes.

Again I saw its long black tongue whipping in and out, tasting the air, testing for an unfamiliar smell in the green world. Its eyes looked like black jade, and it moved over the ground in a smooth sinuous motion, sliding majestically into the water where the sunlight poured down through the leafy vegetation. For a moment its coal black scales gleamed with beauty until this rare and endangered creature vanished, spiritlike, into the mangroves.

The snake here was a strange coincidence, for over and over again in Chinese motifs a tortoise and a serpent appear intertwined. And even in American folklore it is said that if a turtle crawls through the marsh, it will be followed by a snake. Rattlesnakes routinely inhabit burrows made by gopher tortoises along the southeast coast and the two live together in a comfortable symbiosis of some sort. How much of this was coincidence, piling up fragments that might have absolutely no connection with each other, and how much was real, I had no idea.

I took another reading on the black snake head, and still nothing. Then I started methodically pointing my compass at all the other rocks and altars.

"Go ahead," said the professor in a bemused tone. "Do them all. You won't find anything else magnetic. When I first found this thing I must have checked half the cobblestones in the ball court, but nothing else here is magnetic. But the turtle's about twice as strong as the monuments we found in Guatemala yesterday."

I looked wearily at all the other basaltic boulders strewn around the site, some carved, others not. I tested them; all were negative. A nearby river was filled with rocks, many the size of the turtle head and just as black. I waded out and tested them also until I finally came back and sat down, weary of pointing my compass at every mineral and getting nothing.

I sat on the turtle rock, running my hand over its smooth water-polished surface. "You really don't think there's a chance that all this could be coincidence?

"You see how much luck you've had finding a magnetic stone. Sure it could be random, but I doubt it, now more than ever, especially after what we just saw in La Democracia and El Baúl. As I said before, I think they deliberately fashioned this rock so the magnetic lines of force came to focus in the snout." On this point, Vince was unshakable.

Anne ran her hand over the smooth black rock. "The stones are going to keep their secrets," she mused. She looked at all the other stones, stelae, and monuments. "How did you find this thing?"

Vince said, "It was the sheerest of accidents. One of my students was doing her research paper on the role of the sperpent in Mesoamerican art and we were checking to see if the snake sculpture had any particular orientation. Even though that turned out to be negative, when we checked the turtle sculpture behind it, the compass needle went crazy.

"You can imagine it's been pretty controversial. A lot of people don't believe it. There's even some dispute as to whether it's really even a turtle. The archaeologists who first excavated it in 1963 called it a frog. What do you think?"

I looked back at those rigid down-turned jaws. "It looks like a turtle to me. Since the guy who carved it isn't around, and isn't in a position to say, and I've come this damn far, it's a turtle."

Suddenly I wondered who the priest was who first hauled this rock down from the mountains or dragged it up from a dry riverbed and chiseled out those features. Whoever he was, he went to a great deal of effort to chisel and polish it so the magnetic lines of force were centered in the nose. Not in the eye or the side of the head or the lower jaw, but specifically in the nose.

I looked at my wife questioningly, hoping she'd have some answers or at least some observations, since she was our resident scientific skeptic, always prepared to come up with a rational approach. "You could read it either way," she said matter-of-factly. "It looks more like a turtle than a frog to me."

We wandered around Izapa for hours, until the sun was starting to set. "Well," Vince said at last, "Paul and I have to be pushing on. You're welcome to accompany us up the coast if you like."

Anne and Nikkie looked at me, awaiting my decision. A great feeling of hopelessness swept over me. I had no idea what to do next. Had we been on a collecting trip, to bring back some weird shark or speckled nudibranch, I could have coped. I could ask questions, explore new habitats, try a different kind of trap or net. But now I was lost. Certainly there was no real story here. All that happened was the rock made a needle jump. I could have predicted that before I left. The logical part of me said go home and cut off these outlandish expenses. But I couldn't do that. "I don't know what to say," I admitted. "I haven't found Turtle Mother, or a magic rock that revolves. I can try to whip this into some kind of story, but nothing happened. The truth is, we haven't learned any more about this turtle head than what you wrote in your article. So I don't know where to go from here."

"There is another possibility," Malmstrom said thoughtfully. "There's an old civilization up in the mountains about a hundred miles further up the coast called Tonalá. I understand that they have some primitive-looking animal sculptures up there and there may be turtles there too.

"I've always wanted to go there," he said, his voice turning wistful. "Several years ago I tried to climb that mountain and take readings on the pyramids. But I got hopelessly lost. We're short on time, and I've got to be in Oaxaca the day after tomorrow for an appointment. But if we get lucky and find a guide, and we could get up there and back in a day's time. I'd like to try it again and you might find a turtle rock."

Once again we piled into our vehicles and headed down the highway. Never had we spent so much time on the road, searching for God knows what.

"Well, you found a compass needle that turned," Nikkie said optimistically, as we settled down for the long drive ahead. "When you put it next to a magnetic rock, the needle turns just like the Turtle Mother does in the legend. That's something, isn't it?"

5

TURTLE ON TONALÁ MOUNTAIN

W E SPENT THE NIGHT IN THE MEXICAN town of Tapachula and the next morning drove to San Cristóbal, stopping at the New World Archaeological Foundation to look at the field notes of the archaeologists who had dug up the magnetic turtle head in Izapa. There was nothing remarkable about it in their observations. It was just another carved stone to them.

The next day we took the Pan American Highway up to Tuxtla Gutierrez, stopping at more museums, and looped back down toward the sea on a coastal highway. We drove and we drove and we drove. The terrain became more mountainous further up the coast, changing from agricultural land to dry rolling scrub to cattle land. Our destination was yet another museum at Tonalá, which we reached at midmorning. The display cases were filled with nonmagnetic figurines, pottery, monuments, and other artifacts that had been dug out of the coastal lowland sites and hauled down from the Old Church Mountain, *Iglesia Vieja*. An old man we met in front of the museum came from "up there." He said he'd be glad to take us up and show us the ruins.

Anne looked up with trepidation at the burning sun, which was already turning the air into wavering shimmers of heat, and the bare fangs of the mountain that seemed to rise forever into the sky. Everywhere the land looked parched and dried out. Here it really was the dry season. "We need horses," she pleaded. "Without one I doubt I'll be able to make it to the top. Is there any way we can rent them?"

In halting Spanish, Nikkie asked Oscar, the wiry old man, if that were an option, indicating that we would pay extra. But the old man pessimistically shook his head. "Not this late," he said in Spanish. "It could be arranged if we had just a little more notice. Tomorrow," he told us brightly, "we can rent horses from my son-in-law and start at dawn."

But Vincent couldn't wait another day. He was back on his frenetic schedule and insisted that he and Paul still had lots of archaeological sites yet to be examined, hundreds of miles to travel, and they had to be in Oaxaca the next day. And if we didn't make it to the top of Iglesia Vieja, the Old Church Mountain where the ruins of Tonalá lay today, the trip was off.

Oscar grinned affably, giving him that knowing look that said all gringos were crazy, and pointed the way. It was a long, long winding narrow path through an arsenal of bullthorn acacia and dry scrub forests. At first I was grateful to be out of the automobile and getting some real exercise. But by the time we made it to the foot of Iglesia Vieja, even though it was early afternoon, the hot dry desert heat was already beginning to dry our throats. Sweat was pouring down our faces and we had hardly started.

Oscar looked at us with such pity it made us laugh. He practically skipped along the trail, encouraging us to keep moving, getting ahead, beckoning us with his hands. He was 65 years old, but he was as spry as a young man and better at climbing mountains than most. Oscar was brown-skinned from a lifetime of being in the sun, short, wiry thin with a bushy mustache. His big sombrero and khaki pants made him look a bit like Pancho Villa, but with a warm, genuinely friendly smile. The old rancher was happy to have company. As we moved along he pointed out medicinal plants, told us the names of cows we passed and their personalities, and didn't show the slightest sign of fatigue while we sweated and clutched the rock facing, pulling ourselves up.

"It isn't far," he said encouragingly, "only a little ways up to the top—an hour at most." We continued up the incline, staying on the narrow footpath lest we be skewered by the bristling acacia thorns that grew among the sun-baked granite rocks—the only greenery to survive the overgrazed landscape.

The broiling afternoon sun rose into the center of the sky and we were still climbing. Up and up we continued, our muscles aching, our feet blistering inside our hiking boots. The air temperature was easily 100 degrees. We had been climbing for only two hours and half of our water was gone.

Long ago we had left the rain forest behind, and now there was only scrubby growth. Being Florida flatlanders, we were having a bad time of it. "Now how much farther is it to the top?" I croaked. My thirst was tormenting. For a while all I could think about was a cold beer and how good it would taste.

When Vince translated my question, Oscar grinned, took off his sombrero, and fanned his head. He pointed to the top of the first peak and responded in a cheerful deluge of Spanish.

"He says its just a little way up," panted Vince, "a half hour. But I don't think he's got any comprehension of time. Oscar is just like the Olmecs, he divides his days up from the time the sun peeks over the mountains until it sets in the sea. Anything in between like hours and minutes are only twentieth-century abstractions."

We came across a bunch of cattle grouped together, and I thought about grabbing a couple and riding them the rest of the way. But clearly the cows would have the upper hand. They gave us dirty looks and were slow to move. Oscar barked at them, and with the greatest of reluctance they moved out of our way except for one recalcitrant bull who glowered at us. But the rancher tossed a stick at him, and when it bounced off his hide, the bull gave ground.

We continued our trek. "He says there's a rancho up at the top where his daughter lives. We can rest there and be comfortable," Vincent said, breathing hard. That gave us a little hope, but we gazed up with trepidation at the jaws of the mountain above, rising up into the sky from the backbone of Central America. Ascending it in this heat seemed an impossibility. Oscar chatted on in his continuous monologue about his nine sons and three daughters here on the hillside, each managing a ranch.

By the time Anne and Nikkie climbed up to us, I was worried. My wife was soaked with sweat and breathing heavily. "I can't make it," she said collapsing, sweat beading up on her forehead. "I'm going back," she gasped. "I'm starting to get chills." Her teeth were chattering.

She rested beside a large black slab of granite that gave a bit of shade while we figured out what to do next. "You'd better do that," said the professor. "Heat prostration can be deadly. People have died out in the desert after a few hours. There's just too much stress on the body. But we've gone this far, I have to go on."

"It's just that I've been trying to get to Tonalá for such a long time," he said apologetically. "Two years ago, I tried to follow directions and ended up wandering around all over the place and getting hopelessly lost and caught in barbed wire. I had a bad case of diarrhea and was too weak. I had to turn around and go back. That's why I have to go on now. It's an important part of my work; I have to check the alignment on those temples."

"If you want to go on," Nikkie volunteered dryly, "I'll go back down with Anne, and we can wait for you. We'll get a motel, or find a place to hang out until you get back."

I wasn't sure I would last much longer than she did. What was the point? I had accomplished my mission back in Izapa: I had seen the magnetic turtle head. All Tonalá had to offer was the possibility of another zoomorphic rock that could or could not be a turtle. With my wife sick, it really made no sense to go on. Tonalá was Malmstrom's Holy Grail quest, not mine. I could follow this legend all over Mexico, and we could all die of heat stroke and still never find anything.

Off in the distance the blue horizon reached to infinity. I gave the mountains a final look as I prepared to retreat. Yet for some strange reason I felt regret, and I didn't understand why. Wanting to scrape up every bit of information possible, I turned to Vincent: "Ask Oscar if he knows anything about the sea turtles on this part of the coast." We were gazing out at the vast ocean and the string of barrier islands along the coast. I was already thinking about getting a boat and exploring them. From up here, a good thousand feet above sea level, we could see for miles, and the shoreline was a thin pale line that separated the land from the sea.

He told us that there were still a few turtles here, how he used to catch them in gill nets, and how as a child he gathered their eggs on the beaches, and how good they were. How they were an aphrodisiac and made a man strong. But it was the same dismal story as at Ayutla: the turtles had diminished to a rarity.

Just before we crossed the border into Mexico, we had taken an excursion down to a depressing little town called Puerto de Ocós, where waves pounded on a bleak, black, sandy beach. Back in Aztec times, it was known as Ayutla—land of the turtle—but the turtles had been killed out and no longer nested there. There was another Ayutla up the coast near Oaxaca, where hundreds of thousands of olive ridleys nested until the leather factory turned their hides into boots and ground their bones into fertilizer.

My mind wasn't at all prepared for what happened next. In a continuous deluge of words, familiar in tone and rhythm if not in vocabulary, the old man pointed to the mountaintop above us and I heard the word *tortugas* periodically as he spread his arms a good four feet apart. It was a big turtle. That really puzzled me; up here it made no sense.

"Good news, you'll like this!" said Malmstrom smiling, his eyes suddenly bright. "Oscar says there's a big stone carving of a turtle up there—a sea turtle! He'll show it to us."

The old man abruptly rose to his feet, beckoning us to put an end to the conversation and to keep moving. He pointed to the sun overhead and said that it was time to go, unaware that we were about to break up and go our separate ways.

"Ask him if the rock moves," I insisted, "or if there are any stories about the rock turning?"

He looked at me as if I were nuts. "It's a rock. How can a rock move?" he said incredulously.

Then he explained it all over again, that it was not a live turtle but a statue, carved by the ancients, thinking that I had not understood the first time. And when he again bent over and spread his arms four feet apart and said *la piedra*, I really perked up. That was the same span the Miskito Indians used over and over again when talking about the Turtle Mother rock.

A flash of excitement shot through me, a sudden burst of energy. Was it possible that this was the origin of the myth? But with Anne on the verge of heat stroke, I couldn't go. Vince, seeing my chagrin, said to me, "Look, I promise that if I see anything that even looks like a turtle, I'll take a compass reading and I'll take a picture of it for you."

Anne looked at me and grinned wearily. "You have no choice now, do you? I'll be okay. Nikkie will be with me to translate. And it will be a lot easier going down. We'll take our time, and we'll meet you at that little restaurant across from the museum."

Reluctantly, I agreed. I watched Anne and Nikkie descending, headed for a grove of trees and shade at the bottom. Oscar waved goodbye sorrowfully, saying that if we had only given him time to get horses, and started at a reasonable hour before the sun came up, it would have been no problem.

As they headed down the trail, we continued up, up, and up the narrow steep trail that lead to the top. The dry yellowish scrublands were monotonous, broken only by jagged black rocks that looked burned. Long ago I had stopped wasting energy taking readings on them—all were negative. The rocks seemed to go on forever, until they turned black and forbidding against the cloudless blue sky.

Oscar trotted cheerfully over the rough terrain, talking about his life up here and what it was like to scratch a living out of this bare soil. He wanted to learn English so he could become a guide and take people up here to see the ancient things.

Vince and Paul translated his running conversation, breathing heavily from the strain. I kept pace at first, then gradually fell behind. My strength was draining away from me in the heat. I felt dizzy, and the sound of cicadas buzzed in my head. My lips were parched, my breath came in deep gasps, my muscles were aching, and my feet were beginning to blister. I could hear my own panting like a dog's and still we kept moving. Oscar moved up the trail ahead of us all, chatting away. Paul, the athletic 20-year-old, was next, in good shape from mountain climbing and skiing; Malmstrom followed, huffing and puffing; and I took up the rear. The terrain was beginning to change. It was getting rougher and harder to climb; the sparse vegetation was changing rapidly into grasslands with boulders strewn about as if they had been belched out of a volcano. But Vince said that was not so. The boulders were just old igneous rock pushed up from beneath the earth—the very bones of the Old Church Mountain. When I took out my compass to take a reading, Vince shook his head. "Save your energy. It's all granite here; there's not much chance of magnetite. It's possible a few crystals might get incorporated into the stone by inclusion, but it's not likely. So far, all the magnetic statues have been basalt."

What a fool I was, coming all this way after the Holy Grail. So what if there was a stone turtle up there? There were lots of stone turtles in the world. There was the great monolithic stone turtle in the Appalachian Mountains in North Carolina, far from the sea. I first saw it just outside the little town of Murphy, and wrote about it. It looked like a Stonehenge ceremonial site: the sandstone turtle was part of a circle, with a great flat snake pressed up against its tail following it—just like the snake head in Izapa. After *Time of the Turtle* was published, the enthusiastic town fathers of Murphy got the U.S. Forest Service to send a bulldozer up the hill to scoop it up and haul it to the town square, where it sits today in front of the Murphy museum and police station for display and "safekeeping." All I had done was interfere. Without a doubt I had destroyed the turtle's astronomical alignment.

Climbing upward beneath the scorching sun, I was starting to get delirious as my brain and body dehydrated. The hideous two-headed turtle of Copan swam before my eyes with its monstrous claws and devilish skulls. The archeologists left that one in place, and it sat in the middle of a ball court, on a precise north-south alignment. In Uxmal, Mexico, a whole temple was devoted to the turtle. Why was I killing myself to see yet another carving of a turtle?

Voices from the past came to me as I fought with myself to take only the tiniest sip from my diminishing canteen of water, voices of villagers in Costa Rica: "No mon . . . dat is stories. Dat is a lie. I have hunted de whole woods of Tortuguero, and I nevah see dis rock! History have it dat de rock turn, but I nevah see it."

I kept moving, clutching onto rocks and shrubs, pulling myself up the trail, seeing the three men getting further and further up the slope, wondering if I'd ever catch up.

Archie Carr's voice admonished: "Don't go up that mountain looking for a stupid revolving stone, because it doesn't exist!" My heart was pounding. I was hyperventilating to the rhythm, "doesn't exist . . . doesn't exist."

Chunks of rocks protruded from the worn cattle trail. I stumbled over every one of them, my eyes stinging from sweat. I leaned against a rock to keep from collapsing, stealing a rest. Reality and fantasy merged.

"Well, what do you have to say about that!" I demanded of the renowned professor, holding up Vincent Malmstrom's paper and the photograph of the magnetic turtle head. Now I was back in Gainesville, at the University of Florida, sitting in Dr. Archie Carr's cramped little office amid the great clutter of papers, books, and mountains of correspondence. Baby green turtles flippered about and floated in the glass aquarium.

"It's a fantastic piece of archaeology," he conceded warily, growing weary of this crackpot, who continued to intrude into his life with this ridiculous legend. "Look, Jack, I'm a zoologist," he said defensively. "This isn't my field of discipline. My whole life has been studying the biology of reptiles—not their mythology. I can't help you!" His words echoed through the hollows of my mind. "I don't know who can."

No one can. It was my cross, I had to go on. There was something more powerful than my weakness, something drawing me like a magnet to the myth, up the mountain. The rock face above was slowly growing larger, and the winding trail went on and on and on. The climb was growing steeper. I watched my comrades disappearing up the slope. It was quiet now, and I was alone, feeling the dry winds gusting off the sea, listening to the buzzing of insects, and watching the sun god expanding in the sky into a white heat.

Suddenly a large black cow came along, moving slowly up the trail. It stopped and looked at me as I sat there, breathing deeply. The heat and dehydration had burned away any higher functions of my oversized, much-too-complex human brain. At that moment in time we were equals. If anything, the cow was my superior—far better able to cope with this harsh environment than I.

No longer a human, I was just another animal living and dying on this earth, nothing more, nothing less. We stared at each other for a long time, and then something happened. The cow gave me a deep, penetrating look that transgressed the boundaries between our species and penetrated into my medulla, the primitive part of my brain that was

buried somewhere beneath the part that wrote books and listened to music and schemed up expeditions and turned the world upside down to satiate its ego. The cow gazed into my soul. If I were a Buddhist, I would have called it a moment of enlightenment. Then I heard her hoofs plodding over the dried, baked clay of the Old Church Mountain and saw her heading up the slope.

I got to my feet again and continued on, knowing that never again would I be able to view other forms of life from my lofty human perch. Suddenly I understood the Olmec carvings of animals, and their zoolatry. We were all living things, propelled and animated by the same life force, whatever it was, all trying to survive.

Ten minutes later I caught up with Vince, who had also decided to rest. We sat next to a small mountain stream in numbed weariness. Its water flowed by, but we dared not drink—with all the cattle walking around and the dried black cow pies baking in the sun, giving off a pungent odor, that was out of the question. The only thing that could make sunstroke worse would be a case of dysentery. We splashed some on our hair and faces, washing away the sweat.

Oscar had stopped to wait for us. The old man was highly amused at my fatigue. He pounded himself proudly on the chest and said encouragingly, "I am sixty-five years old. If an old man like me can make it, you certainly can."

He moved in front of us, only once in a great while taking a sip from the canteen, swinging his machete, hacking away at the bullthorn acacia that grew stubbornly out from between the rocks. An hour later we crossed into a cow pasture, ascended another ridge. We burst through a picket fence with barbed wire and finally made it to a little shack where Oscar's daughter, husband, and two small children lived. It was a simple adobe hut with clay baked walls and a thatched roof. A cow, lying in the shade with its newborn calf, gave me a dirty look as I approached, and the woman told me to keep my distance.

I didn't have to be asked twice. We sat on benches under a thatched roof, and the wiry old grandfather talked about the man who owned all this land. He spent his entire life riding on trains, and that he thought was odd. Oscar's sons and daughters tended cattle for the wealthy absentee landlord and scratched out a living with their goats, turkeys, and chickens. They cut brush and hauled it down to the city to sell for firewood.

Our rest over, we trod along the dusty trail, stepping over growing numbers of sun-baked piles of cow dung around and on top of the rocks that thrust up in the middle of the trail. A half hour later, we passed through some mysterious stone and earthen walls. Suddenly the scenery changed. I felt a mystical, overbearing force in the mountain rising higher before us. Vince wiped the sweat from his forehead and looked around at the grassy ridge. His voice was awed. "We've just come into a sacred area. Don't ask me how I know, but I can feel it. I've looked at so many Mayan sites—I just know it. It's not rational or scientific, but that's how I found so many of these ceremonial sites in Central America and in Europe to be aligned to the summer or winter solstice."

The terrain looked as if it had been landscaped: all sorts of shade trees formed an oasis. Malmstrom was right—it was a paradise up here. We walked on, suddenly moving faster as if some new strange energy had entered our tired bodies. Vince puzzled over the ruined stone gates, speculating that they were some sort of fortification—but fortification against whom? Struggling several hundred feet farther up the steep incline, we came upon the ruins of a temple. To me, they were more impressive than anything I had seen in Central America. Hundreds of huge granite slabs, each weighing a ton, had been laid down to form a massive wall that stretched for two hundred feet. Rising up from the brush on the high ridge overlooking the sea, in the shadow of the central highlands, it looked like what it was, a truly wild place where the inhabitants had walked off a millennium ago.

The cracks between those masterfully carved blocks bristled with grasses and bushes that had managed to squeeze into the soil and take root through time, but most of the walls were intact. These rectangular shapes were so well fitted that over centuries only a very few trees had been able to take root and push them apart.

Vince gazed upon the great structures with wonder. "It's hard enough to work in limestone, and these guys were working in granite. In Sweden, Vermont, and Georgia they have a major industry for granite, using huge rock saws to cut it up. And two thousand years ago they were building massive temples out of it. Look how polished it is, how straight and refined. How did they do it?"

Each of the slabs measured eight feet by two feet by one foot thick, each perfectly honed granite block weighing two and a half tons. There were hundreds of them. "Can you imagine them struggling with two-and-a-half-ton blocks," Vince said, "putting them into position way up here? They must have been here for a long, long time to have built all that. And they say these were primitive men," he said with a sardonic laugh. "It was a tour de force to maneuver these blocks."

An awesome presence hung in the air. What a sight, what a spectacular view it was from the top. Huge rounded and egg-shaped boulders were scattered on precipices, looking as if they might go tumbling down with the next breath of wind. The smaller ones weighed a mere 50 tons, the biggest ones between 150 and 200 tons. "How did they get those up here?" I wondered aloud.

"They didn't," Vince said. "They're natural. They're shaped by weathering, by rain and winds. It's called exfoliation. It takes hundreds of thousands of years—perhaps millions—to round them down. The rain trickles down into the grains of granite rocks and it flakes off in a rounded form. You see rocks like this all over the place in the foothills and in the mountains. I often think these rounded, natural-formed boulders might have been the prototype of the Olmec heads. Maybe they saw faces in them and were inspired to build the giant heads. All they had to do was scratch two eyes, a nose, and a mouth in it."

But to me, they didn't look like ordinary weathered stones. They looked as if some incredible force had shaped and polished them into elliptical chicken eggs and artfully placed them on a rock ledge. Did the ancients build their sacred temples up here so they could be next to these incredible boulders, which emanated power? I wondered. Why did they build up here anyway, in this isolated place that was nothing but wild scrub land? Where did their water and food come from? It was a great mystery. It was obviously a hard place to reach, and the walls surrounding the temple seemed like some sort of fortification, yet at the same time it seemed like a religious temple or perhaps an observatory.

A refreshing cool breeze swept through the mountains, making the prairie grass ripple in the breeze and cooling away our sweat. The Old Church Mountain overlooked the distant mountains and the Tehuantepec gap where the fronts swept down from North America and funneled through from the Pacific to the Caribbean coast.

"This is what makes me think I'm right, that the antecedents of the Olmecs began right here on the Pacific coast," Vince said after he rested. "They had to go through the gap; it's ten to fifteen miles wide, and it goes all the way across Mexico. Everywhere else you have to go through the mountains, walking barefooted up in the thorn forests. The Olmecs on the Gulf coast were thought to be the best carvers of jade. But where did they get the practice? There isn't any jade on the Atlantic coast; it all came from the Pacific."

The air was so clear, we could easily see out 30 miles, affording a spacious view of the lagoon. We could see the barrier islands, a huge sand bar stretching out parallel to the shoreline, and sunlight glimmering in the flat afternoon sea. You'd have to think about the sea constantly, if you lived up here—it stretches out and blends with the sky.

If there had been trans-Pacific migration, the people who lived here must have looked at that vast ocean and thought about home, or, if not, wondered what lay on the other side. Chances are, we'll never know which. Someday I knew I would have to cross the Pacific and see if the Turtle Mother legend existed on some distant shore.

In a hushed silence, we explored the long-abandoned ceremonial site. Monuments and carved boulders were everywhere, overgrown with lichens. Primitive, crudely carved figures and barely visible petroglyphs were scattered about, presenting a contrast to the huge, impeccably finished polished temple walls.

"This is really very mysterious," declared Vincent, looking around at the crudely carved figures. "It doesn't make any sense the way the pyramid facings and stone works are so incredibly precisely fitted and polished, and the statues are so crude, so rudimentary. It looks as if each had been done by two entirely different people superimposed upon each other."

This was clearly a culture that worshipped animals. There were carvings of birds, snakes, and jaguars as well as humans, all crudely rendered. What a contrast to the Mayans who spent so much time on art, carving their motifs with intricate detail and flourish.

As we rested in the shade of a tree, watching a leaf-cutter ant crawling along the pyramid wall carrying a piece of green foliage, it occurred to me that zoolatry was nothing new to me. Had I not spent a lifetime worshipping animals, studying them, collecting them for museums and laboratories so others could venerate them? And did I not sacrifice my energies, labors, and peace of mind to preserve their habitats in environmental conflicts, trying to save the bay, stop the cutting of trees, fight the wanton destruction from oil spills, and prevent the drowning of turtles? And it wasn't just me. Our whole society seemed to be concerned with problems such as endangered species, and our public television stations broadcast nature programs ad nauseum.

"All right, Paul," the professor breathed heavily, interrupting my thoughts, "we've come all this way, now let's go to work." Malmstrom rose to his feet, and he and Paul began taking alignments on the pyramids and walls. They didn't seem to align to anything.

I remained collapsed on the ground, my muscles torn and raw, and watched them take sightings on the pyramid walls with their compasses, still not totally clear on what they were doing.

Vince had spent years checking the astronomical alignments of every structure he came upon, trying to learn more about the strange 260-day ritual cycle. He found that whole cities were oriented according to the position of the sun when it passed overhead in Izapa on August 13. He believed that the Mayan concept of time and creation began at the Izapa ceremonial site. Teotihuacan, the biggest pre-Columbian city in the New World; the main doorway of the observatory at Chichén Itzá; temples at Tikal and Edzná—virtually every Mayan known site has structures with the same astronomical alignment.

Tired of watching them measuring, I rose to my feet and wet my parched throat, ready to see the object of my quest. "Where is the turtle?"

Vince translated my question, and Oscar pointed to yet another mountain saying it was just up ahead, across the meadow and over the next peak. Not far. He said the turtle was at a separate site, an earlier civilization, just over the rise, no more than 15 minutes away.

"Fifteen minutes?" I wailed. "His fifteen minutes!" I was shattered. I could hardly go another step.

The old man laughed, seeing my reaction. "What time is it? I bet it's eleven-thirty?" I glanced at my watch, it was almost five.

When Vince finished his measurements, it took everything I had to pick up and push my worn body another step. But somehow I kept going, trudging past the carvings, the immense blocks of stones covered with lichens, and the great rounded uncarved boulders that had a tremendous energizing power about them.

In a numbed daze, I stumbled forward, and up the grassy hill we went. It was cooler; the sun had dropped down lower in the sky. An hour later we arrived at a large earthen temple mound about 20 feet tall, with stones set in earth. Down below at its foot, amid a grove of trees, was the turtle altar.

Next to this great mound of dirt and stone boulders that were scattered throughout the area was the carved turtle. Worn down with age and weather, it was a round flat relief statue four and a half feet long, etched out of a 15-inch-thick black stone. Its human head with Oriental eyes looked out over the blue Pacific Ocean. But there was no question it was a "turtle of the sea," with flippers and a tapered shell, so faded that we could barely make out the details, even though someone long ago had delineated them with chalk marks. Oscar stood there tracing with his fingers the flippers, the rear paddles, the carapace.

"They knew the sea turtle," said Vince, "whoever drew this. It's more of a petroglyph than an actual statue." He looked around at the mounds, and the stela behind it of a large human foot. "And the turtle sits in the center. It must have been an altar."

That foot looked familiar. I remembered seeing a large carved foot in Izapa, not far from the turtle head. The foot had something to do with Buddhist mythology also, or the Taoist perhaps. I remembered the saying, "A journey of a thousand miles begins with a single step." Somehow there was an association, a forgotten legend here also.

Not far away there was another petroglyph of a big serpent, associated with the turtle perhaps like the snake head in Izapa, or like the one I had seen in North Carolina. "This appears to be a viper," Vince conjectured, "and these are stars around it. Probably that's what your turtle is, an astronomical figure. What we now call the 'Gemini constellation' the Mayans used to call the 'turtle stars.'"

"Gemini? Like the magnetic twins in El Baúl?" I chortled, seeing another connection, or making one up.

"Could be," he said distractedly as he traced out the celestial markings—diamond shapes depicting stars. The legend, whatever it was, lived on.

The petroglyph stone turtle that sat on the mountain was positioned at the base of the man-made earthen mound and did not overlook anything in particular. But when I ascended the top mound I could see the world. There were man-made mounds all around it. I was overwhelmed by their mystery. Why would these people climb to the mountaintop and then build a hill?

The moment of truth had come. I pulled out my compass hoping I would see the needle spin off the dial.

The professor said softly, "I don't want to disappoint you, but you're wasting your time. This rock isn't basalt, it's the same granite as everything else around here. It can't possibly be magnetic."

"But look how black it is," I croaked, my throat dry, hell-determined to try, if it were the last thing I did.

"Doesn't matter," he said, shaking his head. "You can't go by color. You have to have volcanic rock to be magnetic. This is granite, igneous rock."

He was right, of course; the needle stayed in its fixed position. Resting on my hands and knees, I ran the compass all the way around the flat block of stone, two and three times, and still nothing happened. A great feeling of disappointment came over me and I sat heavily on the turtle stone.

"Well that's that," I said wearily. "When you go in search of the Holy Grail, you're bound to run out of time, energy, and money."

"What did you expect?" Paul asked sympathetically, after taking a long drink from his canteen.

"I don't know," I replied vaguely, shaking my head. "I sort of had this vision of climbing up a mountain and seeing a great stone turtle up there, turning above the landscape. I don't know what I expected."

"You found a stone turtle on top of a mountain," Malmstrom's student assistant said encouragingly. "That's better than no turtle at all. And it is a sea turtle. That fits part of the legend, doesn't it?"

"Yes," I concluded, "I did find a stone turtle on a mountain. And yes, I saw your magnetic turtle head, and the magnetic Fat Boy statues. But I still don't know what any of this means, or why I'm doing it."

"You'll never know what it means, and you'll probably never solve the Turtle Mother myth to your satisfaction," Vince interjected. "You may never put it all together, because most of the pieces are lost. But you'll probably keep on trying, just like I keep following the sun."

I knew he was right. I would probably never find out why they carved that turtle head in Izapa with a magnetic nose. The weak magnetic field in a rock couldn't influence the behavior of turtles at sea in any way, or could it? Then I thought about the aborigines of northern Australia where there was an individual chosen to perform certain rites and ceremonies to keep the turtles abundant and healthy. He was called "the keeper of the turtles." Dr. Colin Limpus, the country's foremost sea turtle biologist, said the aborigines piled up cobbles and built effigies of turtles and depicted them in rock art to maintain their abundance. The rituals were kept strictly secret, and whites were not privileged to know about them. The keeper was not allowed to kill turtles nor eat turtle meat, although he participated in the hunts. It was an inherited position and had something to do with the family totem. At least three different species were portrayed in the piled-up rocks, including a hawksbill.

Somehow by piling up these cobbles in the shape of a turtle and communing with spirits, the aborigines knew how to influence the turtles' behavior. Perhaps this stone turtle in Tonalá, and the magnetic turtle head in Izapa tapped into those most ancient rituals which provided food and well-being for the community. I hadn't found Turtle Mother, or had I? There was something here, a clue, and I wasn't sure it didn't relate to the aborigines of Australia or the mysterious turtle mountain in Costa Rica.

Then words came back to me from afar, from an old, old man named Bertie Downs in Tortuguero, Costa Rica, when I had asked him about the origins of the Turtle Mother legend: "Well dat was de belief of dose ancient peoples who had it dat way from de creation of time!"

COSTA RICA—1984 AND 1988

6

RETURN TO TORTUGUERO

ONCE MORE I WAS HEADED FOR CENTRAL America—this time to Costa Rica to collect fish for the New York Aquarium and once again delve into the Turtle Mother legend. At least this time, it wasn't my sole focus, as it had been when I climbed the mountain at Tonalá.

Hurrying from one building to another in the sprawling Miami airport, I passed a huge drainage ditch just outside Concourse "H." It passed beneath the guts of the air terminal at this point and looked as if it probably contained some of the most polluted water on the planet. Building an airport on top of what was once a tributary of the Little Miami River was no doubt a great engineering feat.

With each rain, waters carrying oil and chemicals rushed through sewer grates, spilling thousands of gallons of pollution from one of the busiest airports in the world into the concrete-lined ditch. Yet what a contradiction: even in my haste I could tell it was full of life.

Something told me to stop and look around even though my plane was leaving in an hour. That gave me 15 minutes to look around. I pushed through an unlocked door marked "Do Not Enter" and there I was, next to the chain-link fence, looking down at this great slash of water that ran around the perimeter of the airport.

Out on the runway in the bright sunlight, jet engines shrieked. Overhead the skies shook and rumbled with planes taking off and arriving. The air reeked of jet fuel, stinging my eyes as it was carried along by the warm summer Florida breeze—but the ditch was alive.

Life is tough. In the old battle between rocks and roots, plants take root on rock facings and grow among rocky streams. Stubbornly, the rootlets and tubers, thistles, and grasses hung on in the ditch, growing down through an inch or less of oily dirt. In some places there were even delicate ferns popping out of the drainage pipes that spilled into the ditch from the runway. And I cheered for them as I stared down at the unpleasant-looking, oily soup eight feet down that inched slowly by on its eventual trip to pollute the ocean, and saw ripples and shapes of things down below.

Drab little mosquitofish were everywhere in the grasses that edged the muddy walls. There were thousands of them, perhaps millions. They run the whole length of the canal, never venturing out into the open, green-pea soup of the water of the channel. For all its pollution, this ditch continued to amaze me. There was a small green night heron, hidden in the overhanging vegetation, poised and waiting for fish. There was something sneaky about this bird, the way it crouched low to the ground, its head bouncing on its long neck as it moved forward with fixed concentration on its prey. This trip I was looking at live, flesh-and-blood animals, not their renditions in ancient sculpted stones, and yet there seemed to be a sameness between them.

Still as death, the heron waited, studying the black lizard crawling up the wall. Quick as death, it stepped forward and snatched it up with its bill. From my hiding place above, behind the chain-link fence, I saw the eager snapping of jaws pulling the heron's head back and watched the lizard disappearing down its throat, the tail and legs all a-wiggle. The heron flew off in triumph.

The shy endangered wood stork might become extinct, but the crow will hang on. The great blue heron that learns to take fish out of your hand in a city lake or a dredged-up canal will survive, while others of its kind will die of nervousness.

Glancing over my shoulder, expecting to see guards running after me, I drew closer. A turtle baking in the hot afternoon sun on a culvert pipe saw me and plunged into the ditch. Another one floated on the green eutrophic water, its shell trailing filamentous green algae that looked like dirty, unkempt hair. Another one popped up, saw me, freaked out, and rocketed down into murky oblivion.

As I pushed back into the terminal, I realized that the ditch was a symbol of my lack of understanding, the upturning of my assumptions about life, of how and where we fit into the universe, and the dooms-day attitude of environmentalists—myself included. We could not create the water, and we could not destroy the life force, whatever that was, not all of it. Life evolved in a harsh world, in sulfurous slime, and we'll never be able to exterminate all life, probably not even our own.

Despite everything our technology could do to obliterate it, ditches, canals, disturbed lands and waters still seethed with life among the garbage and the flowers, waiting, hiding, to reseed the world of asphalt when the time comes, like white blood cells coming forth to heal a wound.

I hurried on to catch my flight with a nagging feeling that somehow this ditch was an important part of my search for Turtle Mother. I wasn't sure how, but I thought it must have to do with rediscovering the ancient Turtle Mother religion and the veneration of nature. The answers to these sorts of quests are always right under our noses. We just don't recognize them for what they are.

I joined Nixon Griffis, Nikkie's father, and his friend Cary Phillips at the gate. It had been some months since I had seen them in New York, and while waiting in line we discussed the forthcoming expedition and our plans to collect tarpon and other creatures for the New York Aquarium. As we took off, I looked down on the concrete landscape of Miami that had once been barrier islands, mangrove swamps, and the Everglades—that vast flowing river of grass—now so diminished and polluted. Then, several hours later, I was gazing down at Costa Rica's endless agricultural fields that had once been rain forests. It was clear that the creatures who do survive are being increasingly banished to the drainage ditches, unplowable creeks, and ravines, forgotten or inaccessible to people.

And there the Turtle Mother, or life force, waits, adapting and evolving life, spreading seeds across the landscape like white blood corpuscles rushing to an infection, remaining there in spite of our oblivious efforts until it is time for her to reign again. When humanity learns to live in balance with nature rather than pushing it forever backwards, she will emerge from the cave. Legend says that the Turtle Mother rock vanished from the coast of Nicaragua after being harassed and reappeared in Tortuguero, where it was seen for a time before disappearing into a cave on the mountain Cerro Tortuguero. The legend says that only when humankind comes to its senses will the rock return. Until then she works in our minds and psyches against the undertow of destruction, of insatiable, uncaring consumption. Slowly she works as the planet dies around her, the trees fall in the rain forests, and the turtle blood gushes on the beaches.

We spent the night in San José where I caught a taxi to the National Museum, hoping to find a clue about the origins of the Turtle Mother myth. Nothing came to mind as I studied the intricate gold jewelry, the complex stone works, and ornate pottery, but I found myself intrigued by great mystical granite spheres that had been carved by the ancient Indians. What were they?

The next morning we took off in a small chartered plane headed for the Caribbean beaches of Tortuguero, where the green turtles nested near the mountain that people said drew the turtles to the shore. Rain pelted down against the windshield, and the plane jerked spasmodically in the crosswinds. I asked the pilot if we could circle so I could get a good look at the mountain, Cerro Tortuguero, but he shook his head tensely and pointed to the storm clouds that were closing in on us. The ride had been rough, with heavy pockets of turbulence that tossed the aircraft around like a toy.

We were overloaded with all the gear we had brought for fish collecting. So I leaned against my seat belt, my eyes desperately roving the scenery below, trying to soak up every bit of Cerro Tortuguero as we spiraled our way to the ground. Catching a 15-second glimpse, I noticed that this 550-foot seaside hill that everyone called "The Mountain" wasn't all one lump. There was another, much smaller rise separated from the larger one by a few hundred feet at the foot of the jungle. And during that fleeting glimpse, before it vanished from my field of vision, I thought it looked like a big rock, sitting there all by itself. Was that Turtle Mother? The engine roared, we dropped just above the waves, and then bounced along the grass strip of the closed turtle station.

We got out of the cramped aircraft and stood looking at one of the most godforsaken, desolate beaches in the world. As if dropped on an alien planet, we stood on the grassy runway, looking at the ocean and the run-down bungalow where Archie Carr and the Caribbean Conservation Corporation did their sea turtle research. It was never calm there, the sea was always rough, with violent undertows, and enormous bull sharks and hammerheads roamed just outside the breakers. No one swam there.

It was some of the roughest waters in the Caribbean, an endless, pounding, angry roar thundering up on the black volcanic sands. It was a sound that never ceased, an energy that never quit, a reverberation that could be heard for miles. Perhaps that was one of the reasons the green sea turtles came by the thousands to lay their eggs each year— they could hear the low-frequency sounds hundreds of miles away. The whole coast looked harsh; great tangles of sharp logs and sticks were piled up on the beach and matted with rotting hyacinths flushed out of the river swamps.

The official purpose of our trip was to collect small tarpon and, if we got lucky, a sawfish for the New York Aquarium. Nixon, a trustee of the New York Zoological Society, was also here to see if the station could be used for eco-tourism, which was an ever-growing market. But he was aware of my unofficial, but never-ending, other agenda.

"Where's Turtle Mother? I thought she'd be waiting for us." He grinned.

I shrugged. "That's what I'm going to find out."

For weeks, between planning the trip and ordering supplies, I had talked about my unfinished business concerning this persistent Miskito Indian legend. This trip I was going to solve the great mystery. How, I wasn't sure.

There wasn't time to think about this vestige of a legend. The pilot wanted to be out of there—and now. The weather was closing in, and he was busy snatching out our gear and stashing it on the runway. He pointed to the great wall of clouds moving across the ocean toward us. "I must get back quick, or I will have to stay here all night."

With a great roar the plane taxied to the end of the grassy strip, spun around, and zoomed down the beach. The rain pelted down, soaking the groceries, liquor, and stores that had been flown in from San José for the Tortuga Lodge across the lagoon, where we were going to stay.

We lugged our gear over to the now-abandoned turtle station, known as Casa Verde because of its faded green paint. It was obvious that the place needed a lot of fixing up before it would be ready for tourists. Some of the screens were out, and small piles of termite dust lay on the floor. The paint had faded, turning gray and powdery, and there was a loneliness about the place. But soon it would be spring, and staff and volunteers would be arriving to clean the place up and get ready for the turtles that would arrive in June. When I first came here in 1975, what a busy spot this was during the turtle nesting season. In the mornings, graduate students and volunteers would be busily transcribing data from their soggy notebooks from the previous night's beach walks in the drenching rain. Sleeping by day, working by night, they tagged every turtle that came ashore. Sometimes, during the dinners before patrol, they talked about how many turtles they tagged or measured, or about some interesting observation that had occurred, or Archie and his wife Margie would discourse on some scientific aspect of their work. Then when darkness came, it was time to go to work again, hiking the beach. A memory flashed through my mind of the big green turtles heaving their way out of the fiery surf amid the crashing waves breaking into foam, crawling up the beach through the darkness like large, smooth rocks glistening with reflected starlight.

I thought how different this beach had looked when it was torn up with tracks, serrated trails from turtles that made their way up the slope to nest, or changed their minds and retreated, leaving the sign of their

presence behind. And how the fine, glittering black sand was strewn with leathery white eggshells when the little turtles emerged from their nests in the fall or when predators scooped away the heavy layers of sand for a tasty meal, leaving the eggshells behind.

But this was January, months before the green turtles came ashore to nest. The first green turtles would be arriving in April, their numbers would peak in July and August, and a few individuals would nest throughout October. I gazed out over the vast expanse of the rolling Caribbean horizon; there were no boats, no turtle fishermen in skiffs as there had been before, waiting to harpoon the coupled pairs of green turtles as they rode the waves.

It was just as well. I didn't want to be distracted by living green turtles and their biology. I had come to explore the mountain and its geology and hopefully catch small tarpon, rare crabs, and other creatures for the New York Aquarium, while I focused on the myth.

"Hurry up, Jack," yelled Nixon. "The rain's coming." His voice jerked me back into the present. We started to lug our gear over to the turtle station when two helpers from the lodge showed up. The two black men, who introduced themselves as Fernando and John from the Tortuga Lodge, helped us unload the gill net, supplies, equipment, and luggage on the grassy strip and carry it across the narrow barrier strip of land to their waiting boat in the lagoon.

As we lugged the gear over the barrier beach, through a narrow trail that fed through the broad waxy-leafed buttonwood trees to the lagoon side where the boat waited, I asked them about Bertie Downs, the old man who had first told me about the magic turning rock in the shape of a turtle.

"He dead," John said sorrowfully. "Two robber men come up de beach, all de way from Panama dey say, and dey kill him last year. It was terrible thing, dey torture him bad to get his money don't you know. He say he don't have any money, but dey kill him anyway." It was a great shock, for Bertie had been a fixture in the little village of Tortuguero.

"Did they catch whoever did it?" I asked, feeling sick.

"Oh yeah, dey cotch 'em, and hang 'em.'"

The bad news cast a pall over my return to Tortuguero. Bertie didn't deserve such treatment. Changing the subject, I asked them if they worked for the Caribbean Conservation Corporation—most people in the village did. Over the years, the village had seen the turtle factories spring up, harvesting the green turtles almost to extinction. It had witnessed the schemes of numerous exploitive businessmen, such as the copra farmers who stripped the timber out of the rain forests and left in debt and bankrupt. Year after year, the CCC paid the villagers to patrol the beach at night and help tag turtles as they came ashore.

Fernando reluctantly ventured that they were involved in the tagging project and worked at the turtle station with Archie Carr's students when the season was on. But right now they worked for the German, Axel Maynard, who ran the Green Turtle Lodge where we were going to stay. They didn't have much else to say. They seemed tense, almost unfriendly. I remembered that there was a war going on in Nicaragua, and refugees were spilling over the border, piling into the village. That changed things. When I had been here in 1975, Tortuguero was a friendly place.

Nevertheless, as we carried our gear to the boat, I brought up the subject of Turtle Mother, telling Fernando that that was one of the main reasons I had come.

That caused Fernando to laugh, so that he looked more relaxed for a moment. "I heard dis story," he scoffed, "but it is not so. There's no rock here like dat!" He then lapsed back into silence and said nothing further about it.

I turned my head to John, the younger, shyer man, "How about you, do you know?"

He shrugged. "No mon, I don't know."

Perhaps Turtle Mother was an embarrassment, I thought. Perhaps Fernando's rigid denial came from so many years of working with Archie Carr, watching scientists and graduate students walking up and down the beaches with clipboards and notebooks, systematically and methodically measuring and tagging sea turtles, using orthodox scientific method that made the very idea of a moving rock seem preposterous.

Or perhaps it was my idea that was preposterous, I thought, lugging a big styrofoam box packed with the gill net. Perhaps Archie Carr was right: there really is no rock. He never saw the rock, nor did the hundred scientists and graduate students who worked there over the years, and God knows it's a small enough place, with little enough to do on that barrier beach, isolated from the rest of the world. If it were there, with his acute powers of observation, he would have seen it. However, he never dismissed the idea that the mountain had something to do with the turtles coming there. In 1967 he wrote in his book, *So Excellent a Fishe:*

> It is Cerro, the local legend says, that draws in the green turtles each July from all over the Caribbean. It is just folklore, of course, that wild notion about the mountain being a beacon for migrating turtles. But I have spent ten years looking for a better theory to explain how they find the place, so I never argue the point.

Heading toward the lodge, we puttered up the winding river, the afternoon sun suddenly in our eyes as the clouds shifted away from us, rounding the shore where Cerro Tortuguero loomed and mounded up like the back of a colossal tortoise—a shaggy tortoise covered with tropical rain forest. It didn't look like a mountain, or even a volcano. It looked more like an ancient pyramid. Its faces dropped off sharply, more like walls than slopes. It was by no means symmetrical, as one expects a mountain to be. The eastern side, facing the Tortuguero River, looked as if someone had sheered it away with a butter knife, leaving a wall-like facing, and two other sides angled down sharply and steeply to the jungle below. Only the front side, facing the lagoon and ocean, was sloped and that appeared so broad and expansive that it favored the great ramp of a Mayan pyramid. The only possible access would be from this side.

If this had been a pyramid, as some people claimed, it would be the only one in Costa Rica. The Indians did not build grandiose stone structures as their Mayan neighbors did in what we now call Guatemala, Mexico, and Belize. The few geologists who casually looked at it speculated that Cerro Tortuguero was an old cinder cone, the eroded core of a volcano that had blasted up through a weak spot in the earth's crust—a geological anomaly something like Stone Mountain in Georgia, which rises up amid the flatland, miles from the foothills of the Smoky Mountains.

Although geologists said that this volcanic intrusion thrust up through the earth's mantle was completely natural, I couldn't take my eyes away from those suspicious steep cliffs that sheered away down to the water. For a while I thought it might be a man-made excavated pyramid, but it was much too large for that. The largest pyramids in Mexico are less than 300 feet. The mountain was double that, which isn't saying much for a mountain. Some of the scientific papers written about the area described it in passing as a "seaside hill." But I couldn't take my eyes away from that mountain and the steep cliffs that fell away down to the water.

Aside from being a place to take occasional tourists, the mountain itself held very little importance for the villagers. Tortuguero was really just a clutter of huts, a few bars, an inn, and a sort of restaurant. Life here was a constant struggle for subsistence. The little scientific Caribbean Conservation Corporation, with its own ongoing precarious financial dilemmas, was the single long-range employer. The villagers, about a hundred Latinos, Miskito Indians and Creole Blacks descended from shipwrecked slaves, scratched out a bare living from the American and European sports fishermen who came in search of tarpon and snook, sharks and sawfish. Natural history groups also piled in from time to time to see the turtle beaches and explore the National Park.

We arrived at the Tortuga Lodge. I thought, if Turtle Mother is on the mountain, she is hiding deeper in the cave and farther out of reach than ever before. Perhaps deeper than in the days when the slaughter was going full tilt, and green turtles were being carved up for a few pounds of calipee, the cartilaginous part of the belly shell that's boiled into soup. For here nature had been supplanted, the land tamed, and this resort with its quaint wooden villas, neatly trimmed grass lawns, manicured chicken palms, with all the conveniences of a restaurant and bar, dripped opulence. Carved out of the rain forests, it was a playground for wealthy visitors from the United States, Germany, and other countries, who spent thousands to catch tarpon—a fish they couldn't possibly eat—and lounged about in wooden rocking chairs, enjoying their fantasies.

And redevelopment was coming. The Tortuga Lodge, the proprietor told us, was just the beginning. More resorts were being built, and soon it would be one big tourist city. Not far off, the utility company was stringing power lines, clearing right of way, and building a road. He said that with a four-wheel-drive vehicle, you could now drive to within 15 miles of Tortuguero instead of coming up the canal by boat or having to fly in. The remoteness was vanishing,

And Cerro Tortuguero, the wild mountain that rose above it all, was under consideration by a group of businessmen as the proposed site of a grand seaside hotel. In the envisioned redevelopment scheme, it would be flattened and the hotel perched on top, with even bigger restaurants and bars, and yet another green lawn where attractive women wearing swimsuits could sit beside a yet another swimming pool, worship Ra, the sun god, and read. And at night, they could go for turtle walks to watch these ancient reptiles come ashore.

The palms rattled in the artfully thatched roof of the lodge, and the breeze blew down about the mountain, and at that moment there was no Turtle Mother. Even though we were only a half mile away from the mountain, the legend seemed more distant than ever. I thought that here Turtle Mother was really just a wisp, a vapor, an old, old story—one that I'd largely perpetuated through my books.

Talking with Nixon, Cary, and other guests about my quest, Turtle Mother became a dinner table conversation piece, a bizarre curiosity far removed from the lives of most of the people who frequented Tortuga Lodge. To feel superior to these other people was being an ass. If I lived in a mud hut, was lean, balanced, and in control of my life and destiny, I could feel superior, but probably wouldn't. I was born into a society with too much to eat, while across the lagoon, malnourished refugees, Creoles and Indians were living in the shambles of an overcrowded village, overflowing with displaced refugees from the war in neighboring Nicaragua.

As I listened to the idle chatter of people killing time in the bar, clustered around the wealthy young German who held court like a sovereign as he mixed their drinks, and as I watched the pilgrims working so hard to be part of the "in crowd," I suddenly realized how ephemeral all this was, and that Turtle Mother was there on the mountain hiding until it was her time to return.

The earth spirit I sought, the Turtle Mother, was a manifestation of the great Mother Earth beneath our feet, who is the giver of life.

Because of humanity's abuses of the earth, smashing down the rain forests and turning them into pesticide- and herbicide-drenched croplands and grazing grounds for cattle, and the slaughter of thousands of nesting turtles on the beaches, Turtle Mother, this enchanted rock, withdrew into the cave—roughly 50 years ago according to the legend.

With her retreat came the reduction of the evolutionary gene pool, the steady decline of butterflies, reptiles, amphibians, songbirds, and rare mammals along with the reduction of native vegetation and breakdown of ecosystems around the world. As global biodiversity shrinks, the list of endangered species continues to grow. The oceans are stripped of fish from overharvesting and pollution, and the misfortunes of war, famines, floods, droughts, colossal hurricanes, blizzards, and plagues relentlessly rain down on humanity. Is there cause and effect here? Have the parallel lines of myth and reality finally crossed? Only when human beings come to their senses, control their population, and try to live in balance with nature will the Turtle Mother rock reemerge from the cave and life spring up from the ditches and replenish the land.

Archie Carr had become exasperated at my persistence in focusing on this legend. I could hear his high-pitched, forceful voice over the background roar of surf, annoyed that I would consider even for a moment something so outlandish. "There are good hypotheses and bad hypotheses and your Turtle Mother is a bad one. Turtles do come here, and the villagers know they come from a long distance, and that is where the legend might have started, but don't go up the mountain looking for some idiotic black revolving stone, because it doesn't exist!"

Although this dynamic professor, the mentor of so many biologists, including myself, would never have agreed, I suspected that Turtle Mother directed him to Tortuguero in the first place. When she saw this inquisitive, sensitive scientist so enraptured in her turtles wandering alone, she began to work her miracles. It was through Carr's writings and creativity that turtle conservation grew to be the worldwide effort that it is today. Turtle Mother used his dynamic personality, acute powers of observation and lyrical nature writing to let humans know what a mess they were making of the planet.

At the same time, when the young herpetologist from the University of Florida first set foot in Tortuguero in 1947, Turtle Mother vanished into the cave. In accordance with all great myths, Turtle Mother, when blasted with the light of science, vanished. It was just that she didn't want to share her space with the new age of scientific investigation which had taken on its own form of religion, ritualized thinking, and biases.

It was an old story. Before Christianity and its church prevailed, the old nature religions were proliferated around the world. With the rise of the church, dragons, magic, warlocks, and other symbols of these primitive religions faded away. The old belief systems were dimmed and Turtle Mother/Mother Earth was replaced by the Virgin Mary.

I thought back to my interviews with turtlemen in Nicaragua, perfectly coherent and intelligent men who had spent lifetimes at sea and who had acute powers of observation in sea turtle natural history, all talking about the years they saw the rock. Then there were the villagers at Tortuguero who remembered seeing it when they were young. Were they liars? I didn't think so. There was such consistency, but only among the old men who could remember the rock and describe it. But then again, what about old Bertie Downs, who said he never saw the rock. Where did the truth lie?

I didn't think anyone was lying, just that the analytical mind cannot see Turtle Mother; only the accepting mind can. Great myths don't hold up to the light of "scientific investigation."

I took a break from the guests and sat on the verandah, sipping a rum and Coke that one of the waiters brought to me. The wind blew, moving along a great armada of green hyacinths floating on the surface of the river, easing ever so gently and persistently along, headed for the mouth of the lagoon. A small night heron perched on it as a passenger, riding the great mat, which I knew held multitudes of crustaceans, fish, and other life interwoven in the mass of floating roots. Shrimp were here, hordes of grass shrimp seething in the mud and the shallows, but particularly thick under the dock of the Tortuga Lodge. Schools of tiny mangrove snapper moved in careful formation, and here and there a smooth marbled puffer picked and chose amid the mud and the remains of cleaned fish. It was symbolic: nature moving in where people are, despite their pretensions. The old religion of the Indians says, "Man is part of the earth."

Seeing all that life around me, I understood. Maybe Turtle Mother was the force of life. Maybe she did, or maybe she did not, exist in the form of a magic rock. She was, or was not, on the mountain. Maybe she wasn't a physical thing but a part of our psyche, hidden in the inner recesses of our minds. And then again maybe she was manifest in the magnetite crystals that we, along with the turtles, the dolphins, the homing pigeons, and other creatures, possess in our brains, computer chips beeping out not just directional vectors, but also a message telling us that we must live with, and not against, nature if we are to survive.

The Indians of North, Central, and South America all believed that the earth does not belong to us, but we belong to the earth. We did not evolve among asphalt and automobiles, noise and the reek of diesel fumes, and factories with pipes discharging into the rivers. Nor did we evolve with nuclear bombs. We were shaped by forests and greenery and yet, over and over again, be it Panacea, Florida, or San José or Tortuguero, we keep pushing it back.

Maybe Turtle Mother was not hiding at all, but was already at work, repairing the damage or directing restoration of cut-over forests, cleansing the earth of pollution and the sky of filth. Maybe she was in the ditch at the Miami Airport.

7

RIVER OF CRABS

IN THE DAYS THAT FOLLOWED, there was little time to think about Turtle Mother. I spent the first two days setting up air pumps, lines, and tanks for makeshift holding tanks at the Tortuga Lodge. We only had a week here, and I had to catch a large number of specimens. Nixon Griffis particularly wanted a baby tarpon for the New York Aquarium, to see what its growth rate in captivity would be. Always a lively subject of conversation at the fishing lodge, the baby tarpon became the latest Holy Grail, another unattainable quest, for no one—not even the professional fishing guides—had ever seen tiny tarpon anywhere in Tortuguero.

The rivers abounded with adult tarpon that rolled or leaped into the air flashing their silvery scales in the sunlight and landing with an explosion of might and fury. People spent fortunes fishing on lures to catch a fish they couldn't eat, to match their strength against the tarpon's. The old wise fishing guides know how a tarpon thinks, but no one, not even the experts, had any idea where the little tarpon lived. The smallest one anyone had ever seen was about two feet long.

We headed out in the Boston whaler to the open passageway where the swampy tannic waters flowed out into the angry Caribbean sea. I wanted to get the lay of the land so that I could plan my collecting strategy for the days ahead. Maps and charts are one thing—seeing it firsthand was another.

We pretty much had the place to ourselves. A few sports fishermen from Germany were there, and Axel Maynard and his wife, and their little daughter who was fascinated by the strange gringos who collected big freshwater prawns and netted freshwater puffers that aggregated around the mats of floating hyacinths.

Once the wind carried a great raft of hyacinths toward the shore until it bumped against the dock pilings and clogged the boat stalls where Axel Maynard kept all the little fishing boats. I looked carefully among the tangle of green stems, and bulbous floats, and black rootlets not only for freshwater puffers, but also for a particular black amphibious crab, a rare black marsh crab that was last seen in Tortuguero a hundred years ago. Or just maybe I might get lucky and find a baby tarpon, one of the main reasons we had come to Tortuguero.

So I picked among the vegetation, wondering if I was doing it for science, my ego, or both. There were no crabs or baby tarpon, and the raft continued down the lagoon to its doom. Out there where it was headed, the untamable sea hissed and sizzled and frothed with vengeance and ferocity. Did any of those little creatures swimming about know how limited their future was? If the wave action didn't get them, the high salinity would, but it didn't matter.

Every morning at sunup, I rounded up my two helpers and set out in the little Boston whaler to strike our nets. As we approached the open water, we neared two black craggy sharp rocks about six feet tall, which stood at the entrance of the lagoon like fanged guards. The sea pounded them day and night.

"How close can we get to those rocks?" I called out to Fernando above the throb of the motor and the pounding surf, wondering now if they could be the origins of the Turtle Mother myth. "I need to chip off a sample."

"This is as close as I go," he shouted back emphatically above the thundering roll of the sea and the whine of the outboard motor, quelling in advance any notion I might have of further exploration. "Very dangerous, you know." He pointed down shore to the shattered remains of the Caribbean Conservation Corporation's 30-foot fiberglass boat that was lying sunk in the midst of the water weeds and hyacinths, its blue finish faded, a huge hole gashed in its belly. "Dat's what happen when you get close."

The proprietor of the Tortuga Lodge told me how Fernando had taken the boat out of the lagoon to go fishing. In the rolling swells, the motor had stalled. The 20-foot swells hurled it up on the rocks, smashing it to bits, and Fernando had barely swum to shore alive.

The first time I had come to Turtle Lodge, those same rocks had caught my imagination; I felt they might have something to do with that mythical turning rock. Now it seemed to me that they were much closer to shore than they had been ten years ago. Watching the breakers rolling over them, exploding into white foam, I could see shoal between those stony fangs and the beach. In fact, I thought, I could almost wade out to them if the surf wasn't so rough.

As we turned back to the lodge, once again in sheltered water, I asked Fernando and John if they thought the rocks were closer to shore than they had been a decade ago. John said nothing, as was his custom, probably because he spoke very little English, and Fernando shrugged disinterestedly.

So I was surprised when, after we had struck the gill net, he answered my question. Obviously he'd been pondering it on the 15-minute ride back. "I don't think the rocks move, de beach build up," he said matter-of-factly. "It fill in all dat sand here. Maybe that's why it look different to you."

We sat idly in the boat, drifting, hoping to see something splash, to see corks snatched under and some struggling creature ensnared. Later I walked along the shore and swept my dip net through the floating mats of hyacinths, wading up to my neck in the dense mats of vegetation, examining the floating roots, looking between the air-filled bulbs, and still there was no sign of the little black Sesarma crab. The hours ticked by, I took elaborate notes, I pickled specimens of fish and freshwater shrimp and grass shrimp in alcohol and formalin to bring back for identification, as well as live ones for our aquarium, but still no tarpon, sawfish, or crab.

Fernando and John were used to taking rich gringos up the river to hook tarpon, snook, and shark. My guides were not at all enthused about wading up to their necks in marshes and digging up muck, taking sand samples, looking for worms, or pulling seines in the rain to collect crabs and minnows. With me they complained about gill netting all night, then getting up early to go trawling. If these two villagers had any curiosity about their environment, I had yet to see it.

By the end of the day, we had buckets of creatures to take back to the lodge and my guides were tired. "You work us too hard, mon. We all de time, go go go. Last night we pull strike de net, and de night before that too. Then we work all day. We gettin' tired."

I felt guilty. It was true, I had been pushing them and myself, seining the riverbanks, wading the banks shining lights into the vegetation, watching giant freshwater shrimp, trawling along the mudbanks, and collecting bright-colored tropical fishes, all without finding a baby tarpon, sawfish, or century-long missing black marsh crab. We only had four days left, and I still hadn't climbed the mountain, but I agreed to take the night off. They weren't driven, I was.

After each collecting trip, I told Nixon what we caught and what we had seen. Occasionally he and Cary took a boat ride and watched as we hauled back the net, picking out the snook, the small sharks and the freshwater turtles. Now, approaching 70, Nixon couldn't go out in the boats as much as he used to, but waited in the comfortable surroundings of the resort smoking cigarette after cigarette and reading until we returned.

And each day when I came back, tired, sunburned, and ready for something cold to drink, he would laugh and ask, "But did you find Turtle Mother?"

And I would say, "Not yet."

Just as there are wealthy patrons of the arts, Nixon Griffis was a champion of life, a connoisseur of diversity, of color, of form. He spent his family foundation funds traveling the planet to feast his eyes on the green dragonfish from Australia, or black-and-yellow-banded sea snakes from the Pacific. He dipped up baby sailfishes in the Gulf Stream, and sponsored expeditions to the Andes to collect freshwater frogs. He sampled and savored life from the rain forests to the deserts, and paid for expeditions dredging the sea bottoms. He gave grants to the New York Zoological Society to protect woolly rhinoceroses in Borneo and tenrecs in Madagascar, while searching the jungles of Africa for the hammerhead bat. Nothing delighted him more than seeing some new creature, no matter how small, especially if it could make some contribution to science.

He realized that habitats are true wealth. Traveling around seeing new environments, soaking them in, watching howler monkeys in the trees, gorgeous unnamed tropical fish in coral reefs, ferns and bromeliads in the mountains—those are true riches.

Always, during all this collecting and exploring, my mind was on the mountain. It seemed that the forces of nature conspired to keep me from getting up there. Whenever there was an opportunity, the weather was bad, and I wouldn't be able to get up there in the rain; Fernando and John said it was too slippery. And when it dried out, we had to tend our nets. In a few days we would be moving on, and I knew I'd better make the time or lose my chance to once again climb that volcanic cinder that loomed up above the flat swampy shoreline.

So as I sat in the boat looking up at the steep sides of Cerro Tortuguero, thinking that the myth was probably lost for all time, an old man paddling a skiff with a load of coconuts rounded the bend. He seemed to be wearing some sort of old military uniform. "Dat Sanfernoosoo," laughed John, "he crazy man. He live over there, all de time wear dat old Nazi uniform." He pointed to a shack at the foot of the rise, hidden among the scrub and coconut palms. "Maybe you ask him about de rock."

As he approached, sculling his skiff, I could see the wrinkled, leathery face of an old man. Happy for human company, he began a deluge of animated Spanish, talking about how much copra he had piled up on shore and how a man from San José was coming this afternoon to buy it. Even though there was a look of wandering madness when he spoke, he was the sole resident of the mountain, and I wanted to know about the Turtle Mother rock. I waited for him to finish his long, involved monologue about his copra, accompanied by much gesticulation.

When Fernando managed to get in a word and translated my question, Sanfernoosoo listened with growing hilarity in his eyes, nodded enthusiastically, and broke into belly laughter. He began another deluge of Spanish, flinging his arms about a yard apart to indicate the size of the rock. I was encouraged; it was the same span everyone else used when talking about the rock. Maybe he knew where it was.

Fernando interpreted. Yes, he knew the story, he had heard of the turning rock, but he had never seen it. But he had only lived there for three years. He knew about other rocks on the mountain, but they did not turn. The turtle rock I was looking for, he said, was supposed to be down in the cave on the far side of the mountain. Years ago I had heard of this cave, filled with bats, but had been unable to find it.

"Ask him if he'll take us to the cave," I pressed my guide. "Tell him I'll pay him for his time."

The old man looked me up and down with perplexed, deranged eyes as Fernando haltingly translated. And when he understood, he gave a huge grin, nodded approvingly, and pointed up to the top. Tomorrow he would take us. He said the brush had grown up, and that he would first have to cut a pathway, but he had to wait until the man from San José came to buy his copra.

I questioned him further about the other rocks and he said he knew where there were several big rocks but they were all covered with logs and brush, from where the loggers worked felling trees. But he would try to locate them also.

He thought it was tremendously funny that a gringo would come all the way down from North America to look for a rock. He gave me a knowing, conspiratorial look, concluded with a smart military salute, and cast off, talking loudly to himself. A trip up to the top of Cerro with him would be interesting.

I wondered which of us was crazier.

The next morning I awoke to the annoying ring of the alarm clock and looked wearily at the gloomy, rainy sky. I had spent the night dreaming about the mountain, climbing it, trying to reach the top and somehow never getting there. It was all too symbolic of my life. It was getting frustrating. Each time I tried to get up there, conditions weren't right. Well, if Sanfernoosoo found the path, regardless of the weather, today was the day.

I lay in bed feeling stiff and tired, needing coffee and knowing no one would be up in the lodge yet to make any. Now in my early 40s, it wasn't as easy as it used to be to spring out of bed and greet the world with enthusiasm. My guides, though younger, were less than enthusiastic, waiting for me under the thatched roofed verandah where our aquariums lay. I looked at the spider crabs we had caught in the shrimp net sitting in our makeshift aquarium, motionless in the dark tannic water.

I picked one up and it commenced crawling around, embedding its pointed legs into my finger. Pulling it off, I placed it gently back in the tank. It had been 18 hours since we had caught it, and it was still alive. Had it been any of the other species of spider crabs that I knew about, it would have been rotten and stinking by now. None, except this one, could withstand fresh water. Finding this species was indeed a contribution, a living example of evolution. All other members of the genus Libinia dwelled in high-saline environments, but this one had indeed managed to evolve its physiology to invade an environment that had one of the highest levels of rainfall in the world. Each year up to 50 inches was dumped on the coast.

As the rain splattered on the water around us, first lightly, causing small radiating concentric circles, and then showering as the intensity increased, I sat there with my two guides, who were looking less than delighted, wearing our raincoats in the open Boston whaler, the motor straining against the shrimp net trying to catch more spider crabs.

It was our second 15-minute tow with the shrimp net. Although they said nothing—they almost never did, except mumble to each other —it was obvious that they failed to see what was so special about a couple of ugly little brown crabs. With the dreary gray sky above, and the rain beating in our faces, I was feeling introspective. Why was I still doing this after 20 years? Why was it so important to make yet another contribution to natural history? What was I really looking for?

Turtle Mother, I guessed.

I was hoping Sanfernoosoo, the crazy Nazi, would appear so we could get started and find the cave where the rock was supposed to be. I could see his shack among the coconut palms at the foot of the mountain and his boat on the shore, but no sign of him.

Fifteen minutes were up. We hauled back the net, dumped the muck out into a washtub and went through it, finding the usual silver perch, some freshwater shrimp, and some anchovies, but no spider crabs. As we were culling, and picking through the rotted leaves, I glanced at a ten-foot clump of green hyacinths drifting past us. And suddenly the tiredness left me. "Get the dip net, get the dip net!" I shouted.

There it was. A shiny black splotch of crab among the green; the square carapace, the insectlike clinging legs—Sesarma, without question the missing crab. Instantly awake, full of adrenaline, I plunged the net handle under the tangle of vegetation, hoisted it up, and with all my strength heaved it into the boat. Frantically I delved through the tangle of hairy roots, bulbs, and big waxy leaves until I caught sight of the startled little crab, and pounced. Instantly my fingers closed over it, bunching its black insectlike legs together to keep it from pinching me. Then I got hold of its one-inch-long square carapace and held it up proudly before stuffing it into a plastic bag. "This is what I've been looking for," I cried triumphantly. "Have you ever seen this crab before?"

John, the younger and less observant of the two, shrugged with disinterest, finding it incomprehensible that anyone could get excited over an obscure black crustacean that was too small to eat. "I nevah see dis crab here before."

Fernando held it up and studied it. "Yeah mon, I see it here sometime. Not often you know, it very rare."

As I watched it methodically, and slowly, trying to crawl up the walls of its new prison, I noticed that although it looked like the abundant North American black marsh crabs, it was much larger and fatter. But its behavior was entirely different, for it acted sluggish and did not try to scuttle off and frantically escape. I threw in some leaves, and it just clung to the vegetation, blending in, barely moving. The other species of Sesarma were dynamos of action. Why should that genus be so successful in temperate waters—fishermen regularly caught them for sheepshead bait whenever they wanted them—and so rare in the tropics?

Now I knew what I was looking for all along: life itself, discovery, something to become enthusiastic about. Nixon Griffis and I had that much in common, we were both expedition junkies. Nothing compares with the thrill of a new discovery.

Even the rains quit, and a bit of blue began appearing in the sky. And coming around the bend in the river, paddling his pirogue, was Sanfernoosoo, shouting and waving his cap. We motored up to him, and I could tell from the conversation that the news was not good.

"He say it's not possible to get to the cave," Fernando translated. "He say dey cut too many trees, and the logs are piled up so bad he can't find no trail." Then Fernando went on to tell us how he had spent the rest of yesterday afternoon exploring, going as far as he could up the mountain, hacking away with his machete trying to clear a path and find the rock, but it was too thick. It would take three men with chain saws a good week to clear a path.

Sadly I thanked him, paid him for his efforts, and we went back to fishing our net. The rock had escaped again. No doubt the rock he was looking for was just another miscellaneous rock, or maybe it was the magic one that had just turned into a crab.

8

THE CAVE

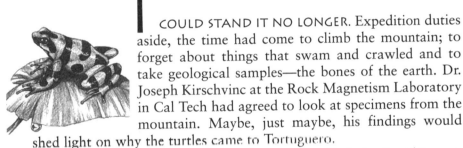

I COULD STAND IT NO LONGER. Expedition duties aside, the time had come to climb the mountain; to forget about things that swam and crawled and to take geological samples—the bones of the earth. Dr. Joseph Kirschvinc at the Rock Magnetism Laboratory in Cal Tech had agreed to look at specimens from the mountain. Maybe, just maybe, his findings would shed light on why the turtles came to Tortuguero.

My helpers were not thrilled at the prospect. Each day I wanted to climb the mountain, Fernando said, "It's too wet, mon. Too dangerous, you slip down and break your neck. Maybe she dry out tomorrow and we go."

With an ominous bank of clouds dumping rain miles out in the ocean, we puttered down the sheltered lagoon, following the narrow shoreline that eventually tapered out at the entrance to the lagoon where Cerro rose abruptly from the landscape like the domed shell of a land tortoise, covered with tropical rain forests. I told them that if we kept waiting for the rains to stop, we'd never get up there. We might fail and have to turn back, but this morning we were going to try it. It had been raining that morning, but the wind had carried the clouds offshore, giving us a brief respite of dryness.

The world seemed to pause; even the mountainous waves had calmed down. The tannin-stained water reflected the trees above like a mirror. A baby crocodile sat on a log, blending in with the branches in perfect camouflage. It was even calm at the entrance of the lagoon and for the first time, I could even think about getting out to the two black rocks that held my fascination. The waves were breaking over them, but without violence; maybe I could even dive on them and break off a sample of rock.

But right now I had a mountain to climb. Arriving at the closest access point to the Turtle Mountain, we dragged the whaler up on shore and hiked along the black beach until we found the path. From there on it was a fight through the scruffy cut-over woods, weeds, and brambles that crept up toward the foot of the mountain. It was more difficult to reach than I remembered from a decade ago. The land had changed: the rain forests at the base of the mountain had been cleared out, and the luxurious swamp vegetation and coastal forests that gave shade were replaced with a monoculture of coconut palms, now abandoned and giving way to weeds and cut-over scrub.

Grimly, without conversation, Fernando and John moved ahead, watching for poisonous snakes and swinging their machetes to clear the brambles and pioneering wild bananas that had sprung up after the onslaught of slash-and-burn agriculture. Abruptly the scrub ended and a canopy of shaded green rain forest closed overhead. Waxy-leafed vegetation, magnificent tree ferns, palm, and hardwoods engulfed us with dazzling diversity. Rich organic smells from the leaf-covered forest floor permeated the air.

"Hold up a minute," I called to them, and stopped to dig away at the leaf litter until I exposed the soil, that strange blood-red earth that was so unique to this otherwise black basaltic sandy coastline. I was hoping to find the transitional zone where the mountain rose from the sandy soils of the coastal plain, but if there was such a thing, we had passed it. The earth I found was from Cerro, not black sand but sticky, thick, wet, red clay that was so slippery, it was almost greasy. A howler monkey chattered above, made a series of obnoxious noises, and leaped back into the jungle.

The two villagers watched me carefully packing the sticky red earth into plastic bags and writing down the location. Finally, John, the younger of the two, broke his long-standing impassive silence. "What you do that for?" he asked suspiciously. "Why you always hunt rock? You look for oil?"

"No," I laughed. "So I can have it analyzed back in the States to see if it's magnetic. I'm looking for the turtle rock; it might explain why turtles come here," I replied simply.

Once again John shook his head uncomprehendingly as I tried to further explain my quest—how this was the only stretch of the coast where green turtles came to nest. I told him that if the mountain had something to do with the migration, I wanted to find out what it was. But since my compass gave absolutely no movement whatsoever when I passed it over the earth, I wasn't sure it was making any sense to me either.

Fernando, who was anxious to get the climb over with before the clouds turned back on us, snapped, "Well maybe you find rock up here, but I doubt you find de one dat turns! But we look, if de rain don't get so bad we can't climb."

Pushing aside doubts, I sampled the red clay that we mushed through and pondered its origins. No doubt when this ancient volcano —if it were a volcano—first erupted, it spewed forth rocks and debris and sent it plunging into the sea. But why was this red earth so scarce outside of the mountain? I had done my share of exploring, diving down to the river bottoms, hiking out into the rain forest swamps and digging through the roots, and all I found was black basaltic sand and mud. Nothing from the roots of the red mountain.

Shortly into the jungle we came upon two very strange fingerlike geological formations rising up from the base of the mountain. Separated from the rise itself by several hundred feet of heavily vegetated flatland, they just seemed to pop out of the earth like mushrooms after a rain. Set apart, they looked like Stonehenge, or some other man-made monument, or rock antennae. Why hadn't I noticed these pinnacle rocks on my last trip? Perhaps Archie Carr had taken us up a different trail. My mind flashed back to the airplane ride; in those few precious seconds of circling the mountain, I had noticed that Cerro wasn't all one lump. There was another, much smaller rise separated from the larger one by a few hundred feet at the foot of the jungle, and this was it.

I pointed my compass up and down the moss-covered earthen facings, but once again, to my disappointment, the needle never budged. I was able to make a few pebbles rock to and fro, as if they had spirits within them, when I passed my strong bar magnet over them, but all that showed was that the soils contained ferrous materials—no different than soil from any other volcano. As I climbed, my eyes roved the needle palms and ferns hoping to see the large black rock just sitting there.

The wind switched, bringing the clouds back, and it began to rain. We plunged on in the gray drizzle heading higher up the trail that led to the mountaintop. The path went up in tiers almost, the narrow path turning ever more mushy. It was hard going, slipping, crawling, clawing at roots, losing our footing in the sticky red clay and slipping back down.

As we hiked up the slippery incline, shadows of doubt crept in. I felt silly. Did I really expect to see an animated stone? But another part of me wanted to cry out that Turtle Mother was hiding somewhere in the brush, away from human eyes.

And while I was looking for the rock, my guides' eyes were glancing around for trouble. Moving through the spongy, soggy brush, every rustle of a bird or animal made them apprehensive, because it might be a man with a gun in camouflaged military clothing. They studied the trail ahead; there were tapir tracks, but nothing human.

There was war in Nicaragua 20 miles to the north. And while the Costa Ricans generally tried to stay out of it, they sat there watching contras and Sandinistas moving back and forth across their borders like spectators watching a tennis match. Mysterious high-powered boats roared up and down the rivers and waterways, and there were rumors that weapons were being off-loaded at night on the air strip in front of the Turtle Station. Raids across the border were common. Refugees from the Mosquito Coast were flocking into the village of Tortuguero to escape persecution and slaughter.

It began to rain in earnest, and the flow ran down the well-worn trail, further disturbed by our footprints, carrying down the eroded earth, running like blood down the spiraling slope. The trail had been there for years, ever since Archie Carr could remember, attesting to a time when there was much greater use. That in itself was another curiosity; why was such a well-traveled road up there anyway? Years ago, Doris Stone, the renowned archaeologist who explored much of Central America, did some preliminary excavations in Tortuguero around the base of the mountain and found the remains of a small, primitive, coastal Indian village with unmarked pottery. Yet down beneath the jungle floor there was a hard-pan road leading down from the Central Highlands, possibly indicating that Cerro Tortuguero was once a ceremonial site. Since the Indians didn't develop wheels or have pack animals to pull carts, the network of cobbled roads throughout Costa Rica, many of them almost as wide as modern highways, remained a mystery. Yet this was the land where pre-Columbian cultures made hundreds, perhaps thousands, of impeccably carved stone spheres. What were they all about?

We climbed on, getting scratched by needle palms and bitten by soldier ants and mosquitoes. Soon the drizzle turned into a torrential downpour and for half an hour we could see nothing. We huddled under a big tree, my helpers sitting there silently with plastic raincoats pulled over their heads, angry, I imagined, that I had brought them up here where we would get thoroughly soaked and muddy at best, possibly catch pneumonia, or, even worse, get shot! The wind gusted through the jungle, driving the rain harder against us, turning the leaves white side out.

But I had come this far, and certainly this mountain was easier to climb than the Old Church Mountain at Tonalá in Mexico. I reminded myself that I wasn't baking in the desert sun, half dying of heat exhaustion. This was easy! For ten years I had had this mountain on my mind, and I wasn't going to turn back now. At last the rain slacked off to a light drizzle. We pushed on, ascending wet trails, slipping, our clothing and faces caked with mud. It grew sweltering hot when the wind passed, and mosquitoes were singing in our ears louder than ever, but we forged upward, winding higher and higher and higher.

Even though the mountain was only 550 feet tall, the vegetation changed abruptly, leaving the dense tropical rain forest below and giving rise to cooler moister cloud forests with banks of ferns. We passed the sheer drop that overlooked the Caio River, a small tributary of the Tortuga River that flowed around the back side of the mountain. Here a slip could be serious; 550 feet was a long way to fall straight down.

As we approached the top, crawling up a steep grade, the wet clay became even more slippery. Several times my helpers and I went bellysliding down and had to mush our way back up. But at last we reached the top, covered with red mud from toes to eyeballs. Out of breath, sweating, we arrived at the top and stood next to the 50-foot moldering steel tower that rose above everything else. It was supposedly built around World War II (although some say World War I) to spot German submarines. Rust and mold had eaten it up, more so than when I was last here. And ritualistically I climbed it.

It started to rain again, and we were there out in the open with no trees to hide in. Long ago the land around the tower had been flattened, and the vegetation never grew back save for a scalp of weedy crabgrass that looked out of place in this lush jungle setting. I gazed out west over the vast rain forest that extended far inland, and to the east over the whitecapped waters of the Caribbean, just as I had when I came up here with Archie Carr. And just as before, there was no turtle rock.

Back on the ground, I looked through my backpack of weathered brick-red basalt, plastic bags with mud and gravel that I had picked up en route to the top. With a shy smile, as if to appease this madman, young John handed me a beautiful cinder that had been fused into reddish green glass that he had saved in his pocket. Fernando had also picked up some treasures. I noticed that all during the climb he too rooted and grubbed under the vegetation and gathered up different and interesting rocks.

Finally he shook his head and said softly, "You see, there is no turning rock up here. I told you dat is stories. . . ."

I nodded; maybe it was stories. Maybe this was just a senseless quest, an obsession, an escape from day-to-day reality and economic struggle. Archie Carr was probably right, the Turtle Rock didn't exist. Did I really expect to see a large black monolith rock shaped like a turtle sitting up there, square on the top of the mountain where so many had hiked up before, guiding the turtles to shore?

The rain poured down into my eyes and I squatted next to John and Fernando to sit it out. In a way it was a help—it was washing the mud off us all. I tried to think profound thoughts, with liquid mud running down my face, but I was too tired, and scratched with thorns. A childhood nursery tune kept going through my mind: "The bear went over the mountain, the bear went over the mountain." Was I going nuts? Was this the border of insanity?

Before I gave up on the quest, I wanted to see that cave, to crawl into it and sit and think about it. The local people said it was full of snakes, evil spirits, and poison gas. I didn't care about that. But it was somewhere on the back side of the mountain, and no one, including Sanfernoosoo, really knew where it was. There was a mythological quality about it; everyone had seen it years ago, but now it was withdrawn, all grown up with brush.

Caves were very important to the mythology and legends of the Mayans and the ancient peoples of Central America. The "caile," as it is called in the Mayan tongue, is a mythical sink. It is the entrance to the underworld, where the gods and earth spirits dwell. There are many stories in mythology about it.

Over and over again in pre-Columbian sculpture and motif, a priest or king, sitting in a meditation pose, showing extreme serenity, is often depicted coming out of the mouth of an angry, grotesque serpent or a jaguar. Some archaeologists say this symbolizes humanity emerging from the cave. The old Indians believed that Choc, the rain god, and the clouds themselves came out of caves, and at night the sun used it to crawl back down into the depths of the earth.

I envisioned the rock, the Turtle Mother, sitting deep in the bowels of the red earthen mountain, turning in the darkness, directing the movements of turtles far out at sea, and integrating their lives with the needs of humanity. She is a direct agent for Gaia, the earth goddess, the cosmic great turtle beneath our feet that makes the world function. To really find Turtle Mother I knew I must find the cave, crawl deep into the mountain, and sit there and meditate for a long time, as seekers

of wisdom have done through the ages in both Eastern and Western tra-
ditions. But I was not ready to do so yet, and may not be before my life
comes to an end.

Mercifully, the rain quit, and a refreshing breeze swept over the
land, pushing the clouds along. A chorus of acrylic-colored frogs
mewed and chirped and clinked like crystals from the uncleared foliage
surrounding us, and then before our eyes a golden ray of sunlight came
down from the heavens—like the cliché image on a religious picture
postcard. And if that wasn't spectacular enough, a great rainbow with
all its hazy reds, blues, and yellows spread across the sky.

I gazed out over the forested coastal plain, that vast rain forest
interwoven with rivers that extended inland to the west, then back to
the east to the white-capped waters of the Caribbean. I could almost

imagine that I saw the Gulf Stream out there, here called the equatorial current, pushing its blue waters filled with sargassum weed, baby turtles, and creatures of all sorts across from Africa, up from the Guianas, and Venezuela and headed on into the Gulf of Mexico through the Yucatan straits.

Far down below, the waves pounded eternally on the shore, bringing some of the weed with it, shifting and swirling the black sands, battering the two jagged rocks that stood at the entrance of the lagoon. Suddenly I knew that I would have to swim out to them and chip off a sample. Maybe I couldn't find the cave, but I could do that. There was no choice, because if I didn't I wouldn't put the matter to rest. Were they part of the mountain? Or did they belong to the extensive reef system that lay a half mile offshore. Were they one and the same?

But getting down from the summit was the immediate problem. We started down the steep incline, digging in with our feet, trying to avoid the thorns, slipping, running, grabbing onto tree roots, and finally sliding down the rest of the way on our bottoms. It was like going down a giant mud slide, down, down, down, slithering around the curves. Even as the blur of vegetation went by, my eyes roved the jungle for a large black rock in the shape of a turtle. I couldn't help it. All rationality went to the winds. Try as I might to be scientific, and objective, I wanted to see Turtle Mother. In Medieval legends, many men went in search of the Holy Grail, and most perished trying. Maybe I just wasn't pure enough to find Turtle Mother.

It took only a few minutes to arrive at the foot of the mountain. We were laughing and having a wonderful time; it was as good as sleigh riding. Soon the three of us mud men were picking ourselves up on ground level and mushing back down the trail plastered with sticky red earth squishing between our toes inside our shoes.

Then we fought our way back out through the flatland scrub and stood blinking at the open water and angry clouds moving far out to sea. John started laughing as he looked at us mudballs, and even Fernando dropped his grim face and started chuckling at the sight of us: rust iron red covering our bodies from our hair to our feet, caked and sticky in our clothing. We were now part of the Turtle Mountain, wearing it deep within our skin. And as I felt the warm rays of the sunshine, the mud dried on my skin and that felt wonderful too. Women pay fortunes for mud baths to improve their complexions. There is a reason for this; the mud is highly paramagnetic, as I later learned, but that's another story.

My guides waded out into the lagoon just deep enough to wash off, but I started swimming. John became alarmed. "Hey mon, de bull sharks come and eat you here good," he warned.

I trod water and pointed to our tethered gill net out in the lagoon which was as empty as it ever was. "If there were any sharks here, they'd starve to death," I called back. "We've been fishing for four days and haven't caught a thing."

"Dat's why he eat you," he called back emphatically. "He hungry."

I came out feeling cool, refreshed, and less muddy. I sat on a log riddled with the holes of thousands of shipworms and watched a big raft of hyacinths floating down the lagoon, out to sea, riding the brown, coffee-colored swamp water. It was time to try. Carrying my hammer and chisel, I headed north to the two black fangs of rock that stood at the entrance to the lagoon. Fernando hurried behind me. "Mon, you crazy, that's bad place, that water suck you out and we never find you. Dat current carry you way, way offshore. Out there sharks get you for sure!"

"It's okay," I tried to reassure him, plunging in. "I can make it."

It wasn't very rough; the water was the calmest I had ever seen in Tortuguero. And while I knew this was one of the most shark-infested coasts in the Western Hemisphere, there were no nesting turtles to draw them here at this time of year, no steady flow of hatchlings coming off the beach. In the old days, when the villagers butchered greens as fast as they crawled ashore for their calipee and the waters ran red with blood, people would see ten-foot sharks coming through the breakers with their dorsal fins and backs sticking out, fighting over scraps. If I met one now, it would be a chance encounter.

The tide was out also, which was another advantage; sharks feed on rising or falling tides, but they don't like low water. The waves pulled back and I could see every detail, sometimes even the very base of the craggy, weed-covered rocks. It was amazing that any life could survive in such violent sand-blasted surf. Dwarfed and wired to the black, burned surface by a matrix of hairs, or cemented with biological glue, the mussels' growth never had a calm moment. I figured I could wade halfway out before I'd have to swim the gully between the rocks and the shore.

I waded out into the surf line, waited until the next wave pulled back and then strode quickly forward. The cool water foamed around my knees. I felt the bottom sloping off, getting deeper. Another surge came in as I held my ground, and with a sudden unexpected surprise it was up to my chest. I went with the receding wave, focusing on the rocks ahead of me. The next big wave roared in, broke over my shoulders, and suddenly there was no sand beneath my feet. I started swimming with hammer and chisel in hand, kicking through the froth that was more air than water. Reassuringly, my feet scraped over the sand. Then when the breaker drew back, I beached myself on top of the rock and clung like a limpet.

This triangular rock was covered with sharp little barnacles, mussels, and stubbly algae, and it took all my strength just to hold on, grasping my legs around it with a wrestler's grip. Once positioned, I aimed my chisel into a cranny, and slammed down hard with my hammer, smashing the barnacles but having very little impact on the rock. A wave exploded, knocking me backwards, but I hung on, feeling the sting of saltwater in my eyes, the barnacles and fouling growth penetrating and scratching my skin. I pulled myself up, heartened that I had at least remained in place, but also knowing that I couldn't take too many more such poundings. Now that I was out there, fear swept through me, the fright of being washed out to sea, of not being able to swim against the currents. Again and again I struck the rock; it vibrated with resonance, but there was no give. Desperately I pounded and pounded until another wave thundered over me.

This time I was knocked loose, and for a panic-stricken moment I floundered in the sea. A flicker of recrimination flashed into my brain; was it really worth dying for, leaving a wife and two small children behind, just to get a tiny piece of rock which I hadn't the foggiest idea what I was going to do with if I got back? I fought the backwash pulling me out to sea, out to where the dangerous long-shore currents were. I dropped my chisel and beached myself again on the rocks like a seal, never feeling the scrapes.

I pounded the rock with all my fear and anxiety, using the flat end of the hammer, smashing down again and again, crushing the barnacles to a yellow pulp, and finally a sliver broke off. It was small, but enough —whatever enough was. In that moment between the next swell, I saw it wasn't solid black, as it appeared, but burned red inside, just like the mountain.

Then I looked up to see a mammoth wave, bigger than all the rest, coming down, and the next thing I knew I was rolling head over heels, like a log in the flotsam, trying to right myself. I felt sand scraping beneath me, and I swam furiously, clutching the rock and hammer until I bellied up on the beach. My guides waded out to help me to my feet and drag me out of the surf, looking with utter disbelief at this crazy gringo who was willing to risk his life for a piece of rock.

Fernando looked at the chip of stone and turned it around in his large black hand. Finally he handed it back to me. As we walked up the beach he said with a tone of wonder, "I remember something now, long ago when I was a boy, I hear about a rock somewhere down the coast from de Miskito Indians. Dis old, old Miskito man say it was a manatee rock, and they say it turn, you know, like a sea cow."

"Not a turtle?"

"No it was a sea cow, you know, a manatee. They say it turn, and dat's all I know about it. Now we go home."

As I followed along, down the beach toward where our skiff was waiting in sheltered water, I carried my rock, and our footprints remained behind in the magnetic sands. I wondered if those peaceful sea cows that lived in the freshwater spring back in Crystal River in Florida also had magnetite in their heads the way sea turtles, whales, and so many other species did. Maybe someday I'd find one that had been run over by an outboard motor—something that happened all too often—and send tissue to Joe Kirschvinc. So was there now a "Manatee Mother" somewhere?

Why not? It was all part of my endless search for Turtle Mother, trying to blend science and superstition, nature and myth, getting a handle on whatever forces guided creatures across the sea and skies.

I was in a good mood, and when I came back from the mountain I wanted a drink. I pushed into Sabrina's bar where her husband was unpacking a case of liquor and putting the bottles on a shelf. "Be with you in a minute," he said.

Just then bottles started flying off the shelf, shattering, smashing on the floor. They were raining down all around him, sending splinters of glass into his bare torso. He stood there in shock, blood running down his bare, protruding stomach while Sabrina sponged him down and finally waited on me.

I was carrying the rum back to the boat when I met Fernando, looking grim. "Something terrible just happen. The maid's little girl just drowned, she fell off the dock," he said miserably. "They find her floating face down."

A sick feeling of guilt swept over me. The air seemed charged with power, with evil. Did I have something to do with it? The world is a fabric of tragedy that happens all around, all the time. It seems to function on suffering and tears. It was the timing that was so coincidental.

Had I stirred the power by climbing the mountain, by wresting the rock from the sea? Perhaps that little girl paid for it, perhaps not. I thought of my own children at home; Cypress was two years old at the time, and we lived on the water and had a dock. Often I wondered why people live at the edge of the sea or risk their all before the mighty terrifying ferocity of nature where winds sweep across the gray, rolling, white-capped waves, whipping the palms back and forth, stirring the water and sea into turmoil? We stand before the cosmic flow of energy, frail and weak, afraid of the destruction and craving it all at the same time. And sometimes we lose.

Enough of this quest, I thought, it was time to go home with my rocks and put the quest on the shelf. Maybe forever! As we flew out the next day with our fish and our rocks, I looked down at the mountain sitting there like a big lump on the shoreline, wondering if I would ever return to Costa Rica again. Wondering if I should!

When I returned to Florida, I mailed the chip to Dr. Joseph Kirschvinc at the Rock Magnetism Laboratory at Cal Tech. He said it was plain hematite and had no special ferromagnetic qualities. Another friend in the physics department at Florida State University checked my samples in a cesium magnetometer and declared it to be "just plain rock."

For years the rocks and samples lay in a corner in my house, keeping company with a growing clutter of mineral samples from my travels. I had no idea why I was still collecting stones, but I felt it would have been sacrilegious to throw them out. Time passed. I put them away and went on with more practical things in my life. Then one day a young man named Sherrill Thompson, who owned a crystal shop in Tallahassee, visited me. He said he had once lived in the desert and had been trained in the power of rocks by an Indian shaman. Certain rocks were used for healing, others for psychic readings. Like many "New Agers," he was a believer in the power and energies of crystals and minerals. He had lived among the Pueblo Indians, and had learned the ancient art of rock reading.

Telling Sherrill nothing of the legend, I unpacked a variety of rocks and laid them out on my living-room floor: a hunk of obsidian from Guatemala, quartz from Maine, glacial cobbles and white pebbles from the Long Island seashore, chunks of red rock from Arkansas, and a piece of the mountain at Tortuguero. He felt each one, eyes closed, in rapt consideration. When he picked up the rock from the mountain he said, "This is so intense, it's burning me. I can feel it throb all through my body. I've never felt anything like it. You could sell this to Indians for their medicine bundles. What is it?"

I then told him about the mountain, about the legend and the Turtle Mother, and gave him a few pieces. He was a believer. But in this age of science, someone saying a rock gave him strange vibrations through the neurons in his fingertips, transmitting this sensation to his brain and spinal cord, held no credibility.

The credibility finally came from Dr. Philip Callahan, a retired professor in Gainesville, Florida, who studied the effects of microvoltages on insects and had written numerous books about electromagnetic phenomena in nature. The 70-year-old professor had become both famous and controversial in his career for applying scientific methodology to occult phenomena. Unwilling to drench the world with pesticides to control insects, he experimented with ways to repel them using low-energy forces.

When I called him, told him about the legend, and explained the findings of other scientists, Dr. Callahan invited me to come down and test my samples. "Magnetometers measure the magnetic field," he explained. "My instrument measures the susceptibility to the field, and there is a significant difference."

As I unpacked them in his laboratory in Gainesville, I repeated the story of the shaman's apprentice to him and he smiled with understanding. "Whenever I get around big granite rocks, especially at dawn or dusk, I get that feeling. I feel good. I get that happy exuberance that children have, especially early in the morning. There are auras, and they're different at dawn and at dark. The source of radio frequency auras—which can be rocks—changes throughout the day.

"So when the hippies and New Agers say, 'Hey man, the vibes ain't right'—or 'this one's got good vibes,' they're right. There are emissions, frequencies, and electrical currents being emitted from the human body, or from trees and rocks, and we pick up on them. But when they come to me and say, 'It's some mysterious force that we don't understand—something that hasn't been described, Yum-Yum Waves,'—I tell them 'Baloney. Learn some physics. All the emissions are part of the electromagnetic spectrum.'"

He pointed to a big chart on his wall that showed all the complicated spectra of wavelengths. "Don't give up on it. The electromagnetic spectrum runs our toasters and our microwaves. We use them for radio and television. Light puts images on film. We use lasers to shine an image on the moon. That's where we should be looking—not at yum-yum waves."

As we put chips of rocks, or plastic film cans filled with beach sand, into his Barrington MS-222 Magnetic Susceptibility Meter, Dr. Callahan reminded me that we weren't measuring magnetism per se, but the rocks' ability to retain a magnetic field after being blasted with a powerful electromagnet. His instrument, which was built in Great Britain and used by scientists around the world, measured the rate of decay—the period of time it took for the rock or sand sample to become demagnetized. As soon as the machine was switched off, diamagnetic substances like paper and carbonate sands lost their magnetism instantly. However, other types of rock, particularly those doped with iron, were paramagnetic and retained the field for varying amounts of time. Their atoms lined up when the machine was turned on, and they slowly went back to their normal disorganization when it was turned off.

"It measures the torque of the magnetic field," Dr. Callahan told me. "It's just as if you made a pendulum out of a nail and used a magnet to swing it over. This machine measures movement. The electromagnetic field inside this coil calculates it in cgs—centimeters per grams per second." Archaeologists use this instrument to measure magnetic weak fields fixed in fire-tempered pottery, or to determine when land clearing and burning had taken place. The machine was so sensitive it could detect the trace amounts of iron that had been locked up in vegetation and released into the soil after the plants had been burned to ashes.

Dr. Callahan found that my Florida beach sand, where loggerheads nested on the Gulf coast, was typical, measuring around 15 cgs, and my piece of granite rock from the Carolinas gave a reading of 30 cgs. But the real surprise was Cerro soil, which ranged around 200, and rock chips which reached nearly 1000. We watched the numbers rise dramatically. "Wow, this is some of the most highly paramagnetic rock I've ever looked at," he said.

Dr. Callahan was taking multiple readings when all of a sudden the machine seemed to go haywire. The numbers started jumping around wildly, from 800 and 900 cgs down to a 100, then to 10, 5, and then they started climbing back up. The rock was pulsing.

"My equipment isn't doing this; there's nothing wrong. All the standards are met. This is magic stuff!" the retired professor declared in astonishment. "This rock acts just like an antenna. You'll have to rewrite the physics book to explain the mountain's variation. The British talk about 'Ley Lines' and Chinese geomancers lay out their buildings and graves based on Fung Shui—wind and water forces charged with 'Chi' energy. Parts of the earth where 'chi' is intense—certain mountains or watercourses—are called 'dragon spines.' This is one of them. Everywhere on earth, you have diamagnetic and paramagnetic layers, yin and yang.

"The ancients knew that if you move the rock, you can change the local energy parameters. If you line them up they do one thing; if you put them in a circle they do another. Create orderliness and you get a generator. Maybe that's where your Turtle Mother legend comes into it. Keep it up. I think you're onto something."

9

SPHERES OF INFLUENCE

OSTA RICA HAS THE LARGEST turtle population in the world. It has *arribadas* of Pacific ridleys, when as many as two hundred thousand of the small, grayish green, round-shelled turtles swarm ashore to lay eggs. That narrow strip of land between continents also has the greatest number of nesting beaches of any place in the Caribbean. Up to five thousand greens nest in Tortuguero on the Atlantic coast, along with a smattering of loggerheads, leatherbacks, and hawksbills. Of the seven known species of sea turtles, five are found in the waters of that tiny strip of mountainous land standing between two oceans. Only the Kemp's ridley and the Australian flat-back are missing. Through whatever quirks in circumstances, the country has managed to preserve their nesting beaches while most other nations are busy destroying theirs.

This is the land where I first heard about the Turtle Mother myth, and it is the only place in the world that has hordes of giant, man-made stone balls. Although I scarcely paid any attention to it, I saw my first granite sphere in 1963 in the courtyard of Harvard's Museum of Comparative Zoology. On pleasant summer afternoons, I used to eat lunch on the benches next to it. It was a campus fixture. People gazed uncomprehendingly at it for a moment, shrugged, and walked away, wondering why anyone would make a big stone ball. It radiated a giant question mark. The plaque next to it wasn't much help either:

> In Costa Rica's Diquis Valley two thousand years ago, artisans carved hundreds, perhaps thousands of almost perfectly spherical granite balls, some measuring up to eight feet in diameter and weighing sixteen tons. Although they were found at sacred burial grounds and in front of ceremonial buildings, they are a great mystery and no one knows their function.

I saw them when I first went to Tortuguero and became infected with the Turtle Mother quest, and again on this last trip with Nixon, and I couldn't get them out of my mind. The balls could have been oversized soccer balls kicked around by the gods, or renditions of the sun and planets, or fertile turtle eggs. Or all three. But I thought they were sea turtle eggs, a symbol of fertility made to insure that turtles would return to the beaches each year and leave their eggs to feed the people. Perhaps the Turtle Mother religion began with its own version of Genesis:

> In the beginning was Turtle Mother, and Turtle Mother laid the great egg. And the egg was the earth, and the egg brought forth life.

Or something like that.

No one said how the great turtle got there, but then again there wasn't much explanation of how God arrived on the scene either. Maybe people thought the earth itself secreted life. Green growing plants sprouted from the soils; lizards, snakes, tortoises, small mammals, birds, and insects popped out from burrows. And fresh-water springs gushed up from the ground. The earth itself was a giant egg, having been laid by the cosmic Turtle Mother. Watching hatchling sea turtles burst out of the nests often reminded me of the Mayan hieroglyphics of birth. Over and over again on Mayan stelae throughout Mexico, Guatemala, and Honduras, a reptilian creature emerging from the earth is depicted as a symbol of human birth. The birth glyph looks like a frog with teeth, or a turtle head or an alligator with a swirl around its jaws. The swirl or spiral is a water sign, so say the archaeologists, but it could just as well depict the magnetic field, or spirit of life, water, and wind all rolled into one.

Some archaeologists believe that turtle eggs were of the utmost importance among the ancient civilizations who lived along the Central American coasts, and may have been part of fertility rites. Dots and circles, in conjunction with sea turtles, sometimes appear on monochrome pottery. But no one can prove they were eggs.

In a sense, the Giant Turtle Beneath Our Feet did lay stone eggs. *National Geographic* has described hundreds of similar-sized spheres in the National Museum in Mexico, which were made of basalt and had been blown out of a volcano. But spheres in Costa Rica were man-made, pecked and polished out of granite, one of the hardest substances on earth. The balls were first described in the general press in 1927. The author showed pictures of his team of native diggers down in the trenches, the earth stripped away exposing these incredible stone balls. Most were like the Olmec heads in Mexico, buried deep in the jungle floor. There were so many that people practically stumbled over them.

I vowed that one day I'd return to Costa Rica and deal with it. I had images of going into the jungles to look for them. Somehow there was a connection between all those turtles, that shadow of the Turtle Mother myth, and the spheres. However, in spite of their intrigue, the great stone balls remained on the back burner while I struggled with daily survival and making a living. Ruefully I added it to my list of unfinished business and unattainable eclectic interests such as seeing the woolly rhinoceros of Borneo in its native haunts, diving to the ocean depths in a submersible to see Deepstaria, the giant red jellyfish, and catching a great white shark.

But four years later, in 1988, I was invited to teach a marine ecology class in Nicaragua, and I scheduled a few extra days in Costa Rica to investigate the great stone balls. As coincidence would have it, Dr. Bernard Neitchmann, a geographer from the University of California who had first written about the Turtle Mother, was teaching in San José. It had been nearly 20 years since I'd seen him, but it took only a few minutes for the years to melt away.

Over the past 25 years, the professor had blended himself into the Miskito Indian culture of the Nicaraguan coast, studying their subsistence economies and their dependence on the green turtle for food. He published numerous books, articles, and scientific papers on subjects ranging from politics and anthropology to the biology of hawksbill sea turtles. Geography is one of the few disciplines in which people feel free to tackle any subject, from atomic physics to cooking. It was no surprise that Neitchmann and Vincent Malmstrom were geographers. All that geographers seem to have in common is maps.

We were sitting in a neighborhood bar in San José, where a band was playing lively Spanish music in the background. I was telling the professor about my current mania with the great stone balls.

"Yes, I know what you're talking about," Barney began slowly. "To tell you the truth, I've never paid much attention to them. They were just sort of 'there.' I mean, what can you say about a big stone ball? Why are you interested in them?"

I reviewed my quest for Turtle Mother, my trips to Central America, and my archaeological discoveries over the years. I explained how the Turtle Mother rock in the lower Miskito Keys, that he had written about, and the lone volcanic mountain at Tortuguero were still mysteries as impenetrable as ever. I recapped my experiences with Vincent Malmstrom and his discovery of the magnetic turtle head, and how we found the Fat Boys and their magnetic belly buttons. And then I told him about the stone sea turtle at Tonalá in Mexico.

I felt I had to pour it all out to Barney, because it more or less started with him. In spite all my efforts, I was no closer to solving the Turtle Mother puzzle than before. And then there was the personal puzzle of why I was so obsessed with it anyway—I couldn't answer that either.

"One thing I do know," I concluded. "I have to find out where the Diquis Valley is and get down there. The great stone balls are something permanent and tangible. You can see and touch them."

"What makes you think they have anything whatsoever to do with the Turtle Mother myth?" he asked.

"It's just a hunch, a feeling. . ." my voice trailed off with uncertainty.

There was a long silence.

"Do you have any idea of what you're going to do with all this?" he asked with a twinkle in his eye.

"I don't know, but I feel it's very important. It has to do with humanity and our role in nature and survival on this planet. This whole Turtle Mother business has been driving me nuts a long time. I was hoping you'd have some information, either on the Miskito or the Torres Straits. Is there anything new there on Turtle Mother?"

"No, not as such," he said thoughtfully. "The Torres Islanders have a deep appreciation for nature, a lot of gods of the sea, and a lot of similarities to the Miskito Indians, but there's nothing like a rock." He paused for a moment and concluded, "I'm afraid I don't have any new answers for you. No more than I did when you came up to visit me in Michigan 20 years ago. Really not much has changed since we last talked. I still don't know of any place to go for Turtle Mother—no records, no libraries, no scientific references; no anthropologists have worked on it. As you know, it's not easy trying to connect all these things." His tone took on an ominous tone. "And if you get too thin, people will think you a fool. You'll lose credibility."

"That's why I have to function in a framework of facts," I returned. "There really is a magnetic turtle head down in Chiapas, Mexico. It is a fact that sea turtles have ferromagnetic crystals in their brains, and that Cerro Tortuguero has some of the most powerful paramagnetic substances on earth. The whole beach is magnetic. And that's why I'm going to the Diquis Valley, where the stone balls are, to find some more facts. Turtle Mother leaves few hints and only the faintest of trails; they're mostly swept away by the tides of time."

Barney's tone became mysterious. "Well, maybe I can help you there. I'll tell you about a stone ball in the Torres Straits. And it can be documented with facts."

"Oh?" I brightened.

He took a long sip of his beer. The band had stopped playing, as if they, too, were waiting for him to speak. "There was and probably still is a stone ball in the Torres Straits."

I switched on my tape recorder. He leaned back in his chair. Things hadn't changed; he was obviously enjoying keeping me on pins and needles, stringing out these little gems, knowing I had come a long way to get them.

"Go on," I said, settling down, trying not to show such great interest.

"Not a massive one like the Costa Rican spheres, but a perfectly spherical ball made of basalt which the natives venerated. The ball is mentioned in A. C. Hadden's *Cambridge Expedition to the Torres Straits, 1889,* six volumes, and it was found along with stone alligator effigies and other zoomorphs." He waited until I copied down the reference before going on. "It was the definitive work on the islanders there. I managed to get the complete set and brought it with me. It had photographs of all their ceremonial centers nearly a hundred years ago. I went back to the area where the ceremonial site lay at the edge of the beach and found all the figures except the stone ball.

"When I asked my contacts in the village, they said they didn't know anything about a stone ball. Yet I had the photograph of the beach with all the other carvings, in Hadden's book. They were all there. All except the ball. It became a mystery to me."

He told me that it was only after he had gained their confidence, by living in the village, hunting dugongs beside them, netting green turtles, and blending into their society for 18 months that he was able to learn more about the missing stone sphere. With the greatest of reluctance the villagers admitted the sphere's existence and said that it had been moved by their ancestors but that its location was kept secret, the innermost of tribal knowledge.

Barney was packing up and almost ready to leave when one of his informants took him to where the stone sphere was hidden. To his surprise, it was only a few hundred feet away, right beside the steps of the church, in plain view. "It was so obvious, no one would take any notice of it," he laughed, still amazed. "The missionaries never knew anything about it, they just thought it was a round rock—a decoration.

"The islanders knew that their religion, their way of life, was coming to an end when the church moved in a hundred years ago," he and a new religion was superimposed on their old one. All the other sculptures were left on the beach to fend for themselves, but the Torres Islanders didn't want to take any chances with the stone ball."

He grinned widely. "They wanted the ball to be safe, so they put it in a place so obvious that missionaries would never notice it and it could continue doing whatever stone spheres do right next to the most powerful, prominent place of power—the almighty church." We both laughed, though we could hardly be heard over the din of the music, which had begun again. The guitars, caterwauling, and whooping grew so loud I could hardly hear him.

"And they were successful," he concluded, practically shouting. "It sat there unnoticed by the missionaries for almost a hundred years."

We stopped talking until the band finished. "Did they say what the ball did? Why it was so important?" I asked eagerly.

"Not in so many words, no. I got the impression that it was associated with fertility, or maybe it made fishing better. Perhaps it had something to do with the homing instinct of sea turtles. It wasn't something that was talked about. I didn't think much about it at the time; it was just another of those mysteries or quirks about the place. But based on the ball in the Torres Straits, I believe you're on the right track. It meant something."

The next morning I went to the National Museum in San José, walked into the courtyard, and there before me was the biggest stone ball of all—truly a sphere of influence. It was mounted on a pedestal in the very center of the circular concrete walk, on a mound surrounded by green manicured grass with marigolds tastefully planted around it, occupying a place of honor. Off to the side were six smaller granite spheres. Stone or not, I got the feeling that there was something inside —some sort of embryonic rock spirit. I almost expected them to hatch.

Unable to do anything else, I wrapped my tape measure around each one of them. They came in all sizes. The biggest one measured seven feet in diameter. The smaller ones measured anywhere from one to three feet in diameter. After a few measurements, I gave up. Samuel Lathrop, the archaeologist who first described the Costa Rican spheres in 1927, had done a superb job of measuring them and had described the sizes in great detail in his paper. I was just duplicating his work for nothing. Giving up on measuring them, I passed my compass around each one. Nothing.

These balls didn't speak to my compass, but they did something to my fingers. I rocked a three-footer to and fro when no one was looking. The more I put my hands on the stone and concentrated, the more the music rang in my ears. I felt a great sense of relief just by holding onto the stone ball; it seemed to draw bad feelings out of me. It calmed me like meditation beads, as if sucking up my anxieties and fears into its very center. It gave off a feeling of wholeness, of connectedness with the universe—the feeling defied words. No wonder Costa Rica never had a major war, I thought. Even in pre-Columbian times, the country enjoyed relative peace. There were a few battles here and there between kings, but nothing as massive, bloody, and organized as those of their Mayan and Aztec neighbors to the north or the Incas to the south. Costa Rica is a tiny strip of land between two oceans. A few hundred miles away in Nicaragua, war raged. There were no stone balls in Nicaragua; there was no peace, and there hadn't been any for nearly two hundred years.

People walked by, museum personnel and tourists, staring with curious, amused, or alarmed looks at the crazy gringo hugging the bola, seemingly getting some sort of thrill out of it. I didn't care. I had come all this way and waited all these years to do it. I kept on rubbing my hands over them in a slow spiraling motion, consuming their smooth roundness, soaking up the soothing sensation through my palms and my fingertips. The vibrating molecules sped up my spinal cord to my brain, traveling through miles of nervous wiring, synapses, and complex electrochemical switching mechanisms. It fed into my skeleton which acted as an antenna for the collective forces of the universe.

It was that same marvelous feeling you get when you touch a water-polished, rounded stone with no obstructions, cracks, rough spots, or fissures. The perfection of the sphere made it more intense. The sphere is fundamental to life, it is geometrically flawless, with a constant radius that starts at a central point and radiates out equidistantly in all directions.

It took a sphere of a certain size to generate that particular feeling. If it was small, like a marble, it didn't have that property, and if it was too big, you might as well be feeling the wall. The small ones inside the museum that I could lift and cradle in my arms, or hold in my hand when nobody was looking, had the most power. They were smooth and polished as if they had been rubbed and caressed over and over by human hands. Archaeologists have opened the tombs of shamans and found them with their personal spheres lying at their side.

Hugging this weathered sphere and letting my mind go blank, I could suddenly feel the world turning beneath my feet. Could it be that all the great stone balls were models of the earth upon which we live? It brought the world down to something real; by touching it I could feel the great turtle beneath our feet. At that very minute somewhere in China it was cool, damp nighttime with stars shining down from above, while the sun here was blazing higher into the sky over Central America.

Satellite photos of the earth, wonderful as they are, don't convey it the same way as these ancient balls did. From hundreds of miles above the earth, you can see the blue planet with its moving white clouds, the vast matrix of spirals, gyres and eddies linking the oceans of the world. Who knew that the oceans had endless surface gyres interwoven from the Arctic to the Tropics until they were viewed from a satellite? In this fabric of swirling waters that runs from pole to pole, the sea turtles on this Nicaraguan beach, penguins in the Antarctic, and the great white sharks in Australia have a connection.

There were no markings on any of the spheres except one, which showed a simple spiral—nothing more. That, I thought, was fitting: the spiral is the sign of infinity, growing ever smaller as it orbits inward and simultaneously forever expanding outward to the great beyond. All the rest of the balls were carved in stark simplicity without markings.

The ancient people of Costa Rica fashioned some of the most intricate and detailed stone carvings in the world. A few yards away in the museum were intricate monuments carved out of granite, with dragon heads and stone serpents so fluid it looked like the Indians had the ability to turn granite stone into clay and mold it. Certainly they had the capability to embellish their spheres, but they left them unmarked. That in itself made a statement.

I grabbed a taxi and set off to see as many spheres as possible. There was no "guide to the stone balls of Costa Rica," although after a day of driving around San José's environs, fighting traffic and breathing diesel fuel, I could almost have written one.

There was a big one in front of the Ford dealership, looking woefully out of place in the industrial area. I looked at nine balls, traveling past "Pollo Frito Kentucky" and McDonalds to the din of honking horns on the rush-hour-clogged street. There was a medium-sized ball in front of the university, and another six-foot monolith next to a church. They sat there on the green lawns among the marigolds. I passed by smaller ones, in subdivisions, used as front-yard ornaments.

I hoped that if I saw enough of them something would flash into my mind—some blinding inspiration. But they sat there looking neither in nor out of place—a testimonial to their enduring and mystifying qualities. Their grave, silent presence said nothing and everything at the same time. They were just "there." Great stone balls.

Archaeologists said that when *bolas* were first built several thousand years ago, they were placed in the villages, in public places, in areas of importance. And they still are. Now it's big companies, hotels, and public buildings. As far as the great stone ball was concerned, things—societies, cultures that have grown up and died around them—haven't changed.

After two days, I was just going through the motions: "Yup, there's another stone ball!" I would snap a perfunctory picture, get back into the car, and drive off.

Talking to people I met here and there, I got some vague idea that they were the *patron nacional*, the father symbol or protector of Costa Rica. The presidential palace had a good number of balls, all sizes.

One man grinned at me in a bar and crowed, "No other country has the balls that Costa Rica does!" It was clear from the beginning that there was a bawdy side to the balls. At one point, when I was traveling with friends through a small town in the Nicoya Peninsula, I saw two large stone balls sitting in front of a hotel, where I least expected to see them. "Stop!" I cried with urgency. "Let's go in."

Randall Arauz, a young Costa Rican biologist who was helping as my translator, hurried in with me. We had a car full of people, it was a hot day, and we had a tight schedule. Two neatly dressed and very attractive girls stood behind the reception counter and gave us friendly smiles as we walked over to them.

My friend Randall pointed to me and blurted out, "This man is interested in balls!"

Not understanding, I stood by expectantly, with a look of eager anticipation.

The girls' welcoming smiles vanished. They looked as if they were under siege by a couple of lunatics and ready to call the police.

A great red blush came to Randall's face. "*Piedra bolas*," he cried, desperately pointing toward the spheres outside the door and explaining in urgent Spanish. The girls looked at each other and started to giggle, managed to tell him that the manager was out and that they didn't know anything about it, and then lost control and broke into peals of laughter. We fled. Crimson with embarrassment, I followed the retreating Randall and scrambled back into the van, cursing, "To hell with stone balls!"

Maybe they did have something to do with reproduction. Maybe they were cosmic testicles. I knocked at the door of another household that had a ball in front of it, and a young woman answered, two kids peering out curiously from behind her dress. Grinning, she said her father-in-law gave it to her as a wedding present. If he wanted grandchildren, the gift had been successful.

I was getting nowhere in this quest. I had to get out of San José and go down to the Diquis Valley to see the spheres in their "natural" surroundings. No longer was I interested in seeing "tame" stone balls in out-of-place surroundings. I wanted "wild" ones, sitting where the Indians who carved them had placed them.

I arranged to go to the Diquis Valley with Mike Snarskis, an archaeologist who oversaw most of the stone balls' excavations years ago. Finding him was another one of those Turtle Mother miracles. Using all my contacts, calling archaeologists at Yale, at Harvard, and in Florida, I finally located the "king of the great stone balls." Mike was the former curator at the National Museum in San José, but due to budget cuts, he had been forced to go into publishing. We arrived at a mutual agreement. In exchange for his acting as guide, lecturer, and logistics coordinator, I would pay a reasonable sum. "This will be good for me," he said. "It's been nearly a decade since I've been down there. In a sense it will be like coming home."

"I hate to dash your hopes of seeing a ball being unearthed," he said as we drove through the congestion of San José out into the countryside, "but I'm afraid there aren't any more archaeological digs of any significance going on anywhere in Costa Rica, especially in the Diquis Valley. We should be able to find a few on the plantations in Palmar Norte, in their original sites. Most of the spheres had been moved into town, unfortunately."

"I know," I said wearily. "I've been stone ball watching until my eyes are about to fall out. They seem to be everywhere."

We headed south along the Pan American Highway, up into the mountains, headed for the legendary Diquis Valley. At first Mike was intensely careful, quiet, and reserved. He was one of those abandoned academics of the baby boomer generation left to forage outside the universities, without secure positions or tenure.

After a while we were deep in conversation as we sped along the narrow highway, passing cars and whipping around dangerous curves. Climbing up into the misty mountains, we talked of Olmecs, Mayans, and other ancient pre-Columbian civilizations. Careful in his statements, Mike, like all professionals in the field, saw the world of the past in a definite order built upon the discoveries of other scientists who sifted through the rubble of past civilizations.

Because of the scarcity of turtle motifs in Costa Rica, hardly anyone subscribed to my theory that the great stone balls were turtle eggs. "There's absolutely nothing to support your theory anywhere in the literature," he said flatly. "In Costa Rica the turtle was of minor importance in archaeology. I can't think of any motifs where one is depicted or shown as being particularly important. It's nothing compared to the crocodile. Most people think the spheres represent the sun god."

"Is there any particular place that the stone balls have been found?" I asked. "Is there some pattern? A geographic similarity or some sort of astronomical alignment?"

"That's hard to say," he said, swerving around a muddy pothole on the narrow road. "Fifteen of them were found in a straight line at one site. Some were found in curves, and others in groups of three arranged in a triangle. It would be speculation to say they were arranged in any particular line of sight."

A few moments later he added, "The balls that I excavated were not concentrated in or around any particular structure, or in any particular location, for that matter. They were all on the Pacific Plain. We found them in flood plains, up in the mountains, where the elevation was a thousand meters." He shrugged, "They just seemed to be everywhere."

"Any particular context," I asked, "like the center of the village, or next to mounds?"

"I've seen them on top of mounds, which was a good indication that they once stood in the middle of someone's house and were probably walled in. And there were some big ones that sat in front of the long houses. I know that because I dug up the footings; you could see where the logs that supported the buildings once stood even though they had rotted away."

The long houses were enormous public buildings and temples built out of trees, where court and ceremonies were held. Unlike the pyramids to the north in Guatemala and Mexico that were built of stone blocks, long houses were constructed from immense rain-forest trees and had palm-thatched roofs. Although stone abounded in Costa Rica, it was used for constructing ceremonial objects like spheres, mutates, altars, or utilitarian implements, but not for building.

According to Carbon-14 dating, the stone ball era lasted from 200 B.C. to A.D. 900 in Costa Rica. That was the same period when the Mayans, a few hundred miles to the north, were developing much more complex societies, erecting enormous temples of stone that rose above the rain forests. But in Costa Rica the population always remained low. It was a simpler and less brutal time when the rain forests, rivers, and oceans provided for their needs. The estuaries teemed with seafood, the woods were full of deer, and crops sprang up from the ground. Costa Rica means "rich coast." They didn't need complex societies. The rivers were full of gold, gems, and minerals that gave the people wealth for trading.

"Why do you think they built all those stone balls?" I asked after a while, looking down into the green valleys as we climbed higher. The pastures were full of innumerable cows bound for North American fast-food hamburger chains.

He shrugged dubiously. "I don't know. Maybe it was to promote power. The spheres and the long houses were built to impress. Imagine what it must have been like for the natives emerging from this quiet forest into the splendor of a temple where the great stone balls sat and where rulers dressed in finery and feathers presided. To pay homage to the kings they had to walk through the jungle on a two-hundred-foot-wide cobbled road. When they arrived at clearings, giant long house buildings rose up fifty feet tall."

Suddenly the car jolted and slammed down into a pothole, and Mike cursed as we bounced out of it. I glanced down to see if the wheels of my tape recorder were turning. Keeping written notes on those rough roads was impossible.

"But the stone spheres must have done something," I said. "You said people built them for more than a thousand years. Man doesn't usually repeat failure. They must have worked!"

The archaeologist shook his head, wearying of my questions and the long hard drive over the narrow roads with their grinding potholes. "I don't know. No one does. There's no written record. The Spanish chroniclers failed to mention their existence. It's all conjecture."

I gave the questions a rest as we climbed higher and higher into the milky clouds that settle on the mountains and drench the forests with moisture. This was paradise; it was cooler here, high above the tropical swampy lowlands and the muggy wet forests and swamplands of the coast. There was a spot up there where you could look to the west and see the Pacific, and to the east and see the Atlantic. But not today. We stopped and looked out over the mist, stretched, and then went on.

The higher we climbed, the worse the road grew. Our spinning tires frequently dropped into teeth-rattling potholes. I tried to envision the time when there were no highways, when the vast jungle swallowed up all sounds; a time when rivers were full of gold, gems, and minerals. Incan goods flowed up this narrow land bridge from South America. Olmec and Mayan influences and motifs from what is now Mexico, Guatemala, and Belize also turned up in Costa Rican pottery.

According to archaeologists, those famous civilizations of Mexico and Guatemala that built the great stone pyramids made very few stone balls. A few were found in Belize, Mexico, and Ecuador, but they were all quite small. I remembered the grisly limestone ball with a curved channel cut through it sitting in the middle of the ball field of Copan next to a giant two-headed turtle, which was thought to be a sacrificial altar. The guides told people that sacrificial victims had their heads bashed in there, and the blood ran down the great round ball. It was supposed to be a blood sacrifice to promote fecundity.

And while the Costa Ricans, who controlled their population and lived in balance with the rain forests, also performed human sacrifices, they didn't become a massive blood-letting culture as did their neighbors at higher latitudes.

As corruption, power struggles, and warfare reigned among the

Maya so long ago, the forests were cleared away. In Copan, scientists examining the plant pollen found there was a period when there were no trees whatsoever—only grasses and weeds. They had all been cut for firewood, building materials, and ceremonial objects. Like the civilizations of today, they polluted their drinking water and depleted their natural resources. Physical archaeologists examining bones of that era found a population riddled with diseases and malnutrition. As the resources shrank, people went to war over them, just as they do today. If there is a doctrine to Turtle Mother religion, part of it should say, "As the forest decreases, the blood letting and brutality humanity inflicts on itself increases."

Maybe the manufacture of the granite spheres helped keep things in moderation. There was no indication that the makers of these stone balls stripped out their resources, polluted their drinking water, and trashed their own society the way the people to the north ultimately did. I tried not to make any assumptions. For all I or anyone else knew, the spheres were part of an unknown and horrible blood-letting sacrifice. Maybe they rolled them over people in some grisly game.

It was getting dark, and driving in the mountainous passes was dangerous, so we stopped for the night in a small town on the descent. This was modern-day archaeology: speeding over paved roads, staying at quaint little motels with their swimming pools landscaped with regulation hanging ferns, and a bar with a Latin band playing in the background. The tables were set with cheerful red-and-white checkered tablecloths and green napkins. The waiter who brought our coffee wore a standard white shirt and black tie. And of course the food was excellent. It was a table set for rich gringo tourists, and out on the patio was a big blue swimming pool. Three stars!

Early archaeological accounts told of men traveling for days on horseback through the jungle to get to a site. They dug with shovels and trowels, felling trees and pushing them out of the way to get to the history buried beneath the dirt, and sweating in the sun. Those days were gone. Save for the ever-present mosquitoes that managed to get in our room, and a wild cockroach that madly scurried over my legs while I slept that night, there was no wildlife. No jaguars screaming in the trees, no peccaries tearing up the camp, no tapirs diving into the river.

Outside the Costa Rican motel, cars and trucks sped down the highway. Across the street was a car dealership with a great stone ball in front of it. In the morning, before we took off, we inspected it. It wasn't one of the better ones. Whoever carved it had botched the job; it was spherical, but squat and ill formed. Mike said the great spheres, the ones at governmental projects, were the perfect ones, built by master sphere makers. Great skill went into making them perfectly round; at most they were a centimeter or two off.

"On some of the more primitive Caribbean sites," he said, "they just used round river cobbles and put them in place—sort of makeshift ceremonial objects. Most of the really fine ones were found where we're going."

We started our descent from the mountains through remnant patches of rain forest. Now and then we hit a rock slide, the green gouged out of the side of the mountain and the soils and stones exposed. There were rocks and cobbles everywhere—uncountable millions of them, with plants peeking up through the stones. "You said the rocks were made of granite," I said, beginning the morning's questions, "but all I see is basalt."

"There's some granite up here, but most of it is further down, by the river. It is curious that they never used basalt to make them. A couple of balls were found on the coast made of coquina rock, but that was rare." It had to be granite, apparently.

Soon we came to the great river Térraba that rushes through the countryside carrying its riches of silts and rocks, fans out into the boggy swamplands, and seeps out into the Pacific. There were mountains on either side. Mike pointed to the gray stone walls that periodically peeked out from the rain forests: "This, I think, is where they came to get the granite for the spheres."

I looked dubiously at the water-worn rocks in the river and at the fractured gray walls along the banks. "It's at least forty miles to Palmar Norte, our destination," Mike said. "They had to haul them a long way. You'll see when we get there that there are no granite outcrops where the spheres are found. This must have been the place."

I thought of Samuel Lathrop, who had carefully measured the specific gravity of local granite to calculate the weights and concluded that a four-foot ball would weigh about three tons. He guessed that a nine-foot cube would probably be needed to make an eight-foot ball and that it would weigh over 24 tons.

It probably took a whole cadre of artisans an enormous amount of time to shape a single large ball. They had to move the original block from its bed to gain working space, then it had to be turned over and over during abrasion to achieve the desired shape. When they finished, they had the only portable monolith. None of that looked likely as I looked down at the granite walls that ran straight down to the water.

We sped past rushing white water boiling over the stones and cascading into waterfalls. I wondered aloud, "With no pack animals, no transport, imagine rolling one of those things out of the mountains. It must have become a national endeavor; there must have been hundreds of people involved."

"I don't think they did that," said Mike. "I think they transported the blocks first, then carved them. I believe they excavated granite blocks from the riverbeds, floated them down on rafts, and carved them into balls on location. We've found evidence of tailings that probably came from worked spheres down in the Diquis Valley.

"How did they get a twenty-five-ton block cut out of a mountain to start with?" I wanted to know.

"I don't know," he said solemnly. "Maybe they heated the rocks, then poured in cold water and made it crack. It wasn't easy. Massive amounts of effort went into it, that's for sure."

I looked at the shallow river full of boulders, cobbles, and sandbars. Maybe during the rainy season, they could float 25-ton blocks. But remembering trying to ford some Costa Rican rivers that turned into raging torrents with a couple of days' rain, I was beginning to wonder if the UFO fanciers, who thought aliens from outer space had moved the rocks around with tractor beams, might not have something on their side.

Finally we entered the Diquis Valley, land of the great stone balls. This valley was known for tremendous lightning storms and the highest rainfall in Costa Rica next to the Atlantic coast. It was hot, perpetually damp, and soggy. If all the vegetation hadn't been cleared away, it could have been described as swampy, but there were no ferns, trees with drip leaves, or natural grasses—only row upon row of chocolate trees and pineapple.

At last we arrived in Palmar Norte. There were rocks and cobbles everywhere, and rounded water-tumbled stones—uncountable millions of them—but none of them big enough to make stone balls. The granite used to make the stone balls must have come from the mountains.

Kicking up a plume of dust, Mike drove carefully over the dirt roads filled with cobbles, passing paths that fed off into the leafy plantations of croplands. Palmar Norte was a rather typical agricultural town; a producer of chocolate and bananas. It had a sullen slowness about it. The village was laid out with stores, and every house—every building, it seemed—was coated with the cheap, regulation-blue Central American paint that stands for poverty. But it was home of the great stone balls and the center of the sacred Diquis Valley.

There was a plethora of them, dozens in front of almost every building of any importance. Every park bore the *patron nacional*, Costa Rica's paternal symbol. Blackened and weathered they sat there, in the city park. We passed a ball field next to the brick high school and there, baking in the sun, were four great stone balls. Each corner of the field was delineated by a stone sphere. There was a baseball diamond, but no one was playing in the stifling heat. The spheres were each about a yard across and must have weighed several tons.

"Maybe the spheres were part of the ball game. It just took a helluva amount of pushing," I offered.

"No, I'm sure it wasn't," Mike said positively. "There's no indication that it had anything whatsoever to do with the ball game. Even a little one weighs a ton or two."

Mike had excavated sites in Palmar Norte, but it had been ten years since he was here last. The place had changed and he drove through the streets, reacquainting himself with the landmarks. We stopped at a little café for lunch and asked for directions, but no one knew the place he was looking for. Nor did they know anything about stone spheres in the cocoa plantations.

He drew a list of names of people who could lead us to the balls *in situ* out of his attaché case, but after asking questions around town, at the police station, and of passersby, he wasn't able to locate any of them. Crickets buzzed loudly as I sat on top of a stone ball and watched Dr. Snarskis talking with passersby, who were gesticulating in their conversation, shaking their heads, and pointing to the *bolas* where I was sitting.

Then we saw some workers digging up a garden in front of a house. "If anyone knows, they will," he said. Mike spoke to them at length and came away shaking his head. "This isn't good," he said pessimistically, getting back into the car. "They would know if they were here." He was worried. "It sounds like the balls have all been moved out of here."

Next we stopped at a cantina, a bar that reeked of stale beer and cigarette smoke, and asked for directions to a road leading down to the sea. It was one of the hundreds of bars in Latin America where turtle eggs were served as *bocas*. Most of them came from olive ridleys that nested in the village of Ostional on the Pacific coast. The bartender opened the egg, drained off the clear mucus, dropped the yellow yoke in a glass of Sangria or spicy tomato juice, and his patrons gulped it down, believing it was a powerful aphrodisiac.

I asked about the turtles, and a tall young Indian man wearing new riding boots offered to take us to the beaches on horseback for a fee. We would leave in the morning, he said, and it would take all day to get there. Mike shook his head; we didn't have the time. We asked everyone if they knew where any stone balls were still in the jungle, or on the plantation, and they all shook their heads.

While we were talking, a pale young Indian girl with a pockmarked face and an unhealthy look came up smiling sweetly and asked for a cigarette. When she lightly stroked my shoulder, brushing my face with her long, dark hair, it was abundantly clear that she had soft favors to offer. She spoke no English, save for a word or two, but in her line of work, language wasn't required. I declined, thinking of another ball, a submicroscopic one that can only be seen under an electron microscope; covered with hooks made to attach to healthy cells, it was called the AIDS virus. Customers suggested we go to the *finca* and find the old caretaker who might know about the *bolas*. We left, and the quest to see balls *in situ* continued. The bawdy jingle that ended ". . . no balls at all . . ." was going through my mind.

A half hour later, after driving through coffee plantations, we found him. An old man with weathered brown skin, a big floppy sombrero, and stalwart mustache came out of the modest white house. "The balls are all gone," he said in Spanish, after Mike explained what we were looking for. "They were hauled out of here about five years ago. There is only one left, and it's been dynamited, blown apart." The ones Mike Snarskis remembered ten years ago were now in San José.

"If that's the way it is, that's the way it is, " I said, "but I want to see the blown-apart one. Tell him I've come all the way from North America just to see them. See if he'll take us there; we'll pay him to guide us."

Without understanding my words, but sensing the importance to me, the old man nodded his assent, got in, and we proceeded into the canopy of chocolate groves, creeping over the stones that banged the undercarriage of Mike's Toyota. With the old man in the back seat guiding us, we headed over the bumpy roads and washed-out ravines, deep into a chocolate plantation past monotonous and endless rows of agriculture and leafy litter. Nothing was distinctive about the landscape.

This was the farm where Mike had excavated the spheres a decade ago. It looked burned, barren, and scraped. The heat scorched down on the hot, muggy terrain. A few birds squawked from the few trees that stood near the *finca* houses. It was a picture of a destroyed landscape. When United Fruit Company came to the lowlands of the Pacific coast, they took everything: first the trees, then the habitats, and then the archaeological treasures. They cleared away the ancient sites and hauled off the stone balls. And what was left? Bananas, chocolate, grasslands, and cattle.

At last there it was, standing among the leafy chocolate plants, blasted in half, looking like a giant orange cut in two. Only it was black, moldy, and covered with leaf litter. I looked at the desecration and asked "Why?" The old man shrugged wearily and said he didn't know why.

Mike said it was caused by the mistaken belief among the natives that there is gold inside. Even back in the days when Lathrop first described them they were being blown apart. Perhaps it was more than the lustful search for gold; maybe someone wanted to see what they were made of and were no doubt disappointed when they found "plain old black rock."

The archaeologist looked disgustedly at old, chocolate-leaf-filled pits. "Grave robbers," he snorted angrily, with the first real emotion I had seen come into him. "They've stripped the place already." To him, the looted pits were as horrendous and offensive as a bulldozed rain forest or a filled-in marsh was to me. He ranted about how the artifacts sat on the shelves of yuppies in glass cases and make good dinner conversation pieces. How dramatic and poignant it was, looking at the blasted stone and the looted pits. Our age seems so lacking, so empty, even with all its excessive trappings and technologies, that it has to steal from the ancients. But the real owners were dead and in the grave and the stones were silent.

Snarskis looked around at the pits. "This was the valley of the dead. These people were concerned with life and death—this was their burial ground. Some people believe the spheres marked the boundary between the village and the burial grounds."

Mike scratched through the cover of decaying chocolate leaves, exposing the brown dirt, and dug up the soil with the molelike professionalism of archaeologists. It took only a minute for him to produce a broken piece of pottery. After thoroughly wiping off all the mud so that its plain reddish coloring and a dull finish could be seen, he held it up in the tree-shaded light and explained, "This is polychrome. They used this characteristic glaze to create this smooth finish. It tells me this site dates from about A.D. 400. It's one of the more recent ones."

As Mike picked up pottery shards that were all about the place, the old caretaker explained that the management wanted the balls out of there because people would sneak into the place and try to steal them. It was easier to have them gone. A lame excuse, I thought, like developers saying the trees should be removed from a parking lot because someone might dent a fender. Left in their original position, they might have told us something about their astronomical alignments, stars, the sun, or something. Again, I wondered, why would people want so badly to steal these round balls and plunder the ancient graves?

The old *finca* foreman spoke passionately, looking me in the eyes and shaking his finger with emphasis. Mike translated. "He says it is a sin to take away the heritage of Costa Rica, that no one is allowed to take artifacts out of the country now, and he is glad of it."

As I fingered the shattered fragments of stone along the edge of the blasted ball, after that fervid speech, I worried about the ethics of taking a sample, even for science. I wanted the rock tested for magnetism; maybe it would show something. God knows people have been looking at great stone balls for nearly a century, and not much more has been learned about them than when they were first discovered.

The old man pulled off several mossy chunks and handed them to me. "They are only chips of rocks. It does not hurt to take these."

I thanked him, and we went back to the car. Where it might lead, I had no idea. I looked down at the gray slivers that seemed to symbolize the destruction of the ancient cultures, wishing I knew what I was doing. Was the myth I was seeking as shattered and lost as this great stone ball was? Was Turtle Mother lost deep in the cave, never to return?

Somehow it seemed fitting to end this part of the quest in a graveyard. But I couldn't accept the fact that the rocks were lost and the stone ball broken. To do so would be to admit defeat, and that there was no hope for the future. In spite of all that had been done to the Diquis Valley—pillaging the rain forests, the looting, the displacement of indigenous people—something powerful still remained. The shattered ball had a message for me. I suddenly realized what it was that I had been doing all these years. I was trying to find the old world of myth and magic; of a harmonic relationship with nature. And somehow, down beneath my feet, I could feel that the magic was still there.

Perhaps there were remaining great stone balls whose energies permeated up through the clay soils. Or maybe it was the slow, rhythmic heartbeat of the giant turtle—or alligator, or other reptilian god—down below. But instead of dejection, I felt triumph. All was not lost; the rise of Christianity and the abolishment of the old religions was just part of some multi-thousand-year cycle that stretched back to the beginning of time. Listening to that old man, with his strong feelings for his homeland, I felt the tide of exploitation and repression had turned.

And suddenly I knew what I was doing. No longer was this just a quest to find a mythical rock, or a hunch; it was a pilgrimage to restore the ancient knowledge of earth energies and mend the shattered fabric of our environment; to simplify our society and bring Turtle Mother back to life again in the world.

But how? What was I to do next?

NICARAGUA—1988

10

THE HUEVEROS

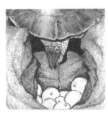

I T WAS TO BE THE FIRST CLASS ON MARINE ecology ever to be taught in Nicaragua through the Jesuit University of Central America (UCA). The plan was to pull students together from all walks of life, from every geographic location in Nicaragua, and give them a crash course on native ecosystems and better ways to manage their natural resources. The 15 students were a mixture of white, Spanish-speaking college students; high-school teachers; government natural resource agency (Direna) people from Managua; and black, English-speaking, commercial fishermen from Corn Island.

The faculty were Ken McKay and Eric Van Der Berger from the University of Maryland; Joe Ryan, a biologist from Veterans for Peace, who had organized the course; and myself. For the first time, these young men and women were going to explore their country ecologically.

Not only would I have an opportunity to explore the Pacific coast and watch olive ridleys nest, I could visit the coral reefs of the Miskito Keys, the land where the legend of the Turtle Mother rock had originated. It was 1984 and this was my chance to see if the myth was still alive. As the years passed, I sometimes thought I had dreamed the whole thing up. At best, it was an anthropological curiosity that had no solid basis in fact. Outside of Bernard Neitchmann in his book *Caribbean Edge*, no ethnographer or anthropologist I talked to had ever heard of it. Had the story diminished here as it had in Tortuguero? Here was an opportunity to find out.

After several days of classroom lectures, we piled into trucks and headed over the mountain passes toward Chacocente, one of the main *arribada* beaches in Nicaragua where thousands of Pacific ridleys swarm ashore in a mass nesting. Of all the sea turtles, these small, gray, round-shelled turtles—the smallest of all the world's species—are the most strongly associated with oceanic environments, traveling thousands of miles from land and feeding on small, red, high-seas crustaceans. While still relatively common, a number of their former breeding populations had disappeared in the last few decades, probably from over-harvest of eggs by humans.

Sun-baked dry forests gave way to rolling scrub vegetation. Suddenly the trees were gone, replaced by an expanse of endless, rolling, treeless landscape filled with under-story scrub. The students said the sulfur from the Masaya volcano killed the trees so that only scrub can grow.

The hilly Pacific coastline was much different from that of the Atlantic. Clouds rose high in the sky as our caravan continued to Chacocente. Each time we stopped, the UCA truck we were using had to be pushed to restart it, but that wasn't hard with 15 people helping. We drove through the village of Nandaime to get malaria pills. The walls were scrawled with political statements and support for Daniel Ortega and FSLM, the socialist government. The whole country was in an election turmoil; it was the biggest party ever. Periodically we'd have to stop for marching demonstrations that included floats with politicos on board and loudspeakers blaring above the crowds.

We waited in the pick-up truck while Maria Mendosa, the biology teacher from UCA, went into the compound and came out with heaping bottles of pills. The medicines were free, as all medical services were in Nicaragua under the Sandinista regime. It was double doses; the doctor there said we needed to saturate our systems. Three white pills a day and one green one, strong enough to treat the worst infections, let alone being a preventative.

The hospital personnel strongly warned that the mosquitoes were bad at Chacocente—very bad. I remembered a warning from the director of the turtle program, Father Adolpho Lopez, that he and all the students who went down there with him had caught malaria. Mosquitoes are the great protectors of turtles, it seems. On virtually every nesting beach around the world there are always dense bushes and swamps behind the sandy nesting beaches that swarm with them.

As we were driving overland, 15 of us stuffed into the rear of pick-up trucks, we knew that hundreds of others, the *hueveros*, the egg hunters, were traveling to meet the *arribada* just as we were, driving in old trucks or riding horses from their villages. Everyone was risking nightmares of chills and fevers to close in on the coast: scientists, conservationists, egg hunters alike. The *arribada* was on, the turtles were coming, and everyone knew it. Were we any different from the coyotes and the jaguars that once flocked to the shores to meet the ridleys?

Father Adolpho had been upset. Last month hundreds of egg hunters overran the beach and stripped out the entire nesting effort. He said people came from as far as Costa Rica to steal the eggs, and the six guards were helpless to stop them. There were half a million eggs on the beach during the *arribada*. The *hueveros* get about a penny an egg and collect about three thousand eggs a night.

Toward the end of that beautiful drive, past volcanoes and dry tropical forests colored by the red evening sky, the land flattened out. Then, just before the coast, rising above it all, was a lone mountain. It stood out, distinct and apart from the terrain, another one of those turtle mountains that I had come to recognize. The road ran behind the coastal cliffs, past a fishing village where people carried fish to market.

Then we followed the bumpy dirt road past the salt flats where the mangroves were diked and seawater evaporated in the baking sun to make blocks of salt. Suddenly we were in a very wild, mature (if not virgin) dry forest, bouncing over pitted dirt roads. For the first time it was shady, with birds calling from the treetops and creatures moving through the trees. There were grunts and screams coming from the forest. A howler monkey let out a series of loud shrieks and growls, and the boys from Corn Island worried. "We're scared of him. That was a tiger." But Joe Ryan assured them it was only a monkey.

Then the forest ended, and here at last was Chacocente after a long day's drive. We arrived just at sunset when the last rays of light blazed orange over the dark horizon of the sea. The scenery was breathtaking, overpowering, and welcoming: the waves rolling on the sandy beach, the blacks rocks silhouetted by liquid fire on the sea, and the dark clouds above. Here we waited and listened to the gentle but endless sizzle and steam of the Pacific Ocean, the big breakers rolling in, gray against the shades of the burning sea.

Ghost crabs ran on the beach, slipping into their burrows, digging down and pulling turtle eggs out of the nests. The beach was covered with eggshells—a white detritus of leathery scraps. Nothing eats the shells; they're like plastic, yet I'll bet they fill some ecological niche. If someone ever found a market for the spent eggshells—say they were found to be some sort of superconductor or energy source—there would be no issue with sea turtle conservation. They'd be saved forever.

The *arribada* beach was pitted with holes and torn up with trails. The four black Miskito students, who remained in a group for much of the trip, looked at the eggshells and gazed out at the Pacific in awe, seeing a different ocean for the first time. "We see turtle all our lives," said Carl, "but never see one lay eggs." It occurred to me that greens nested in Tortuguero, far south of where they lived, and hawksbills, which nested widely, had been so decimated for the Japanese tortoiseshell jewelry trade that these teenagers must have missed seeing most of them.

Not so for Balford Welcome, who was a good 15 years older and had fished all over Central and South America. He looked happily at the vast litter of empty eggshells. "We eat plenty eggs tonight," he grinned. "I eat them until I bust." Then he looked at the pretty young students from Managua who were unloading gear from the truck and crowed, "Mon, I love those turtle eggs. Makes me feel mannish."

Stiff from eight hours of riding cramped up in the back of Joe Ryan's pick-up truck, I raced down the beach, hoping to see an early-arriving turtle before dark, but there were none, just last night's tracks and spent eggshells everywhere.

I was offered accommodations in one of the few bunks that wasn't occupied by the guards, but they seemed to be prime habitat for tiny arthropods with a propensity to suck blood. So we stashed our gear inside where it could be reasonably protected from theft—a chronic problem in Nicaragua—and headed out to the stars and the beach to set up tents.

My flashlight bulb burned out. It was a mini-disaster, particularly since I had to struggle with unfamiliar metal tent poles in the dark. Joe produced his flashlight, and between it and the car headlights, the little community of tents slowly rose in the darkness. At least it was not raining.

There wasn't much room. Our tents were on the upper beach among the turtle pits. There was no other place to put them, and we were warned that during a heavy *arribada* the turtles would crawl right into the tents. Eric tested his strobe, talking hopefully about a turtle coming into our tent and what a good picture it would make.

Food was coming. Jocunda, the high school teacher from Managua with four kids and a lifetime of homemaking, took charge and began cooking a big pot of red beans and rice and some pork over a brick oven in the cottage. Some of the women managed to get things going in a make-shift kitchen. Everybody was ready for food.

Fortunately the breeze was blowing, keeping the mosquitoes away, and we worked under the lights of the pick-up truck with grasshoppers and bugs peppering us as I tied down the tents. It was a great asset to Eric, who grabbed them up and put them in specimen bottles as fast as they rained down. As soon as the young professor from the University of Maryland got his little pup tent together, which he did quietly and efficiently, he was out with his butterfly net, catching the myriad bugs that were swarming around the sudden influx of lights.

Carefully he put his insects in plastic envelopes, inserting a tiny pre-printed data label, bearing the date and the place, "Chacocente," into each one. At every stop on the way down, he had been out of the truck, butterfly net in hand, swooping up insects. Everyone got big laughs out of watching his gymnastics. While working to make camp, he grabbed leafhoppers that fluttered around the headlights and grasshoppers that pelted us. His butterfly net had a practical and immediate use: it was great for scooping up mosquitoes inside the tents—much better than insecticide and probably more effective.

We worked feverishly to get ready, to grab a bite, and then hit the beach. The *arribada* was starting, and the *hueveros,* the egg harvesters, were waiting beside their tiny fires up in the dry forest above the beach. After supper we started down the shore toward the pile of rocks that separated our camp from the nesting beach. Periodically we got a whiff of the noxious smoke from the *hueveros'* fires where wood from the sour apple tree permeated the air. It smelled like creosote, but it kept the bugs away. The 15 students split up into small groups, joined by work-ers from Direna and volunteers from Managua. The mission was to protect the turtles from the poachers and relocate nests to the guarded hatchery. Looking at the number of pinpoints of light on the beach, I thought it would be an easy task.

Shortly after dark, the first of many of the small, grayish-green, round-shelled olive ridleys came ashore. In the image of blackness there was an even blacker spot that moved up the beach out of the sea—a dense black mass heaving itself over the sand—seeking that right spot, wherever it was. We didn't see our first emerge, but followed the trail up, up the beach, the scuff marks standing out from the rest of the dark sands. And there we met the mother turtle digging away, and several young men, plus an older, fiftyish *huevero*—all sitting on their haunch-es behind her.

Flashlights illuminated the eggs that fell like pearls—giant wet pearls. The mucus poured down into the hole and covered them. The old man had his sack in hand, waiting to scoop her eggs up as fast as she laid them. Technically it was the *hueveros'* turtle, if not for this lit-tle matter of law and seasons. They had arrived first.

It began as a friendly meeting. We sat there in the darkness watch-ing the turtle lay eggs, following its ancient ritual. It scraped out the body pit by reaching down, cupping a flipperful of sand, and dumping it out, crouching forever downward into the pit. The mother turtle spread her rear fins apart, then out came more gleaming white spheres

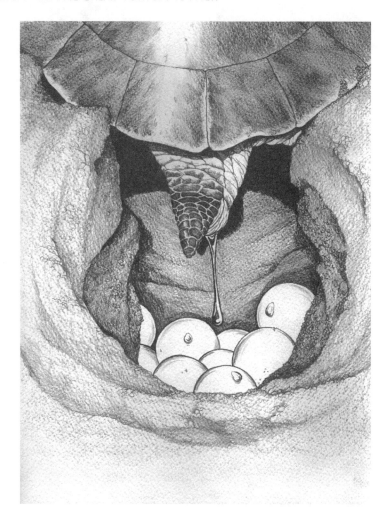

tumbling through the air. The students peered curiously down into the nest chamber watching the clear mucus, the goo of life, pouring down and covering them. The crystal-clear, viscous mucus flowed from her gaping cloaca down into the hole and covered the eggs.

She rested, then out came another flash of white, another batch of small round spheres tumbling through the air. The students tried to count them: . . . 51, 52, 53. "They drop so fast I cannot keep up," Carl, the 14-year-old from Corn Island, exclaimed with delight.

Each time the mother ridley pressed down, another barrage of four to eight spheres tumbled into the bottom of the hole. Then she blew— a loud hissing gasp. Her whole body contracted and her bubbly sounds filled the night above the eternal wash of the rolling surf breaking on the sands.

For a while all the egg laying stopped. She had exhausted herself. She rested a moment and started again. There were short pauses between batches of eggs being laid, brief periods of rest. When she paused for quite a few minutes, the old egg poacher sprinkled sand on her tail to start a new burst of egg laying. He told us that it stimulated her, speeding up the process.

She seemed oblivious to the crowd of people around her; preoccupied with something far more ancient and important than humans. Occasionally she pressed her neck and nose into the sand, as if sensing something or checking something. Periodically she raised her head, seeming to focus momentarily on this strange collection of creatures who were crowded shoulder to shoulder, gawking and shining flashlights into her nest.

We sat beside her in the darkness beneath a blaze of stars; conservationists on one side, egg takers on the other. We watched the waves roll up on the shore. The water reflected the blaze of a billion points of light from a clear sky. What an explosion of stars there was. This was supposed to be the week of the harmonic convergence, when all the planets lined up and the forces of the universe came together. And indeed they did, for you could almost read by them. Venus was rising, throwing a shine on the sea that almost hurt the eyes. It was as if there were a mini-sun up there. I looked up at the Milky Way stretching out into an arc over the heavens, thinking about the people a few hundred miles to the north who made all those great stone balls, and wondering if the balls weren't meant to be stars and planets, or even the universe itself.

Sitting on the beach next to this cosmic sea turtle whose shell was rounded like a dish antenna was a peaceful thing to do. In Greek and Roman mythology, turtles were among the favorite animals of the goddess Venus. Watching the turtle's giant living pearls tumble into the pit, sticky with goo and black sand, planting the seeds of new life, I felt a great sense of connectedness with the stars and the sea.

The old man had lots of interesting things to say about the turtles. Catching a glimpse of his rugged, weathered face, I could see him grin as he spoke affectionately about these creatures of the sea. For a moment there was a bond, for all of us were interested in turtles. It was the same affection shown by the Corn Islanders when they talked about how delicious green turtles were to eat and how turtles were wary and smart. They spoke with the same admiration as the scientists who studied them.

Several volunteers from Direna appeared and sat in a circle with us. The students continued shining lights into the nest and counting the eggs. Then suddenly, as if a switch had been thrown, the digging stopped and the mother turtle began kicking sand into her hole, covering the eggs, and packing them down. She started rocking vigorously; it was like a dance—a burst of energy that went "thump, thump, thump" in the night.

As soon as she had finished laying, the *hueveros* began reaching into the nest, pulling out handfuls of white spheres sticky with black sand, and stuffing them into their sacks.

A young woman wearing a khaki military uniform from Direna told him firmly that the season was closed, and that it was not permitted to take the eggs. Most of November had passed. In another week it would be December and the season would be open, but until then they were to be left alone.

Balford and the other young men from Corn Island translated the conversation for me. But I almost didn't need it. I could hear her righteous and persistent tone; her heart was filled with sincerity and commitment. The girl continued in her firm, authoritative voice.

"She tell him it is for his own good," Balford Welcome translated, "so there will be eggs in the long run. She say if too many turtles are taken now, there will be no more turtles in the future. She say they're here to make sure that won't happen."

But the old man didn't agree. This was *his* turtle, and since he was here first, the clutch of eggs belonged to him. He looked sullen and complained bitterly at the assault. The old man and the younger fellow with him were going on with a long emotional diatribe. Finally I tapped the big Corn Island fisherman's shoulder. "What's he saying now?" I inquired, feeling frustrated and angry at my inability to understand.

"He say he come here to get something to eat, that there is so little money, it is the only food they have. He say, 'there is no freedom any more.' He say, 'you are trying to take away my rights.'" As he argued, the old egg man reached down into the ground beneath the turtle's rear and stole another handful.

Several of our students, including some of the teenaged boys from Corn Island and girls from Managua, protested. I didn't need a translator now. The intensity of their voices transcended the language barrier. The *hueveros* listened, and anger and injustice grew in their eyes as they waited for the words to stop so they could go on arguing. "They say they can't live in the future; they want it now. The turtles have always been here, and there is no shortage. He say he not killing the mother turtle, he just taking her eggs, and she can lay more. And if he didn't get them, the birds, the beasts, and the fish would," Balford hastily translated and tuned back in to the conversation.

I could feel the tension; the confrontation was similar to that over the turtle excluder device. I had just gone through a year of hearings with shrimpers furious at being forced to use a contraption that would save turtles but make them lose shrimp, complicate their fishing operations, and harm their livelihood. In Florida, Louisiana, and Texas great fights were going on, and fishermen were blockading ports. Both in Nicaragua and in Florida it was a time of conflict, and here in the midst of it a handful of students and government workers were trying to protect the sea turtle breeding beach—not to stop, but just to slow down the harvest of eggs.

I had come on this trip to get away from it all, and I realized that there was no place to go where I could. Suddenly I felt a great weariness. I was tired of the same arguments that go on and on through the ages.

Suddenly there was a volley of distant pops which sounded like someone was setting off firecrackers. But as I saw the dark shapes of men approaching, I realized they were soldiers firing a short bursts from their machine guns to let the *hueveros* know they were coming.

Suddenly there were more people standing around this turtle. A muscular young man, carrying a machine gun, also dressed in khaki, stood over us, the symbol of authority. The talking abruptly stopped when the soldier grabbed the turtle, wrenched it up, and dropped it off to the side. Grim with determination, he got down on his hands and knees and began scooping the eggs out of the hole and putting them into his bag.

What an interruption! What was going on? Was this some sort of insurrection? Was this jerk stealing the eggs himself? Watching the abortive attempt of the mother turtle to cover her nonexistent eggs, brutally thrown off her nest, a flood of resentment swept over me. I felt shock and anger. I wanted to belt him, and might have if he hadn't had that machine gun. There was a great moment of confusion. Everyone had been engrossed in watching this great wonder, discussing the issues of conservation and need, and then this armed soldier stormed in, tore the turtle off her nest, and helped himself. Several of our university students raised their voices in protest.

No, we had misunderstood. After Joe Ryan and Balford spoke to him for a few minutes, they learned that he was a fisheries officer and was protecting the eggs. With so many poachers on the beach, the only way to save them was to move them to the *vivaro*, a fenced-off, protected rookery in front of the Direna station.

Meanwhile, the turtle, thrown off the nest, mechanically went on, acting out the breeding ritual by making a great camouflage: filling in the empty, eggless hole, packing it down over the nonexistent nest, going on with its programmed behavior. The eggs were gone and the turtle thumped loudly, covering the sand: "thump, thump, thump." It reverberated through the night. A living powerhouse with a domed shell, she beat her leathery flippers, rocking loudly back and forth, back and forth, then thumping hard upon her belly, using it like a pile driver to pack the sand. She twisted side to side, now covering the eggs, rounding out the nest chamber. We had to move back to keep from getting sand flung in our faces. I was engrossed with her ancient ritual, that far overshadowed the human squabbling.

The *hueveros* snarled some final angry words and faded off into the darkness. And the drama ended with the turtle catapulting herself down, down, down the beach, back into the water. In a flash she was gone.

The government had tried everything to protect the turtles and still allow the *hueveros* to take eggs for commerce. There was a newly posted sign on the wooden barracks at the Chacocente station stating the seasons that egg harvesting was permitted: throughout the spring, summer, and early fall; it was closed for only one month, in November, which was right now.

The nesting season for the Pacific ridley starts in June, when anywhere between one and eight turtles crawl out and nest. The early arrivals are almost certain to have their nesting effort succeed, because nobody is there to bother the eggs. July is about the same; sometimes they don't come at all. A few turtles may come in August. Sometimes there are none in September. Then it picks up dramatically in October, and by November, the season at Chacocente explodes. More than five thousand Pacific ridleys flock to the shore, scrambling up the beach head, digging up the beach. But those numbers are tiny compared to two remote Pacific beaches in Costa Rica where more than a hundred thousand turtles nest in a single night. It is one of the most spectacular sights in biology. They lay more eggs than the *hueveros* can take. But they take all they can. The guards and volunteers do what they can to protect them, but their success is limited.

After the revolution, and before the contras got cranked up, the new energetic revolutionary government of Nicaragua started a turtle protection program that involved employing the poachers to protect the eggs. Before the U.S. embargo forced them to fire nearly everybody the year before, Direna had two thousand employees. Now they had only two hundred. In the beginning of their program, Direna controlled the markets. Because peasants could sell eggs in Managua for ten times what they could locally, Direna went into business, buying them from the local people and selling them in Managua. The profits were used to fund the project, paying for transportation, biologists' and harvesters' salaries, and so on.

After the U.S. imposed a trade embargo and cash stopped flowing into Nicaragua, they couldn't get spare parts when the trucks broke down. One time they had too many eggs and no transportation, and all the eggs they bought rotted.

The project fell apart. They tried to keep it going, using high school volunteers at one point, but they couldn't get enough people. So now it was a skeleton of an operation and the *hueveros* were back to being poachers taking an uncontrolled harvest. Still there were a lot of people willing to volunteer for the turtle watches. Now they sent volunteers for a free beer, or a weekend at the beach.

More turtles were coming ashore; they were all over the beach. It was ten o'clock and the *arribada* was on. Dark shapes were rising up out of the waters, creeping up the beach, and making their trails. Turtles, turtles, and more turtles: huffing, flinging sand and climbing on top of each other. Turtles piling up in traffic jams. Turtle faces emerging from the water, white with fixed, down-turned smiles. Tails of turtles going back. Shelled creatures full of determination, excavating their body pits, flinging sand high into the air, laying eggs, covering them, and returning to the surf.

All through the night the turtles came in waves, dozens of them at a time—at least several hundred altogether. The students gathered around the hard-shelled creatures to shield as many as they could, while the *hueveros* moved in the darkness, grabbing the unguarded. It became a race with the poachers, and they were almost outnumbered that night by a beach full of energetic students, volunteers, and staff members digging up eggs, moving them to the *vivaro* where they could be protected, and asking questions.

Trudging down the beach through the dark, Direna workers and our students—Carl, Lisa, Fernando, Maria, and Juan—carried the eggs in plastic buckets to the impoundment, a stretch of sand in front of the station inside a fence where they buried them under beam of flashlights, making an artificial nest. The guards showed our students how to scoop out the sand and build a chamber that approximated the mother turtle's, expanded in the bottom, with a narrow shaft. Then carefully they placed 80 eggs in each hole. The Corn Islanders worked together, sculpturing the artificial chamber with care. Father Adolpho, a Jesuit priest at the University of Central America in Managua who oversaw the hatchery program, maintained that 65% of the eggs survived the relocation; without moving them, because of the *hueveros*, it would be zero. Part of the fascination of sea turtles is their unswerving dedicated urge to brave the dangers and unknowns of the dry land to nest. It's a dedication that puts their life in jeopardy and exhausts them, and we can't help but sympathize.

I was wondering how many times, over my lifetime, I had peered down at a turtle's behind—loggerheads, greens, leatherbacks, ridleys, and hawksbills, in all parts of the world—watching them do essentially the same thing.

But if I was feeling a shade jaded, the students were full of enthusiasm, as they lay on their bellies, shining lights down into egg chambers and counting eggs. Joe Ryan scooped away the sand at the edge of a nest. "It's a full hole," he announced as proudly as if he had laid them himself; then he began scooping out eggs and putting them into the bucket, counting silently as he went. Sticky with sand plastered onto the mucus, the white eggs piled up.

Lisa, one of the real beauties among our students, reached deep down into the pit, pulling out handful after handful of eggs. Until now she had spent much of her time grooming herself—doing her hair, fussing with her earrings; her dresses always matched. Now she was getting into it. Something had caught fire. It was a chance to put away the notebooks, the textbooks, the evolutionary theory of the university, the ecology movement in newspapers and journals. It was a chance to be involved, to do some good, to help out with nature. She and the other students from Managua were taking it seriously. Everyone worked to exhaustion. The night passed without sleep. The students burned out slowly from the long, long hours of patrolling the beach—an activity that would to go on for the next day, and the next day, and the next.

In the *vivaro* the baby turtles were hatching out of the ground and coming out of the pens. As at all hatcheries, the newly emerged hatchlings were often imprisoned in the wire cages for most of the night wasting needed energy trying to escape. The little black creatures frantically beat themselves against the screen and piled up on the end that faced the sea. Between hauling eggs, the students were having a party—telling jokes, lying on the beach, and sitting around the fenced-in pen watching until the babies emerged, and then ushering them down to the sea.

It was four o'clock in the morning, and there was a fire going in the cook shed. Balford and Carl were boiling up turtle eggs to give to the workers on the beach for nourishment so they could go on relocating and protecting the eggs. When Joe teased them about being hypocritical, Balford replied unabashedly, "No, mon, it don't hurt to take a few eggs just to eat. That's not going to make a difference. It's when you take dem all dat you hurt. Besides, it make me feel mannish." The big fisherman slurped down an egg and grinned at the girls, who broke into giggles.

Now the excitement of all the turtles charging up the beach had passed; most of them had gone back to the sea. It was a time to relax and rest. Sitting around a fire, Balford began spewing forth a stream of bawdy jokes in Spanish that had the students howling. Although I couldn't follow all the details, the whoops, the hollers, and the laughter got the idea across.

A little bawdiness was appropriate, for there was an almost world-wide belief that turtle eggs are reputed to be a powerful aphrodisiac. Women bought them in the marketplace "to make their men strong."

While the *hueveros* made speeches about feeding their families, only a few of the eggs went into the cooking pot; most were sold to the juke joints and bars throughout Nicaragua and Costa Rica. Many middle-class, North American turtle conservationists openly questioned if it was worth jeopardizing a species for a bunch of drunks and philanderers. And looking at the stars above and the eggs below, I had no strong opinions either way, except that I too loved turtle eggs! It wasn't hard to sort out the ethics. I didn't eat the eggs of scarce turtles—leatherbacks, hawksbills, greens, or loggerheads. But with millions of olive ridley eggs available, I didn't have a problem.

Balford brought out a steaming batch of eggs, and they were delicious. Savoring them, I slurped down the rich yokes, leaving the empty eggshells in the sand. The sea thundered in the background. It seemed a primordial thing to do—something humanoids have been doing since the beginning of time. To me it was just another way to commune with the great Turtle Mother: to partake of her gifts. And it was instinctive on some level to save the environment that produced such good things so we can go on enjoying them.

In his 36 years of fishing the Caribbean, Balford Welcome had seen pollution grow, reefs die, and sea turtles being pushed to extinction. Like many people in Latin America, he was addicted to turtle eggs and loved to eat green turtle. Conservation wasn't theoretical to him, it was inherent. He had shrimped all over Nicaragua, he'd run boats in the Cayman Islands from Colombia to Mexico, and he'd watched the lobster fisheries stripped out wherever he went. That, he told us, was why at four o'clock in the morning he was working hard to save the ridley turtles and at the same time boiling turtle eggs—to give nourishment to the workers on the beach so they could go on relocating and protecting the eggs. He saw no conflict. Neither did the guards who came by, wearing their military khaki uniforms and carrying their rifles, to rest and eat some before they continued walking down the beach.

Eric refused to eat any. "I eat a lot of things," the young scientist said, "but I can't see myself eating an unborn baby turtle." And when he said he ate a lot of things, he was telling the truth. As we hiked up and down the beach, helping move the nests, he told me how he had eaten sea anemones in California, tunicates in France, squids and cuttlefish, and many other things. But what was different about the turtles? I asked him.

"I don't know," he said, yawning. "I guess it's like the abortion issue. It's just a feeling. I don't mind eating turtle meat. It isn't rational.

It doesn't make any sense." It was four o'clock in the morning, and I was numb with fatigue. This beach patrol business was a lot harder than I remembered it. It didn't help any when I learned that I was the oldest member of this class and expedition, as I savored one of Balford's delicious eggs grabbed out of the pot, feeling the energy it brought to my tired body.

Eric turned in. I walked down to the Great Divide, a great pile of rocks at the end of the beach, and sat there by myself. I watched the empty sea, half dozing off, half wondering what I was doing with my life and why I was here. Then, in the image of blackness, an even blacker spot appeared in the surf and slowly advanced out of the sea and up onto the beach, a dense black mass heaving itself over the sand. With the surf breaking over its rounded flat form, it looked like a rock. A moving rock. Was this Turtle Mother?

No, I decided after a moment, it was yet another flesh-and-blood ridley. Like all of her kind, she nuzzled the sand with her nose before emerging, scanning the beach with mystifying sensory mechanisms, seeking that right spot, whatever that was. And then she came forward, up the slope, moving with great determination.

My mind switched back and forth between mythology and science like a ping-pong game. One minute involved in the great occult mysteries, the next hard science. Was she sniffing? Was there an olfactory cue she was seeking, some scent or odor in the sand? At this moment, were her olfactory lobes and nerve endings scanning the organic molecular maps and charts of the area or reading the imprints of the earth's magnetic field on rocks beneath the sand?

Not only Pacific ridleys, but all sea turtles did that: loggerheads, greens, Australian flatbacks, leatherbacks, hawksbills, and Kemp's ridleys. It made me think about Joe Kirschvinc's work at Cal Tech and the millions of infinitesimally tiny ferromagnetic crystals found in the turtle's nose—biogenic lodestone touching even tinier, submicroscopic neural receptors that looked like pimples. They were much too tiny to be called nerves.

Was this mother ridley scanning the geomagnetic field, reading the magnetic imprints laid down on the soils and rocks when they blasted out of the volcano thousands of years ago, feeling the torque as the crystals turned, sensing the most subtle of energy forces with internal gear far more sensitive than electronics yet developed by our technology? Or was it a force of life that we would never be able to measure?

I wondered whether the developing embryos down in the natal sands forming their bones, nervous systems, and digestive and reproductive organs were aligning the developing ferromagnetic crystals in their tiny brains to the magnetic fingerprints of the Chacocente beach.

Maybe all that mucus that bathes the eggs as it gushes out of the mother was not just a lubricant, but a complex biochemical glue that held the sand to the shell so the embryo, while coalescing into a turtle, could better absorb, imprint, and bond to the minerals.

There were problems with that theory. There wouldn't be a consistent magnetic field on a beach; sediments shift, and storms and currents rearrange the sand, piling it up and eroding it away. A shoreline can change dramatically from one year to the next, and the magnetic field from magnetite grains would not only be weak (intensity falls off with the square of the distance), it would also lack a consistent magnetic lineation.

Yet a mile or so beneath the sands, deep down in the crystalline bedrock formed back in the Mesozoic Era two hundred million years ago, there exists a very stable and constant magnetic field as distinct as your fingerprints. The rocks have their own individual paleomagnetic patterns created when the sea floor erupted and the north or south alignment of the geomagnetic field in existence at the time imprinted on the cooling rocks, creating invisible magnetic stripes. And these patterns, detectable to oceanographers pulling magnetometers from ships, at the sea surface, many thousands of feet above the sea floor, are even more detectable to the turtle. Fixed magnetic anomalies emanate from iron deposits buried miles deep in the sediments and in seamounts rising up from the sea floor, providing consistent signals throughout the world to the creatures that can sense them. It's tough being a sense-dulled human, unable to sense forces that we cannot see or touch, such as gravity, electricity, and magnetism. To us, the ocean appears as a homogenous water body, yet there are currents, gyres, and eddies spawned by differences in the continental shelf creating almost constant electrical fields that we cannot see.

Watching the mother ridley nest, I found myself thinking about the magnetic turtle head in Izapa on the Pacific coastal plain of Mexico that we visited so long ago, and how it represented the only possible bridge between the world of science and that of myth.

I walked on and soon came across a log, a dense, dark shape with a cut-off branch. It looked like a massive rock in the darkness, with a head protruding from massive turtle shoulders. Turtle Mother, I thought sleepily, and for a moment it was, raised up and pointing up the beach.

Sitting next to the great log that pointed to the sea, starting to doze off, I realized that I had indeed found her. Turtle Mother was no particular rock, or log, or entity, but was a spirit within the depths of our collective minds. She could take any form that suited her. She existed in the innermost reaches of my mind, as she does in the mind of all humanity, if only we allow ourselves to reach deep into our subconscious. If we tune in to the more primitive parts of our lower brains, there we'll meet her.

With a great yawn, satisfied with that last piece of philosophy, I rose and started the mile-long trek back to my tent. I passed another turtle emerging from the water and saw the shadows of men moving in the darkness. When I got back to the camp, only the Corn Islanders were awake. I told them about the turtle, and Balford took off with them to look for it and to get the eggs for the *vivaro*. They searched, walking all the way to the rocky divide at the end of the beach, and still there was no turtle. I was getting ready to crawl into my tent when Carl and Fernando came back.

"We found a fresh trail, but the turtle just disappeared," Carl said. "It's very strange. The trail goes up but does not come back."

Balford was storming mad. "They come and not only take de eggs. Dey take de whole turtle! Take him away, eggs and all. I see them do it and it make me mad. Furious. I tell them we don't have a damn thing left, but they don't care. They call me a black bastard, and say I'm from the Atlantic coast coming over here telling them what to do. They don't want to take some eggs, they want them all. Every last one of them."

I crawled into my tent wondering if it would ever change, and slept the sleep of the dead.

11

SHOWDOWN AT CHACOCENTE

AT DAWN, I AWOKE AND WALKED THE BEACH in the starlight, the sea golden and glassy and the beach streaked with tracks. Torn-up beaches, ripped-up trails everywhere, signs of the *arribada*. Seeing it for the first time in daylight, rather than in the shadows of night, it was awe-inspiring. Off in the distance, a group of men and several horses were walking slowly along the shore, and ahead of them was a distressed Balford, running up the beach.

When he came within range, he shouted, his voice full of distress: "Mr. Jack, they come with de horse and loaded up sacks of eggs. We been working all night long to save the eggs, and now they're digging them up and taking them away." He was agitated, out of breath, and speaking rapidly. "They can't do that. There wouldn't be no turtles, cause they take too many eggs. That's too many turtles, mon. Jesus Christ, they leave no eggs at all. They leave nothing for the years."

He wanted me to do something about it. He stood there expectantly, imploring me to take action.

"Well, do something about it," I urged decisively, instantly assuming my long-standing role of environmental activist. "After all, it is your country. Go get the guards up, go with them, and get them to do their job."

Without hesitation he barged into the little shack, shaking the exhausted guards awake, yelling like Paul Revere, his ire shattering the morning calm. They were all asleep in the little bunkhouse, lying in hammocks and on bare, worn mattresses. "Get up mon, dey stealin' de eggs," he commanded. The old guard in charge of the station slowly got up and stood there in his undershirt, sleepily rubbing his eyes, listening to this ripping-mad black man from the east. Two other guards shuffled out, tucking their drab military green shirts into the regulation frayed matching khaki pants, and blinking at the rising sun.

Anger swept across the old man's face who was in charge of the station; a confrontation was brewing. As he looked at the distant figures, his jaw tightened and his lips pursed, accentuating his salt-and-pepper mustache. He was sick of *huevero*s and their poaching. The audience of students looking to him made it worse.

On several occasions the intruders had broken into the *vivaro* compound, dug up the incubating eggs, and smashed the little turtles to show what they thought of the efforts to regulate them. Many of the eggs were at least 42 days old and inedible, with half-formed embryos several weeks away from hatching. Anything they couldn't sell they stomped on.

There were only seven Direna guards and a mile-and-a-quarter-long beach to patrol, thousands of turtles, and hundreds of men. It was next to impossible to do this job. I suspect that if this had been the first incident, or the guards from Direna were alone, things might have proceeded differently. But the combination of previous raids and our presence demanded a response.

Balford and the guards stormed off to confront the band of *huevero*s. Balford's big hairy barrel chest expanded, his unbuttoned, brown ragged shirt agape. The men in uniforms followed, the old man gripping his machete. Another less-enthusiastic defender of the turtle shuffled along, half carrying, half dragging his equally sunbaked, sandblasted weapon while fiddling with his ammunition clip. They were used to being outnumbered, underfunded, and isolated, and looked at this as yet another hopeless confrontation.

The three black teenage boys from Corn Island came out to see what all the commotion was about and stood there watching Balford and the guards storming down the beach. "Go with them," I urged, and Glen and Fernando took off, followed reluctantly by Carl, who picked up a gun as an afterthought, carrying it like a hiking stick. All the varnish was gone; it was worn to the bare wood from the years of being handled and sandblasted on the beach.

Joe Ryan came in from the well and the scorpion-ridden outhouse, carrying his toothbrush and towel. He looked up and saw the distancing crowd headed determinedly for the *huevero*s, and asked what happened. He had spent much of his life trying to stop the war, to help bring clean water and hygiene to the country, and he was responsible for this idealistic course teaching Nicaraguans about the ecosystems of the country. When I explained the most recent conflict, he looked alarmed and took off after them at a run.

The morning sun had burned away the night chill when the delegation closed with the small army of *hueveros*, who were leading their pack horses. There were at least 20 shabbily dressed men, brown-skinned from working in the sun, with strong, muscular bodies and rough hands from swinging a machete all day in the sugar plantations or hauling in lobster- and fishnets. They were barefoot and wore threadbare brown or old military green baggy clothing. Two egg hunters were working about six hundred yards from the camp. Each had a stick three feet long which they would stab into the ground 18 inches to feel for turtle eggs. They probed for soft spots, and when the stick came up with yoke, they dug the eggs up.

When the protectors caught up, the *hueveros* stopped.

"It is illegal to take the eggs. We have told you before, the season is closed," the old gray-haired guard began. "We are doing this for you, for all of Nicaragua, so that we can have *psaminos* [olive ridley eggs] in the future. This is November twenty-seventh, you've just got five more days before the season will open back up. It's only five days, not five years, five days you have to obey the law. Is that too much to ask?"

"We are hungry, and we are just taking enough eggs to eat, to feed our families. We don't hurt the turtle, all we do is take her eggs," one of the men wearing a big sombrero said defensively.

"You don't hurt her?" the older guard exclaimed. "You take the female, flip her off her nest right when she's laying, and she gets up confused and ends up in the mangroves, and you expect them to live?"

As they spoke, there was a turtle swimming around in the big hot mangrove systems above the beach that were full of cow flop and polluted water, unable to get back to the sea. We had tried to catch her earlier and failed. Who could say how many of the skulls and bones that lay scattered on the beach were the result of such disorientation?

Balford chimed in, his voice shrill: "Last night I see someone come and take de whole turtle away, and steal de eggs." He was both pleading and outraged at the *hueveros*. "We move de eggs all night long and you come and take them away. There's a limit to everything. You fish everything and then you have nothing. You should rotate, have a time when you fish for something and let other things go. But you keep coming back, stealing off de eggs until you got nothing to do but sit there on the flat of your ass. It be just like Jamaica, mon—no lobster, no fish, no turtle, nothing."

Most of the *hueveros* sat there either showing little expression or scowling, but some were obviously enjoying it, amazed at this black man from the Atlantic coast ranting and raving. The Pacific coast of Nicaragua was all mestizo and Spanish-speaking. Seeing a *moreno* here, much less four of them, was a rarity. The *hueveros*, the guards told us later, were from three different villages, two up the coast and one back in the mangrove swamp. Some had come from Costa Rica. Even at a penny apiece, what they received for the eggs was far more than they could get working in the fields. And in a desperate, war-torn economy where food is scarce, nutritious and tasty turtle eggs go a long way augmenting a steady, unending diet of red beans and rice.

One of the *hueveros* had a stick splinter between his teeth and set back on his haunches, grinning. "I am not taking these eggs to sell," he announced grandly. "I only take enough for my family."

"Come on, how come you have the horses loaded?" Balford retorted. "There's more eggs than you could feed to ten families." Balford was warming up, putting all the flair into it that he was famous for. "It's not enough that you take the eggs. You bring your horses and trample them."

"I'm taking some to a friend with a broke leg, he was sick and couldn't come and get his own," another poacher put in, and they all laughed again. There were moments of levity mixed with tensions. Several *hueveros* stood there glowering, clutching their machetes. It was inconceivable to them that there would ever be a shortage of turtles coming up and bringing them eggs. Unlike Balford, who had traveled the oceans widely and seen the declines in turtles elsewhere, they stayed in the same place and watched the turtles come year after year.

After more than an hour of standing in the sun, a small lean man glowered at the black man, his hands truculently on his hips. "What business is it of yours?" He turned angrily to the guards in uniform. "Now the government is bringing in *morenos* to keep us from making our living." The others nodded in agreement, grumbling.

In his fluent Spanish, Joe Ryan told them that the *morenos*, the black men from Corn Island, were here to help Nicaragua. "The reason the *morenos* are here," Joe went on, sounding like he was giving a political speech, "is because they have seen their fisheries collapse on the Atlantic. They have over-fished their lobster on their coast, and they took too many turtles, and they don't want it to happen here. They are Nicaraguans, and they're doing it for the good of everyone."

"It's easy for you to say, you're all getting a salary, and we're starving," grumbled one of the *hueveros*. And the rest nodded and repeated it. More than turtle eggs were involved here; there was bad blood between the English-speaking black people from the Atlantic coast and the Spanish—a battle that has been going on for three hundred years.

Joe shook his head. "I am not being paid one cordoba to be here." His voice rose in challenge. "What are these boys being paid? How much? Ask them." He pointed to Balford: "How much are you getting paid to be here?"

"Nothing," the black fisherman said righteously.

Then Carl: "Nothing," and likewise Fernando and Glen.

Then the *hueveros* pointed to the Direna guards. "But you get paid, we know you do."

"You think we like being here?" snapped the guard who was holding his rifle by the barrel, leaning on the butt. "We don't get paid to do this work, we have other jobs that we're paid for. We do this for nothing. We don't like staying down here, getting bit by mosquitoes, baking in the hot sun, and having to deal with crazy people like you."

That got another round of chuckles. The gray-haired guard with the big mustache, who was obviously in charge, interrupted. "You come last week, and you take the eggs, you break into the *vivaro*, steal eggs. And now you come again. It doesn't stop."

"This is the first time I have ever come here this year," said the heavy man with the broad straw hat. He grinned, showing a gap in his yellow set of teeth.

Another of the Direna guards stepped forward, shook his head, and pointed an accusing finger at him. "Oh come on now, you were here last week!" he hooted. "I saw you here Friday, Saturday, and Sunday." The *campesino* just grinned at him appreciatively and held his ground and they all laughed.

The older guard from Direna, tight-lipped and obviously not enjoying his role, wearily tried again. "We're here, and we talk to you like brothers. We try to reason with you, but it does no good. How would you like it if we came in with the military? In the old days when Samoza was doing it he'd shoot you down like dogs on the beach."

Some of the *hueveros* looked guilty and cast their eyes down to the sand, saying nothing as the guard went on: "If you keep on, we will have to have the same military presence that we have in La Fleur. In Chacocente you don't come to the beach in fear!"

La Fleur was another big *arribada* beach on the Costa Rican border where tens of thousands of ridleys nested. The Sandinistas kept a large militia present. The threat of more power, more troops if the *hueveros* persisted was implied. Even during the argument on the beach, the tone of the guards was conciliatory, trying to tell them why they were doing it. They talked through it over and over again, trying many different approaches, hoping something would sink in.

But it did little good, for the *hueveros* were used to having it their own way. The morning sun rose higher and the heat intensified. They saw that the guards, the gringos, and the black men from the Atlantic coast weren't going to budge and reluctantly started packing up. It looked like the law was finally going to be upheld.

Then one egg harvester slapped the flat side of his machete loudly on his leg. He walked past Balford and hit the back end of his gray-spotted white horse, causing it to jump. Then he walked a few yards away and started digging for turtle eggs.

Balford bellowed in outrage, "What in the hell are you doing, mon? Haven't you listened to a thing we said?"

"You black man from the Atlantic coming here to tell us what to do." He spat contemptuously. "It's no business of yours. Go back to where you come from. We'll take all the eggs we want, to hell with you. This is my living!" He jammed a wire down into the sand in the midst of turtle-torn ground.

Balford grabbed the gun away from a startled guard and fired shots into the sand in front of the *huevero*. The bullets exploded and bursts of sand erupted from the impact ten feet in front of him.

The lean and sullen *huevero* turned stiffly and faced him. "Go ahead and shoot me," he jeered contemptuously, and continued defiantly digging into the nest.

Balford flushed with anger, his bluff called. "You keep on and I will shoot you," he stormed back. Deliberately the man kept digging. Balford raised his rifle and blasted off three more rounds, this time about three feet in front of the man, each explosion coming closer.

The guards looked alarmed. It was a dangerous situation of machismo that could quickly get out of hand and mushroom into a bloody incident. Rumors would fly all up and down the coast if someone got shot, and before long it would be said that someone had been murdered over eggs, and that the government had come down heavy-handed with a militia of ruthless men from the coast bent on blood and destruction. It would create a bad taste that could explode into a big revolution, all because of these outsiders from the Atlantic coast.

Balford pointed the rifle dead at his middle. "I give you a nest or two, but you want it all. While I'm here, you're not going to take no more of de eggs. When I'm gone, do what you want to, but dese little tor-tels is gonna go back to de sea." If the Nicaraguan man from the Pacific coast had had a gun, there might have been bloodshed, but the bullets kept him at bay. He rose to his feet and backed away furiously.

The group finally went on down the beach, leading their horses. After they had gone a few hundred yards, two of them started digging again. This time the guards rushed forward firing shots in the air, and the small army of *hueveros* moved on. There was another volley of shots in the distance when they stopped again.

The authorities were still herding them along when Balford and the teenagers came back to the camp. Balford was still angry as he explained his actions to the Managuan students in Spanish and then in English to everyone on the beach. The girls laughed appreciatively, amused at how agitated the easygoing Balford was. "I tell them that long as I'm here, they can't take the eggs. I talk for an hour and they don't want to get up and move. So I fire a few shots in front of them, and they get up and walk off. I take the gun and make them go. They weren't going to move no other way."

He was chattering in his high, excited voice breaking off into a semi-ritualized chant. "I was in de revolution. I was in de war, I carry a gun all over creation but I never fire a shot in de whole time. Dat was the only time. I told them, and told them, and beg them not to, and man they make me vexed. I'm a lover, not a fighter."

Off in the distance more shots were fired; the police were doing what they were supposed to. Balford Welcome had made a point, and had either shamed them into action or infected them with righteous conservation ethics.

12

TO WHICH GOD
DO I PRAY?

THE SUN ROSE THE NEXT MORNING, casting its eerie orange light on the gray sands. Groggily, I walked down to the beach near the hatching impoundment, sat on a rock, and blinked at the sea. It was our last day in Chacocente, and basically the end of the trip. Each morning, when the tide was low, I hiked down to the estuary, the *estero*, around the rocky headlands where no turtle could nest. But what a spectacular bluff it was, rising above the land with a giant dome topped with cactuses, looking like the Sonoran Desert. A great mass of stone jutted out into the sea, the great craggy rocks like a fallen mountain lying on its side, with the gentle swells breaking over it. It was a world of geological color, interspersed with magnificent botany.

I was compelled to go down to the rocks and sit on them, to feel their energy seeping into my spine, to smell the rich organic smells of life, to soak the sea into my bones, and to feel the rock energies permeate my body. It was called the Great Divide, a headland that separated the ridleys from leatherbacks on that nesting beach.

Ever since I had heard people talk about the Great Divide with amazement, I wanted to see the place. Like most olive ridley nesting beaches, Chacocente was a small beach, about a mile and a quarter long, that seethed with olive ridleys during an *arribada*. As was typical of most of these nesting sites, it was bounded by rocky headlands on both ends, and if you went past the rocks, no ridleys. However, a small number of leatherbacks nested on the other side. It was a magical beach with magical boundaries.

Did this mass of stone that separated the two beaches have anything to do with all those ridleys swarming to the shore? This morning I was not hunting flesh-and-blood turtles with their hard shells and tender insides. There were plenty of people doing that all over the world. I came armed with my notebook, compass, and geology hammer. It was the mystery of the minerals, the turtle rocks, I was after; insight into this magical beach with its magical boundaries.

The beaches were covered with stones, and there was a constant quest for just the right one to take home. The most desirable were the ones that were round and polished—as spherical as possible, and preferably brightly colored. Here at Chacocente, they were easy to find. There was a smorgasbord laid out of wet polished stones glowing in the morning light: red ones, brownish red, some stark white like moonglow. Some were square, or elliptical, or heavily riddled with boring clam holes, all competing for attention. Well, I reminded myself, they were not competing at all, they were just there.

Everything made tracks on this beach: the turtles, the hermit crabs dragging their snail shells, and the ghost crabs that left a scamper of footprints. So did the rocks. Those pebble trails really bothered me. I had spent a lifetime sleuthing burrows, trails, and marks on the tide flats and figuring out what made them. I had hiked the pebble beaches of New England, up to Newfoundland, and waded tidal flats in Madagascar, Central and South America, the beaches of California, and New England, but I had never seen rock trails before.

Just walking along, it looked as if every one of the stones made its own imprint. Sometimes their trails traveled around and around randomly over barren sand, for six or ten feet—even 30—before terminating at a rock. Surely the stones rolled over and over as the water receded. But no matter how hard I looked, I never saw the first imprint being made.

After staring at them in the bright sun long enough, I began to doubt my sanity, especially when they were leaving trails when I wasn't looking! Was this Turtle Mother, fulfilling the story of moving rocks? Was I being teased by animated stones that picked themselves up and moved from place to place, appeared and disappeared, and turned like a compass when no one was looking?

Rocks are naturally propelled by the forces of nature, moved by waves and wind. Hurricanes have lifted boulders from the tide flats that it would have taken four men with crowbars to move a few feet and hurled them a hundred yards up onto the dry beach.

And there are well-documented cases of rocks that inexplicably move. Among the best known are the rocks at Racetrack Playa in the Sierra Nevada mountains that slide across a dry lake bed and leave trails behind. And, like the Turtle Mother rock in Nicaragua, no one has ever managed to see them do it.

Over the course of seven years, Dr. Robert P. Sharp of Cal Tech described 28 rocks that meandered around. He measured their progress as they inched forward in primarily a north-northeast direction, the direction of the prevailing winds. Dr. Sharp determined that the large black stones didn't roll, they slid, pushing up little heaps of dirt and debris in front of them and leaving furrowed trails behind. But not a soul has ever witnessed one move.

The geologist speculated that it took just the right combination of wind, freezing, and thawing to cause motility. He conjectured that it was the result of high winds and slippery substrates that occurred after rare rains in Death Valley, which is one of the driest places in the world.

Seeking a logical explanation of the stones I was observing, I decided to spend some time on the tide flats. The tide had dropped, but there were still six inches or so of water covering the littoral zone. I sloshed through the water, half afraid that I would see stones scampering about through my sleep-deprived eyes.

With slow resoluteness, the sheet of water receded, sand bars became exposed, and, as I expected, a few light rocks tumbled in waves and tidal currents, but they left no trails. Naturally there wouldn't be; any imprints would be washed away by wavelets. Walking a few yards back up on the flats that were covered by an inch or two of water, I found those long, sinuous, jagged trails, with serrated edges again. They wound along from rock to rock.

Then I saw a hermit crab making the trail. Then another. I watched the culprits, stalked eyes erect, scampering around on their pointed legs carrying a variety of snail shells going directly from polished stone to polished stone. It was embarrassing after 30 years of collecting to be fooled so. What threw me off was the directness of the trails—hermits usually meandered around wildly.

The hermits seemed drawn to the rocks as surely as if they were iron filings being sucked in by a magnet. But why? Surely it was not for shelter, they were too small. Food? What possible food value could they find on those smooth, sandblasted, wave-polished pebbles? They practically shone with cleanliness. Maybe some microbe, copepod, or green algal scum collected there that hermits love, but I couldn't see anything, even with my magnifying glass.

Something had to make them behave that way, because they didn't miss a single one. Dare I think it—Hermit Crab Mother? I walked off, shaking my head.

This was the age of science, and science I would do. This was my last day here, and there were geological samples to take back. I climbed around the rock facings of the Great Divide, over to the next beach where only a few straggling ridleys ever nested during the height of the *arribada*.

When I climbed over the headland, I found myself looking at the expanse of beach beyond, hoping to see the beach torn up with leatherback trails, but there were none, so I focused on the stones. They were different here than on other parts of the beach. The usual brown, sandy, compressed stone that formed the sea cliffs along the Pacific stretched out over the tide flat and jutted out from the shoreline. That created the headland and set it apart. Interspersed in the grayish brown sand, there were great drifts of coal-black, large-grained, almost metallic sand that glittered in the sunlight like black ground glass. The grains seemed to stick together. They had such attracting force that they clumped together as if they were wet, when in fact they were dry.

Although they clung to my pocket magnet and looked like Blackbeard's beard, they made my compass needle move ever so slightly—definitely not with the strength of the highly magnetized turtle head at Izapa on the Mexican coast. Perhaps if the grains were all fused back into a single lodestone, they would have. Still looking for a natural lodestone, I swept my compass over the great slabs of sedimentary rocks.

Negative. Negative. But some of the stone felt powerful—not magnetic, necessarily, but there was something else, something mystical, another force that spoke to my neurons, my spinal column, and the nerve endings in my fingertips just as the great stone balls had. Dr. Philip Callahan, a friend in Florida, who studied weak electromagnetic fields, had promised to measure them for me. His instrumentation found all sorts of low-frequency energy wavelengths emanating from granite rocks, and he believed they acted as antennae, storing and releasing energy from the sun.

Without a doubt the glittering black sand and many of the basaltic boulders all would have sent a highly sensitive magnetometer's needle flying off the scale. I continued taking geological samples, scanning the cliff facings with my compass, hoping to find something as strong as Vincent Malmstrom's magnetic turtle head in Izapa or the Fat Boys in La Democracia, and jotting down ideas and notes as they came to me.

After taking samples, I turned back toward the station. The tide was coming in, and I hiked along a higher zone of the beach, looking at the litter of hatched and unhatched shells on the trampled, scratched-up sand. The high beach was littered with eggshells. Many of the shells had a developed turtle inside, half-formed in the dried-up, sunbaked yoke; they stank and were full of ants. They were victims of other turtles digging them up and destroying them while making their own nests. Last night ridleys had been so thick they were digging up old nests and crushing little turtles still in the eggs. Life was cheap, revolving on a giant wheel, easily expended, easily replaced.

I picked up a dried-out hatchling baking in the sands. This was nothing unusual; there were always a few who got crushed in the madhouse of laying females on *arribada* nights. But this one gave me an idea. Years ago, Dr. Joe Kirschvinc, the geologist who had found ferromagnetic crystals in the heads of sea turtles, had suggested that I try an experiment. Get a dead hatchling, he said, dry it, hang it from a string like a pendulum, and see if a magnet would move it.

The trouble was, it wasn't easy to come by a specimen. There were plenty of little turtles in museum collections stored in formaldehyde, but Kirschvinc said that wouldn't do because the magnetite would probably have oxidized or rusted away. I would never kill a hatchling, so it had never been possible to try the experiment.

Until now. I grabbed the shriveled little turtle, brushed off the ants, pulled some fishing line out of my knapsack, and tied it to a rear flipper. Fortunately it was a calm day; not a breath of wind stirred, so I went up into the vegetation of the dry forest, away from any possible breeze, and tied the turtle to a branch, and waited until it hung motionless, the mosquitoes whining in my ears. As it dangled there three feet above the ground, I brought the magnet near. The little turtle suddenly sprang to life, swinging nose first toward the magnet. The nose was where the ferromagnetic crystals were located in living sea turtles. The nose was where the magnetic field was in Malmstrom's stone turtle at Izapa.

I laughed in delight. Something was clearly overcoming the inertia of the turtle. Then it lost the field and swung back. It swung back and forth until it lost its momentum and hung straight down. I moved the magnet back toward the turtle and the same thing happened again.

I tried not to get too excited. This could easily be a false reading caused by magnetic sand grains sticking to the turtle. Even though I had cleaned it as carefully as I could out there on a beach, there were doubtless still plenty of grains on it. To be acceptable science, the experiment would have to be repeated over and over, using many different hatchlings that had been meticulously dried, cleaned, and inspected in a laboratory. The strength of the field and the amount of movement would have to be measured.

Nevertheless, I had a promising lead. I hiked on down the beach, picking up as many dead hatchlings as I could find, anxious to show Eric Van Der Berger and Joe Ryan who would shoot holes in my theory if my conclusions were wrong. Suddenly I saw a group of *campesinos* scrutinizing me suspiciously. One led a small brown horse loaded with saddlebags. Some of them were the same *hueveros* who had been poaching the night before.

As I saw them talking among themselves and pointing at me, I began to wonder how smart it was being out here all by myself, a mile away from the base camp. I doubt they were pleased with my friend

Balford and his shooting spree. I felt some anxiety as all eight of them approached me, especially since I recognized the heavyset old man I had met the other night when the guard snatched the turtle off the nest, took the eggs, and chased him off. People always get very angry when their traditional livelihood suddenly gets taken away. Part of me wanted to flee, to streak off back to the station, but they were blocking my escape, and behind me was the Great Divide.

They all gathered together in a little group around me. I tried to remain calm, tried to put myself in their shoes, watching me climbing around, running my compass over boulders, digging up sand on the beach and stuffing it into plastic bags, then writing like a lunatic, and picking up dead hatchlings and hanging them up like voodoo dolls. Perhaps they were worried themselves, wondering if I was mad, or dangerous.

Turtle eggs or not, they were not villains, they were just men trying to get by in a country that was torn with war and desperate with poverty. At the moment they were hunting and picking the good things that live in the rock crevices, moving slowly with their heads down, no different than I had done when searching tide pools for specimens. They were picking up snails, chitons, and crabs.

I gave the warmest smile I could and waved, *"Buenos dias!"* All I got were some strange glances and uncertain smiles. I had exhausted most of my Spanish, right there.

Looking intent and curious, a spokesman began asking questions. I surmised they wanted to know what I was doing. Was I lost, shipwrecked, a spy, or a just total madman? I told them I didn't speak Spanish, so he asked questions even louder and more slowly trying his best to get me to understand. Several of the others joined in and they repeated their questions over and over again; some were getting exasperated.

I told them I was with UCA and pointed to the station, and that I was an American, here to study the *tortuga*, and after much frustrating conversation back and forth, pointing to the Direna station and *vivaro* up the beach, they finally nodded with understanding and started to drift away.

I pointed to their sacks, wanting to know what they were catching, but they wouldn't let me see and abruptly walked off. Possibly they had some turtle eggs, but most of their sacks didn't bulge suspiciously. They were afraid I'd want to take away the snails and things they'd been gathering for soup. Maybe I was some new breed of law enforcement agent, here to hit them with a barrage of new rules.

Balford had established a presence. On our final night there were no horses and no *hueveros*. But someone had broken in and spitefully dug up some of the nests, scattering and smashing the eggs. It made quite a feast for the scavengers. Wondering what all this had accomplished, I headed back to the compound, my pockets bulging with rocks.

When I got back to the fenced-in enclosure, a half-dozen ghost crabs scattered at my approach. They had been feasting on a number of well-developed eggs and dead black embryonic turtles. A buzzard circled the beach looking for turtle eggs or hatchlings emerging from the nest.

Suddenly I saw a ghost crab, or rather the movement of a crab streaking for its burrow. But it looked different; there was a blur of something dark, something alive with frantic motion of its own and as big as the crab itself. I changed direction, heading up the beach in time to see the crab bolt down its burrow. It was too quick, and for a moment I couldn't tell what it was carrying. Then I saw; it was a baby turtle, and the crab was dragging it into its lair. Desperately it tried to pull it down when I approached, but the turtle got stuck. The crab dropped it and vanished below.

I picked up the black three-inch-long turtle with the diamond markings on its carapace. It wasn't mutilated and fortunately its eyes hadn't been plucked out. It struggled for a few minutes, then all motion stopped and it became passive, inert. Perhaps that was a defensive reaction, to retain its energy for a possible future escape. Or perhaps it was an acceptance of death, that a far larger ghost crab had hold of it, and the end was inevitable.

I carried it away from the ghost crab burrow and set it down on the beach. The little gray hatchling turned, and circled, and then it felt the slope of the beach, or felt the draw of the sea, and it headed for the water. I stood beside it, a giant looking down like God. The cast of my shadow made me look even bigger, a moving darkness on the grayish beach.

When it hit wet sand, the moisture seemed to put even more frenzy in this little one. A wave came in and washed it back up, turning it over; instantly, with turtle fury, it flipped back and fought its way down. What a struggle! It was the struggle of life, but at least this one had the experience of going down the beach.

It felt the sea and saw the white waves and knew exactly what to do. Suddenly the little shelled reptile became a frenzy of activity. It dove for the water and so began a journey that was fraught with danger. Already saved from the claws of death, would it live to adulthood or would its life end with the snap of a king mackerel's jaws, or a shark's?

I couldn't protect it from the fish or the fowl. Like Nicaragua itself, it must go on its own power, its own resources and spirit, and take its chances in a difficult world where difficulty was the norm. As the baby turtle dove in, the opaque waves swallowed it up in clouds of freshly churned-up silt, swirling particles of fine soils right at the edge, bringing life, protection, and shelter. That was that.

Or it should have been. But it wasn't. I wanted to know where the little turtles went, and what guided them, and how. If I were a Miskito Indian, who fished for turtles with nets, I wouldn't need to ask a thousand questions, because the existence of a magic rock named Turtle Mother answered them all. There were no such stories among the *hueveros* or anyone else on the Pacific coast. The legend, if it had ever been here, had vanished long ago.

Once again the running battle between science and myth raged through my mind. I was stubborn. Turtle Mother was a rock, not a flesh-and-blood turtle. Maybe it was a myth and maybe it wasn't.

I had to prove to myself over and over again that sea turtles were attracted to rocks, by amassing circumstantial evidence. Last night I had seen that many of the females bore scrapes on their backs, probably signs that they had been lying under submerged rocks before coming out. These scrapes did not look like mating scars, where the male's plastron and foreflippers sometimes scratch the female.

Father Adolfo had said that right before the *arribada* one could stand on the shore and see ridleys swimming up and down the beach, just out beyond the breakers, popping their heads up, treading water, as if looking about and waiting for night to fall.

Were they looking for landmarks, for headlands, for turtle rocks? If lying on a granite or rock face feels good to us, what then does it feel like to a turtle?

The late Douglas Robinson, at the University of San José, said rocks are associated with estuaries, where all the *arribadas* along the coast of Central America take place. And while it was possible that the turtles were guided by the sound of the waves sloshing up on the headlands, he felt the main draw was the odors coming from the rivers, which dumped fresh water and decaying vegetation out to sea.

Looking out over the dark rolling Pacific with its great rolling swells, I wondered what turtle rock lay out in that murky ocean. We were leaving in a few hours and it was my last chance to find out, so I went back to my tent, grabbed mask, fins, and snorkel, and waded out into the eternal swells. I had tried it several days ago, and visibility had been poor, but I planned to swim out briefly and look around anyway.

It was still murky; I could barely see anything except shifting sand, but it was no worse than diving in the Gulf of Mexico. I saw a few black rocks through the green waters as I swam out into the swells. Save for a little bit of algae and an anemone or two, the Pacific coast had little marine life. Nevertheless, I kept looking, hoping to see a turtle down there beneath the rocks.

Suddenly I felt I was swimming all too freely, with no resistance, no effort, and I looked up and saw that I was being pulled away from shore.

Yesterday we had been swimming out there in the same spot and there had been no problem. Something had changed. I started stroking back toward the hill, found that I was getting nowhere, and then I realized that I was caught in a vicious undercurrent. I popped my head up and the shore was even further away. I could see our tents, the camp, and people on the beach. I cursed myself for not getting several people to swim out with me.

Frantically I swam against the current, stroking and kicking with all my might, but making little headway. All my efforts were failing. Panic started to seize me. My heart was pounding, I was getting out of breath, I was swallowing saltwater, and my eyes were stinging.

All the alarms were going off in my body. I fought to take command and not explode into hysteria that I knew would be death. "Relax, stop," I ordered myself. I recited the creed: "Don't fight it, just go with the flow, sooner or later it will drop you, and then you can swim back."

But how long was that sooner or later? If it carried me far out to sea, with no one knowing I was out there, how long could I stay afloat? I forced myself to concentrate on the Chinese tale of an old Taoist master who jumped into a deadly whirlpool. Those watching him were sure he met his death and were shocked when he came up alive and in total control. He knew the way of spiraling motion and told me, "Go with the flow. Go with the flow."

Floating along, conserving my energy, I watched the shoreline passing horizontally—the trees, the hills, the brown beaches, the camp—and I knew I was headed toward the headland, the large pile of jagged rocks that jutted out into the "life-giving and life-taking sea," as the Polynesian peoples called it. And there it was, with the swells breaking over it.

"I'll take it, I'll take it," I said to myself.

As I drew near, I stroked with the current, cutting across it, swimming as I had never swum in my life. The black rocky fangs were coming closer. I had to make those rocks, take my chances with the seas, jump onto them and scrabble up like a seal, or that would be that. I saw them drawing closer, but I was a good hundred yards away. If I didn't make the rocks, and cling to them like a limpet as I had in Tortuguero, then there was only the sea beyond. At least when I was in Costa Rica, there were people watching me, ready to help if they could. How stupid I was to come out here alone.

Terror shot through me. I started to pray. Did I really believe in Turtle Mother, facing my death? Or did I believe in God—the God of the Christians and the Jews, Yahweh or Allah, or a just a generic God? Right now I needed a personal god who took a personal interest in my carcass. The giant serpent in the earth that drove the currents and the winds and made the earth turn couldn't be bothered with this microbe. Neither did I want a god who created and managed millions of galaxies.

I didn't take any chances; I didn't analyze it, I beseeched whichever one it took. All of them. Any of them. "Let me make the rocks." Knowing that if I missed them, with my endurance waning, I would find out what it was all about.

I wanted to stay alive. With all my strength I began kicking, swimming, slamming my flippers down, thrusting my body forward against the rip tide, getting closer to the jagged fangs, being swept along across the current. I saw waves pounding on them, breaking into whitecaps. I saw the murky green sea pull back and expose the sharp barnacles and oysters, and I stroked as never before.

Suddenly there were rocks beneath me. I felt hardness, and my legs were getting battered as the surge threw me forward and dragged me back across them. I thought of the stories I'd heard of Pacific coast turtle beaches: how fishermen in capsized boats were thrown up on shore and slammed back and forth until every bone in their bodies was broken. I got a fleeting glimpse of the rocks beneath me through my mask, with the seaweed swaying in the surge. Then all of a sudden it was shallow again. Had it not been for the surge and the sweep, I could have stood up. I was catapulted over those submerged rocks, stroked the distance to an emerging rock face, and grabbed on. The waves pulled back, trying to dislodge me, but I held fast to a crevice.

Then the wave came back. I was tossed forward, hard into the next series of rocks, feeling the hardness of stone against the surge, against my bare legs, my chest being scraped by barnacles. But I hung on, crawling forward hand over hand, gaining ground, and slid over the first row of rocks.

The receding wave pulled me backward, hard. It hurt, but I didn't care; now there was hope. The next wave surged and I bolted ahead, grabbing onto the next rock which was rough and sharp, with no polish. I held on until the next wave shoved me over that one. Madly I swam forward until I finally beached myself. Trembling, I wrenched one flipper off and then the next. Every inch of my body was alive, shaking. I waded ashore through the water foaming around me, stepping on sharp shells and stones but hardly noticing them until I walked out on the sandy beach away from the waves onto dry land, and I dropped to my knees. And sat there, my heart pounding.

Sitting on the dark sands, shaking, I realized that I had just had a face-to-face look at my own mortality. Nothing dramatic—no wrestling with crocodiles, no being carried away in the jaws of a great white shark, or eaten by a giant squid—just almost drowned. Had the rip tides and currents carried me just a few feet further out, my endurance would have been overcome and that would have been that.

So is that how death comes—suddenly, completely, and without question, without preparation? One minute you're alive, the next you're not. Only this time I had cheated death, or it had let me go. Looking out over the dark rolling Pacific, with its great rolling swells, I wondered if I would have met Turtle Mother out in the great beyond.

And if I did, would I have believed it then?

Probably not!

13

TURTLE BUTCHERING

THE BIG-BELLIED PROP PLANE TOOK OFF, overloaded by five hundred pounds. It had trouble clearing the mountains but in a short while we were headed toward Nicaragua's Atlantic coast. Down below was Lake Managua, the vast freshwater body with giant volcanic islands and freshwater sharks and sawfishes. Eric, Ken, and Joe were glued to the window shooting pictures of the countryside. Eric wanted to document his trip for his classes at the University of Maryland. The rest of the students looked on also, anticipating the forthcoming trip. For them it was the trip of a lifetime. We were going to Pearl Lagoon to explore jungles and mangrove swamps. A boat was waiting in Bluefields to take us out to the remote Miskito Keys to explore sea grasses, coral reefs, and lobster and green sea turtle habitat.

It was a charter flight in an old DC-3, and the pilot told us he would go anywhere we asked to photograph except over the Pearl Lagoon area. "Too much risk from attack," he said. That wasn't very comforting since that's exactly where we were headed after Bluefields.

And the reality of it impinged even more. When we approached the little town of Rama, the plane angled sharply upward, climbing higher and higher into the sky, almost vertically.

"The contras are armed with surface-to-air missiles," Joe Ryan announced ruefully. "They have an eight-thousand-foot range. But cheer up, there's a truce on. That means they only shoot once in a while."

Down in the jungles there was war, and it was not safe in Rama, where Anne and I had traveled ten years ago while searching for the origins of the Turtle Mother myth. The contras sowed the roads with land mines. Fear permeated the countryside, *campesinos* were shot as they tended the fields. It wasn't safe to travel up the rivers, we were told; you don't go here and you don't go there.

A German and Swiss had been kidnapped the previous week and then released. Twice a month a peasant got killed. The presidents of Central America met and drew up peace accords, and the war was supposed to be over. That meant that instead of a dozen deaths each month, now it was only two. Women were carried off and raped at night; if they returned at all, their future in the Latin machismo culture was permanently ruined.

So we flew on, looking at the countryside, the dense rain forests that had been flattened by a recent hurricane, and the vast rivers, wondering in the back of our minds if there might be a giant explosion that would end it all. I thought about my visit with Father Adolpho Lopez just before we left for Chacocente. He was a Jesuit priest and a member of the university faculty. A gentle, quiet man of Spanish descent, he spoke excellent English. He was a professor of computer programming, but his real love was the seashore and collecting shells.

Father Adolpho took me to the monestary and showed me his vast collection of shells, which he kept in his little stucco-walled room. There were shelves from ceiling to floor filled with sea shells from the Atlantic and Pacific coasts, all neatly identified and catalogued. An old and frail, thin-boned man, he showed me his most treasured possessions: the rare cowries and whelks.

Between discussions of malacology, we talked about the political turmoil in Central America. During tea in the austere dining room, one of the other Jesuit priests sat with us in a daze—he had just returned from the monastery in El Salvador; the day after he left all his close friends and their housekeeper and her daughter had been murdered by the Salvadoran Army. Father Adolpho put his arm around the grief-stricken priest's shoulder, trying to comfort him.

The country was on alert. Everyone was afraid that U.S. troops would come storming into Nicaragua at any minute. The telephone lines were out; no international calls could go through. News was precious, yet life in Managua seemed to go on much the way it always had. People were still selling things in the markets, and traffic was the usual bustle.

Happily our plane landed safely and we arrived in Bluefields without incident. We dragged our freight into the run-down little airport and eventually stuffed it all into a truck that took us into town. Joe

Ryan had received a donation of food for the trip from some church groups—great heaping sacks of beans and rice—and that is what we ate, sometimes with fish and occasionally with a piece of meat. We were well fed by Nicaraguan standards. Joe was quick to point out that there are children who have never known anything but a straight diet of red beans and rice, with the exception of maybe a plantain.

But we hoped to do better in the Bluefield's marketplace. Eric Vanderberger and I set out to buy some fresh fish and vegetables for our group. Going anywhere with Eric was always an adventure. Although he was in his late 20s, the assistant professor of zoology looked as if he were barely out of high school: tall, loose-limbed, and lanky. Eric was first in the water, first in the woods; soaking up the environment as he went. He came from a line of old 19th-century naturalists on both sides of the family. To him there were no wasted minutes or opportunities. He collected moths, butterflies, snails, or whatever, whether it was in the dense woods or downtown Managua.

Carrying on a conversation with him was difficult in the woods or on the beach. One moment he would be deep into a discussion about some evolutionary theory, and the next he would see a big blue butterfly fluttering along and be off leaping over bushes trying to swoop it up. Often he came back with his prize, which he carefully placed in a bottle, and then wrote down the locality data in his notebook in a careful, practiced hand.

He reminded me how he liked to eat strange foods: sea anemones in California, tunicates in France, squids and cuttlefish and other ocean delectables. "I've never eaten sea turtle," he said, "but if there's an opportunity, I'd like to."

"Not if we have to buy it," I protested. "That's against environmental ethics. It's creating a market for an endangered species and that's what causes their real demise. The population can probably take harvesting a few green turtles by indigenous people, but we're not subsistence fishermen."

"I still want to try some."

"Well, if someone gives it to us, it will be okay. Then it's a gift, and it fits into the doctrine of Turtle Mother. Besides, how can you justify not eating turtle eggs, but be willing to eat the turtle itself?"

"So it's not rational. We'll buy some fish!"

We continued debating as we walked down to the waterfront. We wanted to see the turtle docks where the butchering took place. "I want to get pictures so I can show slides in my human ecology class," Eric said.

Our expedition to find fresh seafood didn't hold much hope for success. The few snook we saw looked stale, their eyes sunk in their heads;

nothing we'd want to eat. Here in the clutter of moldy old market stalls, women and children constantly flapped towels to keep the flies off the moldy vegetables piled in worn, soiled baskets: green bananas and over-ripe black plantains. As with any fresh market, you have to know when to come, and we had come too late. It was now sunup, but we should have been there in the darkness—a prospect that in the crowded and somewhat dangerous waterfront didn't seem too appealing.

We gazed around the food stalls to see what else we could find. Open-air, tropical marketplaces are one of my great joys in life. I can spend hours, days, meandering around the stalls. But the Bluefields market was depressing. Bluefields was surely one of the grubbiest little towns anywhere in the tropics. Squalor abounded in the muddy streets and decaying buildings. And the previous year's Hurricane Joan hadn't helped; the town was infinitely worse than I remembered. Not even the bright colors of the fruits and vegetables that were heaped up in the stalls did much to cover the shabbiness and despair of the place. Looking around at the emptiness, I realized that it was the vibrant mul-titudinous hues of any marketplace that give it life: the yellow bananas and plantains, the red tomatoes, the oranges, and the explosion of flowers that draw you in.

The war economy and the recent hurricane had reduced this place to despair. The water on the streets was tepid and slimy, running into gutters and slime-filled puddles. The restaurant walls were all warped; hardly a building didn't show signs of swelling boards and plywood, and drying mud. It was doubtful that it would ever dry, for Bluefields was the land of rain, rain, and more rain. But this was the dry season, which meant it rained only once a day and then for only an hour or two.

Hurrying past us, a young boy balanced a freshly butchered green sea turtle shell upside down on his head. Possibly he was cleaning it up to sell for a souvenir, or more likely, we were told, to make turtle-back stew by boiling the shell to get the residual oil and scraps of meat the knife couldn't scrape off.

From this we surmised that we were getting close to where the tur-tles were butchered; maybe I would be able to learn something about the fishery and Eric could get pictures for his class. Roberto, a fisheries biologist who had joined our class in Bluefields, said that if we had a chance during our travels throughout the Miskito Keys to see a village butchering a green turtle, we shouldn't miss it. It was a cultural experience.

With Eric asking questions in his halting Spanish, we were direct-ed along the cluttered waterfront of shops and wharfs to a collection of run-down piers—the place of turtle termination.

What a hell of a place for a turtle to meet its demise. Set among the

industrial wreckage and oily soaked mud, it was nothing like the small scenic villages with thatched huts on the Miskito Keys that had been described by Balford, the boys from Corn Island, and Barney Neitchmann. If you took all the clutter of man's assaults on the sea, piled it up on the shore, and pieced it together into a wharf with tin, and planks, and lumps of concrete, you'd have the Bluefields waterfront. It, and the rest of the town, definitely needed urban redevelopment.

We had missed the butchering. The docks were littered with old plastrons and carapaces from previous butcherings, and the fresh oil-soaked shell remains bobbed in the waves. There were older ones that had deteriorated, and piles of disarticulated bones. A dog gnawed the flesh out of the freshest green turtle hull, and a couple of old fishermen sat idly on a piling, staring off into the muddy estuary that led out to Bluefields Bay.

A few men sat on fish boxes, just hanging around the docks as if they had been there since the creation of time. They told us that we were too late if we wanted meat. All the boats came in before dawn, and the turtles were butchered and the meat gone before the sun got up. We'd have to come back tomorrow.

Our planned departure for the Miskito Keys that afternoon was delayed—the boat wasn't ready. So we spent the night at a boardinghouse, where there were plenty of insects for Eric's collection, and came back to the waterfront the next morning to try again. The shadowy forms of men and women stood by the cluttered docks of Bluefields, on the turtle pier. People assembled carrying their plastic bags and waited while the butcher worked. The boat captain stood by with his crew. The butcher, a thin, mean-looking man who'd been drinking, sliced the meat into chunks. The bloody hatchet slammed down hard, chopping through the white bones and white ball joints.

"Five pounds, five pounds," cried the owner, and he reached in and selected a chunk of flesh, and handed it to another who weighed it. There were a dozen people there, standing by with cordobas in hand. The people pointed to the pieces they wanted, chattering in Spanish and English. They were serious, wanting their pound of flesh—literally. Some pieces were bloody, others pink. Every piece has a different flavor and is cooked a different way, and with reverence.

The carapace made a great bowl for holding the meat. It was piled up with rich red chunks of meat and yellow-green turtle fat.

The heads and flippers were off to the side, not scattered helterskelter, but neatly aligned in pairs. There was something ceremonial about all this.

Our presence was soon noticed as Eric moved about in his khaki shorts; his camera's explosion of strobe flashes broke the morning dawn.

"Hey mon, you have to pay me," the butcher snarled, when he saw he was the star of the show. Eric blithely ignored him and went on taking pictures of the butchering and rotting bones. The crowd of people were too involved in demanding meat, pointing to the pieces and cuts they wanted, for the butcher to keep focused on Eric. The meat continued to disappear, carried off in plastic bags by men and women.

The young professor moved closer, his obtrusive camera pointing down at the bloody flesh. "Hey mon, you take my picture, you pay me," the butcher yelled again when the hands reaching for the meat momentarily slacked off and Eric once again caught his attention with his blasting strobe.

"What's wrong with taking pictures?" Eric asked casually.

"Where you from, mon?" The butcher demanded suspiciously, staring at us with bloodshot, alcoholic eyes. Most of the crowd seemed to focus on us with curiosity, though some looked suspicious. There I was with my script-filled notebook and Eric with his cameras—expensive, shiny, representing the Yankee dream. I clutched my notebook with insecurity, glancing down the narrow wharf where we were, looking for an escape if the bloody hatchet in the butcher's hand were to be used for anything besides turtle.

"I'm from the U.S.A.," the young professor responded, stepping back and stealing another shot. I could sympathize with the butcher; Eric's incessant picture-taking was getting obnoxious.

"From America?" someone else in the crowd asked.

"Yes."

That impressed the sinewy derelict. He stood straighter in his ragged clothing, encrusted with old and new blood. "Oh, that's okay man, if you're from there," the butcher said, nodding in approval. His eyes were bloodshot, and there was a whiff of stale rum in the air.

"Ah yes, America's good," another joined in, nodding affirmatively. Somehow I sensed our gringo presence was, in their minds, considered some sort of defiance to the Sandanista government. Though we were far away from the larger contra war, we were in the midst of another nasty little civil war that was going on between the central government in Managua and the English-speaking black and Indian people of the Miskito coast. They probably thought we were with the U.S. government. Yet our ecology class was using Sandanista government planes and vessels. I felt like we were in a world of political fun-house mirrors.

"What you doing here?" he asked, his voice more relaxed.

What could I tell him, that we'd come to gawk? That we were conservationists, out to stop the green turtle fishery or regulate it, here in a crowded marketplace with suspicious and hostile people.

"We would like to buy some meat," I said hastily, thinking fast on my feet, "but we didn't bring anything to put it in."

"Sure, sure you can buy meat. You can get a plastic bag too. It only costs ten cordobas. You can get next door at the marketplace."

"How much is the meat?"

"You pay American dollar?" he asked, looking at us hopefully. I gave an affirmative nod, and he looked delighted. "One dollar a pound," the Creole butcher announced, after giving it deep thought. "One American dollar for a pound of meat."

The talking in the crowd ceased; there was a shocked silence. Some of the women looked disapproving. It was obvious that the price was an outrageous rip-off. The grimy alcoholic butcher and the crowd looked expectantly at me to haggle with him.

But I just wanted a graceful out. Compromised ideals or not, the transaction gave us a reason to be there. It softened our intrusion and the picture-taking. The truck was waiting to take us to the boat and we were holding everyone up. There was no time for face-saving bickering.

"A dollar a pound, huh?" I said, pretending to ponder it as a shrewd shopper would. "That's a little steep."

Even allowing for inflation, I well remembered that turtle meat sold for a quarter a pound. It was also obvious to everyone that the turtle butcher was making his own deal, trying to make a killing on the side.

"Okay, we'll take four pounds. If you can find something to put it in."

I was hopeful he couldn't. I really didn't want any part of the bloody flesh. I just wanted to get out of there.

"Not to worry." The butcher smiled at us, showing yellowed gaping teeth. "I'll get you a bag." He called one of the young boys over and gave him a few bills and sent him off.

This started an argument with the owner, or boat captain, which developed into a shouting match in pidgin, with others in the crowd joining in, all protesting the deal the butcher had just made. I guessed it was because he didn't cut the owner in.

We stood uneasily by in the middle of the ruckus, waiting for the bag to arrive while he continued hacking the meat up. "Ain't none of your fockin business," he retorted angrily to the people standing around him, his calloused hand tightened on the hatchet handle that was slimy with coagulated blood. "I sell him my share."

Bad feelings were brewing. The man who stood on the docks overseeing was getting angry and pointing a finger at the butcherman. He issued a loud stream of recriminations and warnings. The derelict lowered his head in subservience, grumbled at the injustice, whatever it was, and went on passing out chunks of dark red meat to the crowd. Handfuls of cordobas were exchanged, collected by yet another man, and the chunks of dark red meat continued to drop in the carapace.

It was ten painful minutes before the boy dutifully returned with the plastic bag. In the interim, the arguments wound down and the focus turned back to the distribution of the meat. Finally the turtle butcher piled our flesh onto the scale; the needle hit four pounds.

Then he asked, "Mister, you want four pounds of meat for the money or five pounds?"

Eric looked surprised at the strange question, shrugged and said, "We'll take five." The butcher scooped up another pound and put that on. The owner and the crowd watched the needle intently and with suspicion to see that it was fairly weighted. The men and women crowded around, watching the transaction, as Eric paid the butcherman four one-dollar bills, and he passed over the bag.

Then trouble really broke out. All during the cutting of the meat an argument about the exchange rate raged between the boat owner and the butcher. The crowd seemed to be quarreling with him also, shaking their heads, and he was arguing and fighting back, with a stream of pidgin intermixed with "fock you mon, it ain't yo' fockin' business. I get what I want for my part and I can sell it or do what I like."

Angry voices were raised. The owner pointed a finger at him and issued an ultimatum, the gist of which seemed to be that if he didn't come clean he was fired. Now I really felt uncomfortable. We had put our noses into their business, disrupted the economy, and were causing bad feelings. It wasn't clear how much focused on us and how much was other ruckuses.

Anxious to get away, we said thanks and started down the wobbly wharf, with its missing boards and an occasional piece of rotten plywood covering the gaps. But the owner shouted after us, "Hey Mister, you wait." We kept walking, anxious to be out of there.

Just as we reached the end of the wharf, he hurried up behind us looking very concerned repeating, "Hey mister, you wait. He pay you money, you wait."

The butcher shuffled up behind him looking chastised and a little defeated. Grudgingly, and looking uncomfortable, he reached into his pocket and pulled out a wad of newly printed Nicaraguan bills and paid Eric the equivalent of about two dollars in change. We thanked him and walked off thoroughly confused, with our change and an extra pound of meat, wondering what had happened but glad to be out of there.

Everywhere else we had been on this trip, there were hands reaching out for money. For air fares, taxis, and even restaurant food we paid a "gringo tax." Clearly it was a double standard. But obviously it was different at the turtle butchering. There were some deeply ingrained ethics here, that probably had something to do with Turtle Mother.

When we got back to the truck where everyone was waiting and told our story, Carl, one of our teenagers from Corn Island, smiled knowingly. "It's always that way around a turtle," he laughed.

"Oh?"

"Sure, people always fighting and arguing about the meat. People all de time pushing and shoving to get de turtle, 'cause it never enough of it. They stand in line, this one wants ten pounds, that one wants ten pounds, this one two pounds. Some stand in line for a long time waiting, and someone else comes in ahead of him and gets meat, and that starts a fuss. Sometimes they cut each other up with knives because it's very scarce."

"Is it that way when they're butchering a cow?" I asked, holding onto the sides of the big-paneled cargo truck as it crunched down into each washed-out muddy pothole in the grimy streets. All of us, plus our luggage and gear, were jammed in together, headed for the wharf where we were to board the lobster boat that would take us to Pearl Lagoon.

"No," Carl shouted back over the roar of the truck protesting it's huge load as the driver shifted gears. "When they go to butcher a turtle there is always a big crowd of people standing around, looking. But when they kill a cow maybe one or two people look on—no one cares."

"Why is that?" I persisted.

Seeing that I really wanted to know, Balford joined the conversation. "It's because there's plenty of cow meat and pig meat and no one care about it, but turtle is scarce, maybe get one or two times a week. The meat is alive, you know. It move, and it has some special spirit about it. A cow is just dead meat, mon, but a turtle meat move."

I began to laugh. There was a contentious nature to turtles. Governments practically go to war over turtles and their breeding beaches. Crawling up the beach, flippering through the seas, turtles leave behind a wake of arguments and strife. It permeates its way deep into the scientific community. Turtle biologists criticize each other's manuscripts and review papers with a vehemence that often goes beyond what is scientifically warranted. A few years ago it reached the point where at a marine turtle scientific conference, they were all formally requested to put their egos and feuds aside.

And nothing was more contentious than the battle among shrimpers, scientists, and conservationists over the Turtle Excluder Device issue, the biggest maritime fishing battle of the century.

Fishermen and turtle lovers in the U.S. were arguing about regulations on shrimp fishing, while Central and South Americans were eating every turtle they could get their hands on and stripping the beaches of their eggs.

And yet there is also a worldwide effort to protect these most venerable old creatures that transcends governments. It keeps volunteers walking up and down beaches throughout the night chasing poachers off the beach, relocating eggs, taking tour groups out to see them nest. It's as if there's an inherent knowledge that if we take too much, we'll lose it all.

Roberto Rigby, one of the fisheries biologists who had accompanied us to the Bluefields butchery, said there was a big difference between this butchery and the community butchering in the turtle fishing villages of the Miskito Keys. In Bluefields it didn't represent the community effort; it had passed through several hands, through middlemen who bought it and butchered it.

In the small turtle communities out in the islands, Roberto told us, it was another story. The person who delivered the meat was not the same one who received the money. There was a great deal of trust in the transactions and a lot of talk. When money was finally exchanged, it was done very casually, almost to downplay its importance.

At five in the morning they went to the beach, with the first rays of the sun. The turtles that had been brought in by the fishermen the day before were kept some feet away with their flippers tied up under a thatched roofed shelter, or beneath someone's house.

The people help the butcher haul one or more down the beach. They come with their little pans and wait. The leader of the community uses the time to make community announcements. The turtle butcher has been doing this for so many years, he has a certain sense of the distribution. Everyone has the confidence in him, that the butcher will do what is right. He handles the distribution and sees that everyone gets their fair share. "If you have a big amount of money it doesn't mean that you can get a big amount of turtle," Roberto told me. "Several that go to the fishing are in charge of the butchering, and have a say in who can get the meat as well. The Miskito people say, 'I won't light the fire until they have turtle.'"

As I listened to this 22-year-old biologist, I realized that it wasn't much different on the other side of the world in Madagascar, in the traditional turtle fishing cultures of Nossi-Be where I had spent time as a young man years ago. I remembered reading DeCary's book *La Fauna de Madagascar*, in which he describes the hunting rituals.

As soon as a turtle was landed, in the old system, it was carried before the "Rantsana" of the fishermen, a sort of altar consisting of rows of branches on which are hung the heads and leaned the carapaces of earlier captures. The fisherman gathered his family, who first had to rid themselves of amulets which they habitually carried. They addressed thanksgiving and prayers to "Andriananahari" or God for having favored the expedition. The food was cooked exclusively in seawater, in special cooking pots reserved for this use.

The stem-post of the boat was reddened with the blood which had been set aside; at the same time, a small quantity of blood was poured into a sort of cup hollowed in the bow to assure success in the next fishing expedition. Finally the ritual meal, in which all the inhabitants of the village participated, took place in the open air outside the huts. It was preceded by special ablutions accompanied by invocations to the spirits:

"Let the roads to the north, south, east, and west be and remain sacred and the prosperous coast on which we live keep all its precious gifts." As in all subsistence-hunting cultures, the animal was killed in a sacred way, and the bonds between nature and man were reaffirmed.

With the loss of indigenous cultures, modern society has turned away from venerating and conserving nature. As turtles disappear on the butcher's block, and their populations dwindle away, strife increases. Wars, famine, erosion, and poisoning of the land with pollution and pesticides increase. Volcanoes bury the land with ash, hurricanes ravage the countryside, and earthquakes split the ground. Children die from bullet wounds and the military keeps on building bombs and missiles in inverse proportion to the declining number of turtles around.

The legend told by the Miskito Islanders says that because of humanity's harassment, the gentle, shy, nature spirit Turtle Mother, like all wild things, ascended the mountain and hid in a deep dark cave. For a while some villagers said they saw the rock, but then it vanished entirely, down into a lost mysterious cave as the green turtles were almost pushed to extinction. But if she could direct the movements of turtles and the luck of turtle fishermen, which meant controlling both time and space—to catch a turtle you have to be there with your net and so does the turtle—she also affected the movements of biologists. Perhaps the ancients knew this and ate little turtle meat, or they built great stone balls to balance the energies and keep them stable, so that there would be enough good things.

As we bounced along in the truck headed for the industrial docks to board a lobster boat that would take us out into the Miskito Keys, I mused that we must have a vision of peace and well-being to restore and replant the forests, to heal the wounds of erosion, to purge the earth of poisons and put nourishment back into the sea, to reuse our wastes and consider the balance and well-being of the earth first, ahead of greed and selfishness. Maybe teaching this class would help to restore the balance.

Turtles are part of the balance. Someday the beach would once again thunder with the sounds of nesting ridleys laying their eggs. Their young would hatch and swim through pollution-free seas, free of oil and plastics, without DDT and pesticides. It is an unrealistic vision many will say, but the only one we can have if we are going to survive. If we save the turtle, we save the world. And to really save them would mean putting an end to war, using the money to restore the land, to promote education and control our exploding population. With six billion people on earth eating every day, draining the resources of the land and sea, the subsistence model of taking only enough doesn't work very well.

In order for turtles to proliferate and nest, the world would have to become a global village and put aside global pillage, with a better understanding of the world and its balances. We would have to act with education, with appreciation, and understanding for all the life forms that exist on the shell of the big tortoise. Our socio-economic systems would have to change, and when they did the flesh-and-blood turtle would stay alive and the symbol of the turtle beneath our feet would go on providing nourishment and balance. People would be able to eat turtle eggs and meat now and then, taking them not for profit, but just for the nourishment of their delicious flesh, and only when there was enough to go around.

The Turtle Mother religion represents a long-forgotten conservation ethic. Sometimes I felt ridiculous, and asked myself what I was doing chasing this crazy myth; trying to re-create something that may be just a native superstition—to reach down into the earth and touch the turtle.

Sitting in the back of the truck with my plastic bag filled with bloody chunks of green turtle flesh, I suddenly realized that it was not I who was crazy, it was the rest of the world, with its destructive money culture gobbling up the land, drenching it with pesticides, draining it, scattering the wildlife and people to the wind, wasting everyone.

The Turtle Mother religion offers hope. Even in that drainage ditch in the Miami airport where native vegetation was springing up next to the runway, there was hope. For there, Turtle Mother is waiting for a time when humankind comes back into balance with nature, cutting its population either by will or force, to reforest the earth and bring back the wildlife.

As we bounced down the rough road, away from the turtle docks I felt good. Even though Turtle Mother had withdrawn from daily life, she still lived on, even in the oily grime and harshness of the Bluefields docks. Her way was still respected—sort of.

14

CORN ISLAND

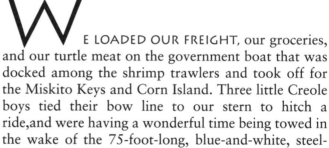

WE LOADED OUR FREIGHT, our groceries, and our turtle meat on the government boat that was docked among the shrimp trawlers and took off for the Miskito Keys and Corn Island. Three little Creole boys tied their bow line to our stern to hitch a ride,and were having a wonderful time being towed in the wake of the 75-foot-long, blue-and-white, steel-hulled lobster boat named *Promar 62* . But when the big boat picked up speed they started to swamp, and the captain hollered, "Cut loose boys, we got to go." Their line was thrown off, and the brown little boys waved and started paddling, looking a little disappointed.

This boat was brand new, one of the government's fishing fleet formed to answer the economic needs of Nicaragua. This was strictly a company boat, with a singular mission: fish more traps, fish deeper, and catch more lobsters to sell for cash. Cash to run a country, cash to fight the contras, cash to buy guns.

It was unusual for a big boat like this one to be seen traveling up the shallow, muddy Miskito Lagoon. The scream of the engine vibrating through the steel hull sent constant tiny tremors through our bones.

Our fishermen students from Corn Island were contemptuous of the young cook in the galley laying the chunks of turtle meat into the pan. "He's not using coconut oil," Fernando complained. "And he don't beat it. When you use coconut oil you brown it all over. You supposed to use certain plants and bushes to give it taste. Dis mon don't know how to cook tortle."

"No, he don't know how to cook tor-tel," Carl joined in, shaking his head with disapproval, after once again stepping into the crowded galley and inspecting the sizzling turtle steaks. "You have to put it in a pot and cook it and pour the gravy water over with a spoon." The meat was sacred, and so was the manner in which it was treated. To the Corn Islanders this cook's method was sacrilege. It was nothing to the white Spanish-speaking students from Managua who sat on the bunks or looked at the passing vegetation through the doorway.

Oblivious of the criticism, the cook was busy chopping up cassava, and pots and knives were rattling and clanging with business. Soon the air in the cabin was filled with the pungent odors of turtle meat cooking. It was a bit strong. The cook also had chunks of red beef being cooked up with rice in another pot, because our five pounds of turtle wasn't going to go very far. It would be just a taste and, even improperly cooked, a delicious one at that. But as I ate my piece, I felt a vaguely uneasy about it. Buying the meat had happened so fast, and I didn't like violating my own taboos.

I had forgotten about it, and was watching white-faced monkeys scrambling through the rain forest trees that rose above the riverbanks, when suddenly we ran hard aground. The *Promar 62* was a deep-drafted lobster boat, designed for traveling the open sea, not the inland waterways. "He knows the sea but he doesn't know this bottom," explained the captain about his navigator, who had been directing the vessel. So there we sat, chopping up mud with the prop, washing out a hole, sliding forward, dredging our way out toward what the captain believed was the channel. The prop boiled the silt into the ever-diminishing water column. It made deep throaty sounds in the hull. Periodically, when the engine almost began to glow in the dark and the smell of burnt oil permeated the air, they shut it off. And we waited and waited and waited for it to cool down. Even a big Volvo diesel engine and steel-hulled boat was no match for a sand- and mudbar, with ever-decreasing water.

Hours passed, the propeller boiled mud trying to push the boat off the flat, and we were getting nowhere. Meanwhile, above the scream of the engine, Joe Ryan and Eric Van Der Berger lectured the students about fish from Pearl Lagoon. We had bought a bucket of shrimp at the last minute, and it was mixed with anchovies, catfish, and other estuarine species. The students were taking notes and saving specimens, pickling them in the formaldehyde I brought. But the hours passed, the lecture was over, and there was still nothing to do but sit there stranded on the mudflats as the sun climbed higher in the sky.

"Bad luck," said Ken McKaye, gloomily. "I think you pissed off Turtle Mother when you bought that meat. Now it's going to be at least another eight hours before we can get back out the pass and see something of the upper keys."

It was a serious setback for him as well as myself, because he was on a tight schedule. He was developing a Central American field biology class for the University of Maryland and had to get back to the States to teach his classes. Perhaps he was right, I thought. By paying money for the turtle meat, we had violated a modern-day taboo among ecologists. I felt uneasy, hoping it was all the bad luck we were going to encounter on this trip.

There was talk about waiting for the tide to rise. But as the day moved on, it became apparent that there was virtually no tide in Pearl Lagoon—a foot rise at the most and, judging from the waterline on the mangroves, we hadn't seen six inches. There we sat, stuck. The students were bored. The girls were all sunbathing on deck.

Finally something happened: a fer-de-lance came swimming by, a beautiful little snake, white with gray diamond markings, undulating towards the boat's hull. It got everyone moving. Tying Eric's butterfly net to a pole, they managed to scoop it up. It came up striking and nasty, showing fangs. It was barely six inches long. Eric grabbed it by the neck and held it up triumphantly.

Balford didn't think it was funny. "Dat snake kill you. One bite and you're dead, Eric. You don't catch no more butterflies," he added ominously. Everybody laughed.

"Do you have some formaldehyde? We'll pickle it," Joe suggested. Jocunda, one of the teachers, nodded in agreement.

"I don't see any need to kill it," I said shortly. "It's minding its own business. It got lost and ended up against our ship. Throw it back."

"Kill dat thing! Don't put no snake back alive, especially a poisonous one like that," the heavy-set captain insisted, looking grave. "He catch you in de bush, and you die. I bit by one just like dat and I sick for three months and almost die!" He looked at it with hatred, his voice rising with anger. "My leg swelled big as a barrel."

In spite of that, it suddenly became very important to me that we let it go. A feeling of dread swept over me. Somewhere I felt in my guts that it had to live; that if we killed it, it would be a bad omen.

"But we're not in the bush," I rejoined. " We're on a big steel-hulled boat, and that's a baby snake that was minding his own business and happened to swim by. We interrupted its life; it doesn't need to die. Let it go. That's the river serpent, the god of the underworld, and if we kill him, we'll never get off this bar!"

Joe Ryan translated my plea into Spanish for the students from Managua who were crowded around watching this little drama unfold, and they laughed.

"You use politics man," accused Carl.

Jocunda spoke rapidly to Joe, in a long stream of fast-spoken Spanish with lots of gesticulations. He said she wanted it as a specimen for their museum collection, that this was a scientific expedition.

But my irrational dread of killing it continued. I wasn't sympathetic to her request. I thought about all those vile-looking, yellowed specimens sitting in jars with rusty lids in the back of the classrooms. I thought about all the specimens I had confined to embalming fluid, over all the years. All were sitting on the shelves of the Smithsonian in glass formaldehyde coffins, not allowed to rot and join the food chain.

I looked at this deadly little living jewel, all huffed up and frightened. I gazed across the expanse of the vast lagoon with its black waters all around us, and the endless uninhabited jungle and rain forest where it could live with the other snakes and never get in anyone's way, and I said, "No, let it go. I've killed enough things for science. Let it live!"

The black crew looked angry, the white Managuan students neutral or sympathetic. Roberto, the fisheries biologist from Pearl Lagoon, probably caught up with the spirit of the impending national elections that would decide whether the Sandinista government remained in power or the new democratic government would take over, urged,

"Let's put it to a vote. To pickle it or let it go free."

It was a solemn moment. Everyone was taking this deadly serious-ly, and at that moment, I think it had nothing to do with snakes any-more. Everyone on board was assembled on the deck.

My hand shot up. "Turn it loose." And several hands went up with mine, including those of Joe, Ken, and Eric. All the Corn Islanders and the crew kept theirs rigidly at their sides. The Nicaraguan students looked uncertain, then slowly Lisa put up her hand, and the other girls joined her—all except Jocunda, who looked angry and fierce. She real-ly wanted it as a specimen. One by one the bulk of the hands went up, but hers stayed down. I counted rapidly.

"The 'ayes' have it; two-thirds voted to let it go." I took the net and shook the snake out, and the stupid thing swam right back up against the bulkhead where we first found it, and stayed right there, with all those antagonistic folks looking down. Nobody said Turtle Mother was clever.

Not feeling particularly victorious, I went back into the cabin to write in my journal. The next time I saw the snake it was coiled up in a jar of formaldehyde. Jocunda's expression was pleased and tri-umphant, as she held the jar up. One day, she said, it might save the life of a child. Her students could see what a poisonous snake really looked like. I shrugged. Who was I to say that the whole event wasn't meant to be?

The day wore on, and the sun was beginning to set. And we were still stuck. Above the shriek of the straining engine, the melodious voic-es of the Creoles turned angry and argumentative. Balford told the cap-tain that he was no seaman, that he should relinquish the wheel and do as Balford told him, because he was too stupid to be running a boat. The captain told Balford where he could put it, and with even more determination, cranked up and dredged even harder towards the chan-nel.

"You supposed to dig a hole out, back her up, and then slide for-ward, back and forth, back and forth," Balford complained to me, "not sit here and dig yourself into hell." And I had to agree with him, hav-ing been in that fix before.

But the captain was the captain. The only trouble was that Pearl Lagoon was in a war zone. If there was contra military activity going on there, and they saw us, no doubt the reason they didn't fire their bazookas was because they were sitting there in disbelief watching this big steel-hulled government boat bellying up even further on the mud flats.

"One doesn't shoot enemies like that. You perpetuate them, because they might be replaced with a brain," Eric said chuckling. Ken looked miserable, and put his head in his hands. Unlike his colleague, Eric was on a much more relaxed schedule.

If we were going to be attacked, it would probably happen after dark. Perhaps worried that it might get serious, the captain finally listened to Balford and dumped the eight hundred gallons of heavy fresh water. To further lighten the load, a number of us, all males, plunged into the water and waded around until we located deep water. We became human channel markers. The Portuguese-built steel-hulled trawler pitched and rolled forward, sliding toward the channel that lay parallel to the mangroves.

At last, with much churning, screaming, and groaning, the great ship slid forward and was free of her mudbank prison. The sun sank beneath the mangrove bushes, and we crept along in the darkness, the big diesel engine barely idling, shining lights on the bushes, trying to stay in the narrow river channel.

As conditions in Nicaragua grew worse, the government fisheries department, known as IMPESCA, with its *Promar* fleet of boats, became a symbol of hated government control. And there we were, a ship of fools, traveling through the thick of contra country—sitting ducks! As I looked out at the black jungle and the shadows, it didn't seem so funny anymore. Rocket fire, bazookas, and AK-47s, could rip us apart as we crept along with our noisy engine chattering, the crew shining lights down from the bridge illuminating the swamp, and the navigator searching for snags and obstructions, fearful of running aground again.

Again that feeling of uneasiness swept over me, first buying turtle meat, then killing a snake. Bad karma!

"If this were two years ago, I would worry," Roberto said, watching the searchlight beaming into the dense mangrove forests. He lived in Pearl Lagoon, in the thick of the conflict. "We were at a point where there were always contras. About fifty percent of the time you couldn't come through here without them shooting at you. But now, after the peace accords, it isn't so bad. They only shoot once in a while now."

Roberto said that, ironically, war hadn't been bad for the environment. During the struggle between the Sandinistas and the Miskito Indians and the contras from 1981 to 1984, no turtles were brought into the market. Nobody fished for lobster or grouper or snapper. Nobody was trapping jaguars in the jungle to sell the hides or shooting crocodiles. It was unsafe to be on the water, because military gunboats patrolled, ready to open fire on anyone they thought was suspicious—which was everyone. The U.S. Marines blockaded and mined harbors to impose economic sanctions. That gave the turtle population a much-needed rest.

But eventually peace accords were signed by all Central American presidents, U.S. military aid to the contras was reduced, and the Sandinista patrol boats no longer fired upon fishing vessels, which made it possible for islanders to set their nets. Instantly markets opened and hungry people were buying turtles from Rio Grande Bar to Bluefields. To make matters worse, European governments rushed in with aid, to help IMPESCA expand the fleet. Soon all the fishing villages had boats under construction paid for by the Belgians or Norwegians. It was the usual response to a declining fishery: build more and bigger and better boats like the one we were riding on to exploit less and less product.

But there were no rockets, or guns, or anything else eventful. We passed the dangerous riverbend without incident and came to the lights of the military checkpoint. By then, most of the students were asleep, crammed into the bunks or lying on pallets on the floor. Some Sandinista soldiers came aboard and checked the passports of the Americans. Balford bummed some cigarettes off them and then we headed out into Bluefields Bay and the open Caribbean.

It was good to leave behind the shallow Miskito Lagoon, with its snake- and mosquito-ridden swamps, and threat of terrorist attacks. The sun rose up from the sea, and the big steel-hulled vessel rode confidently over the waves, with 30 feet, 50 feet, and more beneath her hull.

The Miskito Islands spread out over the Caribbean basin like amoebae. Rooted to the sea floor, they are ringed by spectacular coral reefs filled with dazzlingly beautiful fishes. One of the largest sea-grass meadows in the world is here. Most of the sea floor is covered with turtle and manatee grasses, making it one of the best feeding grounds in the world.

A stiff ocean breeze blew in our faces, and almost everyone, except for four seasick students, was enjoying the rolling sea, and our occasional stops to dive near the islands to look at marine life. We were headed for the "Brancos" off Corn Island, the great rocks that rise up from the bottom like a volcano, a fathom or two above the surface, 15 to 20 fathoms below. They were home to lobsters and green turtles that like to sleep at their feet. Balford was especially cheerful here; the sea was his element. He was a wonder to

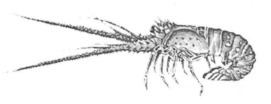

behold as he dove down deep into the reefs, holding his breath, to search for conch and lobster, or to spear a red snapper. In spite of the irritation he sometimes caused me, getting roaring drunk when we were in Managua, and his constant asking to borrow money, I had to admire this half-fish and half-man, for his wisdom and lore of the sea.

He was like a lot of fishermen I had known. The land (or "the hill" as some called it) always brought them trouble, with liquor, with women, and with officious policemen. Balford had managed to disgrace himself on numerous occasions. In Managua we had shared a room. One night he got drunk and fell asleep with a cigarette in his hand. I woke up suffocating from smoke. His pillow was smoldering, and he didn't know it. I flung the pillow out into the street and tried to drag him out of the room. Still he didn't wake up.

But now, as we sat on the bow, he talked enthusiastically about lobsters as we watched the waves breaking into whitecaps. At the Brancos, Balford came back with enough beautiful lobsters and conch to feed us all.

The next day we arrived at Corn Island and we moved into a ratty little hotel on the beach that had been reconstructed shabbily after Hurricane Joan with driftwood. I had fond memories of that serene tropical island with its sky-blue sea and beautiful reefs. Once it had been a small, scenic island with palm trees, a few houses, and a clean blue sea. Anne and I visited there years ago. It used to be a paradise, but it had changed for the worse. Now it was an overcrowded, hurricane-torn slum, and little vegetation was left standing. During the war, Corn Island's population jumped from 2,500 to 6,000. It was one of the few places in Nicaragua where you could get food, and everyone wanted to move to the little island that measured a mere 7 by 13 kilometers.

On that previous visit I had spent long hours talking to fishermen who told me about Turtle Mother and other legends of the sea. I was anxious to see if the myth still survived. Remembering how few people knew about it in Tortuguero, I half expected the legend to have vanished entirely.

A thin, wiry woman named Francis Morgan ran a little guesthouse a little ways down the beach from where we were staying. Years before she had talked at length with us about Turtle Mother and other legends of the Miskito Coast. I was happy to see that she was still there. I found her hanging clothes on the line; she hadn't changed much.

"How are you, Miss Francis?" I said, coming in through the fence. "I was here in 1975, and stayed at the Lundi's place up the beach."

The old woman smiled warmly, and with welcome. "Oh, so you

come back to the island. I don't remember you, there's been so many people, and so much has changed. The hurricane has washed it all away, don't you know."

Before long we were deep in conversation. She told that her father, who had also spent time with us sitting on the beach telling stories, was still alive, but his mind was not too good. She reminisced about the hurricane that hit the island six months ago, about the war, and about life on the Miskito coast and how it had changed for the worse.

But it had been bad before, too, at times. "Life can be hard here," Miss Francis reflected in her high-pitched sing-song voice. "I was one of twenty children, and one day there was nothing to eat. I mean nothing at all! And so my father loaded all of us into his big long boat, and we went down to the Miskito Keys. He said we would fish until we found enough for the family to survive. He caught fish, big snapper, and turtle. And so we had enough food to eat."

"The sea always provides, if you trust it," I said testing. "That's what the Turtle Mother belief is all about, isn't it?"

"Tor-tel Mother?" she said uncertainly. "You mean the rock that's shaped like a tor-tel? They say that rock is broken."

"Broken?" I repeated in astonishment. It was a totally new aspect to the legend. And that was remarkable, because the one thing about the legend was its rigid consistency. On a coast where rumors abound, people repeated it to me over and over again, without the slightest change.

The old woman, sitting there in her sea-worn dress, looked remorseful and shook her head. "Yes, that's what I hear."

"When was it broken?"

"Lately," she said emphatically. "They found it down in the Bogue, and the leg had broken."

In 1975 I had heard no mention of this injury; people talked of Turtle Mother being molested and then moving on. What glimmer I got of it in 1984 in Tortuguero also had given no indication. But now the damage to the rock was physical; the injury has set in. Was this new Humpty-Dumpty condition a symbolism for humankind's destruction and poisoning of the earth? For the war and bloodshed, and terrorism that had taken over the country?

"How?" I cried in dismay. "How did it break?"

"I don't know," she said looking puzzled at my surprised outburst. Then she went on with an open and honest expression, "They say the scientists broke it, to see what made it turn. They say they did some experiments with it." Then she said in a hushed, shocked voice, as if it were the vilest thing someone could do, *They say someone write a book about it. . . .*"

A crushing feeling of guilt swept over me. I had broken the rock. No one else was messing with it beside myself. Had I indeed broken Turtle Mother? The image of the shattered stone sphere in the Diquis Valley of Costa Rica impinged on my mind. Was I carrying this too far?

I struggled to pull my thoughts together, and she looked at me strangely. When I asked her more questions, she shook her head. "Dat's all I know about it. They say the rock was broken, I don't know how."

I went down to the beach where Anne and I had walked before so many years ago; before children, when we were young, before all this Turtle Mother business started. Great thundering waves rolled up on shore, waves of froth, clear tropical blue water breaking into white foam on the rocky headlands of Corn Island. Here the shoreline was sheered away: massive boulders and red cliff facings were exposed to the sea, as sharply as if you took a bread knife and cut a chunk off the loaf. Maybe the hurricane broke the Turtle Mother rock, I thought doubtfully, but that didn't seem right. If anything, Turtle Mother probably made the storm to scour the sea, to shake up things, and to bring about a rebirth.

We took the class diving during the day, swimming around the coral reefs and sea-grass beds, but I preferred the intertidal rocks. I had spent a lifetime turning over rocks, looking into crevices beneath the seaweed, and collecting sea creatures. John Steinbeck had been a big influence in my life. He and Ed Ricketts ("Doc" of *Cannery Row*) worked in the rocky tidepools of the Pacific and once calculated that they moved about 15 tons of rock in a single day; but they always replaced them so as to not disturb the creatures that lived beneath them.

I emphasized how important that was to the students. I showed them how chitons gnawed the rock facing away, their powerful teeth made of magnetite. Joe Ryan translated while they scribbled in their notebooks. But the teenagers from Corn Island were much more involved in foraging, as they turned over rocks. "These very good to eat, Mr. Jack," Carl said, holding up a handful of chitons that rolled themselves up into black segmented balls. "The meat is very sweet; we call them whelks."

"These are also delicious," he said pointing to the multitudes of keyhole limpets clinging onto the rocks. There were so many I had no guilty feelings about eating some. I pick up a rock, one that felt round and good in my hand, and crashed it down on a big nerita snail to crush its shell. I saw the foot coiling up, a naked spiral of snaking flesh, shook off the soft abdomen, tore off the operculum, and bit into the firm muscular foot with my front teeth.

How agreeable and rich it was. It tasted sweet, salty, and like iodine all at once, and there was nothing wrong with eating any of it; that is, if you caught it yourself, and didn't turn it into cash. That sort of foraging was called subsistence by the anthropologists. Unfortunately that word "subsistence" has a bad connotation; it is connected with poverty and despair. But, in truth, it can be the richest of all existences.

I looked at these snails creeping over the rocks, living rocks themselves, and remembered what an old woman, a healer, once told me in Pearl Lagoon, when I asked her why the Turtle Mother manifested herself in a rock. "Can't you see," she said, "the rocks have been calling creatures to them all along. Remember your Bible; God is a rock!"

Standing on the tide flats, watching the disturbed brittlestars snake their way back under the stones, I suddenly realized that the rock wasn't just a metaphor for religious stability, it was fact that life springs from the rocks themselves. The rocks in the sea, like the Brancos, brought us lobsters, fish, and turtle. Put a chunk of quarried limestone into the sea and it soon blossoms forth with sea anemones and seaweed, and becomes riddled with feather-duster worms and clams. Things grow in, on, under, and around it. On land rocks help stabilize the temperature, storing heat and releasing it to prevent abrupt extremes.

Had I not heard of this magic Turtle Mother rock, I would never have paid attention to the seashore rocks and would have continued to take them for granted. Until now they were backdrops, merely substrates, things that creatures lived on. In and by themselves they had no importance.

But now I knew that that was wrong. "This is what Turtle Mother is all about," I told the students excitedly, who had heard me go on about it from time to time. I recited the legend as it was told to me, how each year the great benign rock that sat on the mountain, in the sea, or beneath the earth turned and pointed to the west, and her turtles, which provided sustenance for people, came ashore. And when the season ended, the rock turned back to the sea, and all the turtles left the Bogue and went back out to sea.

"But can you really believe this?" asked Maria in disbelief. She wore a gold cross around her neck. "Can you believe that there is such a thing as a rock that calls the turtle to the shore? That is just an old story!"

Some of the young black students from Corn Island, who were hanging around with our group, nodded, remembering a little of that story from their past. It didn't surprise me that Josefa Montenegro JimÈnez, who worked for Direna, the nation's conservation agency, and specialized in sea turtles, and the other educated Nicaraguans hadn't heard of the legend. Even though she had spent four years interviewing fishermen and butchers in the turtle villages of Tasbaponi, Pearl Lagoon, and Puerto Cabezas, where the myth was strongest, it wasn't something people volunteered; you had to ask.

But to the white Spanish women from Managua, obviously ancient myths and modern science did not compute. Until the government ran out of money, Josefa had been part of a ten-person turtle recovery team doing research on the turtles being butchered, noting their sex, development of eggs, gut contents, and so on. She read all the literature she could get her hands on, and she had won international awards for scholarship.

Her face immobile, but her eyes registering disbelief, Josefa listened carefully as Joe Ryan translated my story of the supernatural rock. She gave me that look that said I had to be joking. But she saw I wasn't. I could see the stare of incredulity in her eyes, the sudden loss of estimation when she saw that I was taking it seriously.

Until I brought this Turtle Mother nonsense up, all our discussions and interviews with the scientists and villagers had been grounded in "reality." We had been discussing problems of cleaning up the environment, the proper use of pesticides, land use, better methods of growing fruit trees, fisheries management plans, catch per unit effort, and so on. She was comfortable with that.

The Sandinistas had laws protecting the turtles for three months prior to nesting season. It was prohibited to take the females because they have eggs, but the males could be taken year-round. The serious young woman wanted to know if this was acceptable, and what the long range consequences would be.

"After the peace accords, they took many turtles," Josefa told us, in rapid Spanish that Joe had a hard time translating. We sat on the black rocks with waves gently washing around the bases, stirring the sea weed. "Too many," the young woman went on. "They had them stacked out all over the place. They carved up meat faster than they could sell it. When the season opened, more turtle flesh came in than the freezers at Promarblue, the government's marketing company, could accommodate. They gave it away and still it rotted. This has happened to the disgust of some of the islanders who complained that fishermen were taking too many turtles. But now they have a new freezer plant to store the meat." She said fishermen were taking between five and ten thousand turtles a year. At that rate, how long could the population survive?

She wanted practical answers from me, not this nonsense about a rock that turned, and I didn't have them. What laws should be put into effect to protect them? The need was so great in Nicaragua, what was

I supposed to do? Tell people not to eat turtle when they were practically starving? It was all they could do to get some red beans and rice, and maybe a piece of fish. If nothing else, this trip had helped me appreciate what it was like to be without food. There were just too many problems, and too little money.

As we headed back to shore, I was thinking that a conservation ethic had to be developed, or rekindled. Unless governments readopted the ethic of Turtle Mother and respect for nature that so called "primitive" people once had, no government, laws, or regulations could save the turtles or humanity.

15

BEACH OF FEAR

BETWEEN TEACHING AND COLLECTING specimens, I tried to get in as many interviews with fishermen as I could, to see if others agreed that the rock
was broken. The legend was repeated with its usual
consistency, but several old men said that word came
from the Bogue that the rock was broken. Most had
heard of the rock, but I wanted to find someone who
had seen it. My quest led me to the Reverend Harold Jones, the energetic Baptist minister. He had a warmth and a personality that almost
made me want to join his church and stay there. After thanking us pro-
fusely for coming and for teaching classes in Nicaragua, he asked me,
"How can we make your stay more effective?"

I told him I wanted to interview turtlemen.

"Then I'll take you to Weddy Ebanks. He is the oldest turtleman in
all of Corn Island. There are several others here, but he knows the
most, and was the best of all the fishermen. Although I think he sold his
boat and quit."

"Weddy Ebanks," I cried excitedly. "I know that name!" And when
the Baptist minister looked puzzled as to how I, a newly arrived gringo,
could possibly know it, I told him that Bernard Neitchmann had
described him as Hemingway's "old man of the sea" in his book
Caribbean Edge. He had been 70 years old when Bernie met him in
1972, with 22 children and uncountable numbers of grandchildren, and
had helped Bernie catch hawksbills for a tagging project.

That evening Harold drove Josefa and me into the interior of the island on his motor scooter. It was a dark, eerie ride with the motor scooter whining over the dirt path, weaving dangerously past dark woods and wooden shacks, some lit with kerosene lanterns. Hordes of people were out walking on the roads, or cooking over open fires.

Finally we arrived at a tiny clapboard shack perched on a small hill where Weddy Ebanks and his wife lived. Like all the other houses that had been damaged or demolished by the hurricane, it looked as if it had been nailed back together with driftwood. There had been happier times for the old fisherman. He and his wife were two out of thousands of displaced persons who had been driven from their home during the war and fled to the already overcrowded Corn Island. For most of his life he had lived in Set Net, a small village that was the hub of turtling in the middle of the Miskito Keys.

When the Baptist minister trooped us into the house, we formally shook hands with Weddy Ebanks. He was a wiry old man, and his wife was a heavyset woman who sat beside him on a wooden chair. I couldn't see much of them, for we were all crammed together in a tiny, sparsely furnished room, with a single candle flickering. We sat in the shadows on the colorless old couch with its cracked plastic and stuffing coming out. Josefa was perched on a wooden chair with her notebook in her lap, awaiting information. Mrs. Ebanks fired up a lantern so she could see better.

"I don't know what I can tell you," Weddy began. "I don't fish turtle no more." "He must have been thinking that I was a turtle buyer. "I sold my boat, net, everything."

The years riding the swells, sailing before the wind, the affairs of the sea—all were etched into his thin, bony frame. His face was weathered with lines and wrinkles. Weddy Ebanks didn't need to recount his life of sailing back and forth across the Caribbean from the Cayman Islands to the Miskito Keys, setting nets over the rocky reefs as the sun sank into the western sea, sleeping beneath the stars, and waiting for dawn for the green turtles to surface and get tangled in the nets. You could look at him and see all that.

"Why did you sell your boat?" I asked.

The old man pursed his lips, "You can't get no help nowadays. People don't work no more. Dey want to get big pay for no work. They steal what dey want," he said with a touch of anger. "You can't keep nothin' here."

"And dey want all de money," his wife put in indignantly. "Weddy take dem out in de boat, own it all, pay all de bills, and dey want de biggest share."

"Do you mind the tape recorder?" I asked. "I like to keep my notes on tape."

"Oh no, you go ahead," he said, a shade nervously, glancing at the little machine in my lap. His expression was somber. Harold had done his best to introduce us as people trying help solve some of the country's problems, but it was obvious that the Ebankses were reserving judgment. It wasn't so long ago that spies were everywhere, checking people's alliances. And the presence of this white woman from Managua, who obviously worked for the Sandinista government, didn't help.

The Atlantic coast had always been separate, geographically and culturally, from the rest of Nicaragua, and Somosa had left the people there alone. Not so the Sandinistas. In order to make "needed reforms," the Sandinistas instituted change with a heavy hand.

"Barney Neitchmann told me about you," I began. "I've worked with him before. In fact, he mentions you in his book *Caribbean Edge*."

Weddy Ebanks nodded approvingly. "You see Mr. Barney, tell him hello. He used to come and talk turtle, just like you. He's a good man. He talk Miskito."

At the mention of the University of California professor's name, he relaxed and a big smile came to his face. Neitchmann was not loved by the Sandinistas. The Miskito called him "Commander Tunki" because he wrote on the side of the Miskito revolutionaries, and he had been banished from Nicaragua as an enemy of the state. "Tunki," it was explained to me, was the Miskito Indian term for the poisonous spine of a saltwater catfish. Getting finned by one causes excruciating pain. That's what the villagers called his pen, because it hurt the Sandinistas when he slipped in behind their lines and wrote articles for American newspapers about the murders and abuse.

Even aside from the war, most fishermen are shy, retiring, and reluctant to talk to strangers. It comes from a lifetime of being on your boat with just you, a few men, and the sea. But it didn't take long to get Weddy talking once I had gained his confidence. Turtlemen love to talk about turtles and their mysteries. Knowing enough to ask the right questions is the key in keeping any discussion going with fishermen. In minutes we were discussing the feeding, breeding, and migratory habits of green turtles. Once, Barney Neitchmann had brought Ebanks and Archie Carr together, and they talked turtle long into the night.

Josefa and the minister sat quietly by while I asked him questions. I began by telling him about our class to teach the Nicaraguan students about their country and to look over the changes wrought by the hurricane. Then I asked him how the turtles had made out.

"De storm was no problem to de tor-tel," he began in his melodic, high-pitched voice. "Dey know long before people do dat it was coming dis way. We catchin' plenty turtle and then, one morning dey all gone. Sudden-like, no one catches 'em, nowhere. We comin' into de dock with sixteen, twenty and sometime thirty tor-tel a week, and den nothin'. And I tell dese boys dat fish for turtle dat turtle know something, dat bad weather's coming. But dey don't have no experience with de sea, dey say, 'Oh no, de weather look fine.' It was calm, pretty, sunshine all right, but three, four days after dat, dey see what happen," he chuckled.

As he talked, Harold was translating for Josefa in Spanish, a sentence or two behind him. In the yellow glow of the lantern, I could see her taking notes across the room.

Weddy Ebanks spoke quickly, almost in a chant. I was having a hard time trying to understand his accent, and periodically the Reverend had to help out. "Where did the turtles go then?"

"Dat tortel go deep. Deep deep down, fifty, maybe a hundred fathom where de waves don't bother him. Dat storm hurt de lobster bad, and tear up de bottom, but it don't hurt dat tor-tel, no sir. Right after de storm, he come back just like before."

The impact of the storm on the grass beds was negligible, and didn't damage the turtles' food supply. It may have even enhanced it, tearing off the old growth and exposing the new green shoots that they like to eat. "Dey don't like to eat de old leaves, dey root around de grass and eat the white part and the young shoots. Sometimes you see where dey root up all de grass, and make a big mud cloud."

We talked turtle into the night: about green turtles running before the wind, about hawksbills eating sponges and hiding under reefs, and loggerheads crushing up crabs and whelks with their powerful jaws.

Because he was a pragmatic, no-nonsense man, he grew impatient when I brought up some of the myths and fanciful stories one hears commonly, such as turtle flesh or eggs being an aphrodisiac. He just chuckled and shook his head. "I hear this but I don't believe it." When I brought up the "turtle book" that Barney Neitchmann wrote about—the extremely rare, thickened, anomalous clump of tissue found in the throats of green turtles that fishermen said brought them good luck—he scoffed: "It's just a thing that grows in the throat. It makes you no luckier than anyone else. It's just something you find."

Periodically the conversation would lapse, and Weddy Ebanks sat there silently waiting until I dredged up a new question. I was dying to plunge into Turtle Mother, but I held back, working up to it slowly. I brought up the problem of how turtles find their way across the ocean.

"Why do you think all the turtles go down to Tortuguero?" I asked him. "What draws them there?"

Weddy Ebanks replied in a slow, considered tone, "It's the rock dat draws them to de Bogue, the Turtle Mother rock in the shape of a tor-tel. I have seen it often, when I was there."

"That's the rock that moves?" I asked, trying to sound casual, to keep from showing the excitement that was building up in me.

I glanced at Josefa as she heard the translation, and saw the puzzlement in her eyes as she waited expectantly.

"They say that rock move, but I nevah see it move. They say it change direction. When I was dere, it all de time pointing de same way."

"You saw the rock?" I repeated in amazement, louder than I wanted to.

"Sure I see de rock, many times when I went down to de Bogue. Many times."

"There are two rocks at the entrance of the channel, two large black pointed rocks."

"Yes, yes, they are out in the water, I know those rocks. Very dangerous to go around them in de boat. That is not the one." He spread his arms far apart. "Dis tor-tel rock sit on de beach. It's about dis big."

It's real! The rock is real! The words screamed out in my mind. The fact that a sensible man like Weddy Ebanks, with his truthful manner and meticulous observations, had personally seen it was a real confirmation.

"Where did you see it in Tortuguero?" I asked, trying not to get too excited. "Was it on the mountain? The beach? Exactly where?" Different people had placed it in different locations in Tortuguero, at different times.

"It was on de beach, don't you know. Just above the rollers. Years ago we go down there every year and buy turtles, and I see it there often, but it always point to de sea."

The Baptist minister's face lit up with excitement. "My old father was a turtleman. He used to talk about that rock down in the Bogue and how it turned." His eyes assumed a faraway expression as he recalled another time and his long-gone family, and a nostalgic warmth came into his voice. "Ever since I was a little child I hear him talk about it. I heard about it all my life among all the turtlemen. And it was a great mystery, because no one ever saw it turn. And no one could turn it. They tried—my father said they used pry bars on it—but it would only turn by itself."

He translated for Josefa. With growing satisfaction I watched this prim young woman, with all her confidence, growing uncomfortable, shifting her position on her chair, impatient at first with this nonsense, and then baffled and amazed.

"Someone told me the rock was broken," I volunteered to Weddy, who sat there waiting for the next question. "Did it have any cracks or breaks when you saw it?"

"No," he shook his head. "There was no break in da rock when I was there. It was solid. Solid rock. I hear also dat it was broken, but only lately."

Then the old fishermen looked at me inquisitively. "But you said you been down to the Bogue. Did you see the rock?"

"No. I went up the mountain looking for it, twice, in 1975 and again in 1984, and I didn't find it. Neither did I see it on the beach." I took a deep breath, held it to calm myself, and unobtrusively exhaled. "When did you see it last?" I asked casually, straining in the dim light to see if my tape recorder was going.

"It was nineteen twenty eight when I first saw de rock down in Turtle Bogue," he said quietly. "I see it there for many years. We go down to buy tor-tel from de people who live in de village, don't you know." Mrs. Ebanks sat on the chair and nodded in affirmation. Obviously she had heard this story before.

"And what did the rock look like?"

"Why it look like a tort-tel," he said simply. "It have a head, and feet, and everything."

Slowly I was building a composite, piecing the legend together—if it was a legend. The rock was on the beach near the foot of the mountain somewhere around 1928. Then in the mid-1940s it moved halfway up the hill, and sometime after that, probably when Archie Carr arrived at the Bogue in 1947, it disappeared entirely. Or maybe the shifting sand on the beach had simply buried it, as it had built a bar out to the rocks where I dove. In any case, it had been there and then disappeared.

I thought back to the dozen or so other turtle fishermen I had interviewed along the Miskito Coast from Puerto Limon, Costa Rica, to Puerto Cabezas, Nicaragua, over the past 20 years, sitting in similar tin-roofed, clapboard huts hearing them talk seriously about the magic rock that turns. Unfortunately, in our technical society, commercial fishermen have little credibility with scientists on fisheries issues—much less fantasy.

I began to wonder deep in my soul whether there really was such a thing as Turtle Mother. It was comfortable as a fantasy, a myth, an idea, a dinner-table conversation piece, a lecture topic, an escape from the less-interesting and romantic parts of my day-to-day reality, but could such a thing really exist?

Harold certainly thought it did. As we talked about the rock, the delight and wonder in the minister's eyes and the enthusiasm in his voice increased, as did the doubt and uncertainty in Josefa's as Harold, this well-dressed pillar of society charged with all sorts of public and church responsibilities, translated Weddy Ebanks's experiences to her.

The young Spanish woman had fallen back on taking notes as

Harold caught her up with the conversation. In the lantern light, as Harold spoke, I could see her expression change from skepticism to worried incomprehension as all the details I had related to her, and showed her in my book, were being confirmed. Now she was hearing the story confirmed by two sensible people, and her incredulous expression seemed to indicate that she was afraid she was entering into La-La Land. Why did it give me such pleasure to tinker with the belief systems of this winner of the Bulgarian Woman of Science Award with her scientific papers, charts, bar graphs, and statistics, and her acceptance of conventional scientific beliefs and assumptions?

The interview was over. It was time to go. Harold announced that he could take only one person at a time on his motor scooter—the ride over had been too dangerous. He took Josefa back to the town hall first and then came back to get me.

I hung onto the Baptist preacher's waist and rode back on his noisy little motor scooter to the meeting hall where our group was meeting with the women's club.

Thinking that the Turtle Mother was a pagan myth that would be inconsistent with his Christian beliefs, I asked Harold when we stopped, "Well, how do you regard this story? Isn't it rather fantastic that a rock could actually move, that it knows when the turtles are coming? Doesn't that go against your religion somehow?"

"Oh no! It's one of God's great mysteries," he said with admiration. "It's all part of the wonderful works of the Lord. The rock is God's creation, and it is a true miracle that it should turn to let people there know that the turtles are about to come."

And with that simple explanation he drove off into the night to attend to the important problems, the souls and sufferings of his parishioners and the islanders. To him the mystery was solved; it went no further.

Josefa and I went back to the storm-battered shack on the beach that passed for a hotel and resumed teaching. Our days were spent exploring the island and diving on the reefs, and we examined tide pools at night. We beamed our flashlights on the rocks and saw chitons that had emerged from their crevices plastered on the rock facings. There were beau gregories and yellow sergeant majors swimming in the tide pools. The place was seething with life, just as I remembered it from my first trip to Corn Island. Sea anemones with their radial symmetry and translucent pastel green and brown tentacles bloomed out from the rocks. Out in the tide flats strewn with black volcanic cobbles and boulders there were purple Cerianthus anemones in tubes. A pale, almost luminous octopus slipped out from among the black boulders, stretched out its arms, and crept over the cobbles. Black pencil urchins

with their armada of spines crept about in slow motion. Grapsid crabs, stunned by the light, stood in momentary stupor, showing all their stripes and speckles, which appear only as fleeting flashes in daylight.

But on our final night in Corn island, no one wanted to go exploring. The students and some of the faculty went partying off to a loud, raucous bar called Club 8. But cumulative exhaustion was getting to me —old age, I guessed. At 47 I was the oldest member of the expedition; that had never happened before! It just wasn't as easy as it used to be. I was exhausted from the sun, snorkeling all day, combing tide flats in the sun, the discomfort of sleeping on the bare steel floor of *Promar 62*, sleep deprivation, and staying in the ratty hotels.

I said good night and went back to the hotel with its naked clear light bulb on a cord dangling from the ceiling in a windowless box of a room. Thinking about going home to see Anne and the kids in Florida where there was running hot water, I crawled under the grimy sheets that covered a padded board and dropped off to sleep.

But I couldn't sleep long. In a few hours I woke up and didn't want to stay in that grubby dark hotel room. That night the air felt thick. Staying in that dingy room with its dirty, unpainted wood walls all by myself only made it worse. I had to get out of there.

Stepping out into the night, I heard the distant beat of the music from the juke joint blaring out over the gentle wash of the ocean. The red-and-green neon lights of the bar screamed out their summons.

I ambled down the beach to the bar—it was no more than a half mile from the hotel—and went in. Our Spanish-speaking students were at the table. The Atlantic kids from Corn Island were home now, and sat apart from the students from Managua. Not much had changed. I bought them beers and the music blasted on.

Then some of the girls in our group grabbed me for a dance to raucous music from the 1950s. The place was crowded, couples practically copulating on the dance floor, pressing their bodies as tightly as they could with their clothes on.

First Lisa grabbed me by the hand, dancing close, then Jocunda, and then Maria. After weeks of being together, even with language difficulties, we had all grown close. I decided that I wasn't college-aged any more. Now my head was throbbing, and I felt groggy and tired. I had had too much to drink, having bought Balford, Fernando, and Carl drinks. *Bed*, I thought, *cut it off, now I'm ready for the room. I'm not twenty years old any more; let the party rage without me.*

Suddenly in the midst of the giant, raucous party, the lights in the juke joint blinked, dimmed, and went off. The music ground to a whine and stopped, and abruptly darkness reclaimed the space. A hundred people or more were in the room, and no one could see anybody else. No one panicked; they were used to it. The generator had to be fired up, and then the party would go on.

Glad for the opportunity, I slipped out into the darkness and started down the beach. I had to get out of there; the air, the sweat, and the noise were becoming overwhelming. I wanted my solitude back. It was midnight, the regular time the power got switched off on the island. All the lights that dot the mountains of Corn Island and define the shore-line and hills suddenly go down, save for a small distant string of lights at *Promar Blue* that keep burning through the nights on the far side of the island.

There were only a few minutes of darkness until the loud, asthmatic spluttering of the generator was heard, and then the lights and music came back on. The fresh air woke me up. I thought about going collecting, to recapture the magic of the night before, but I didn't have my flashlight with me and so I started trotting back to the hotel to get it. The further I walked, however, the more I knew I was too tired. It was going to be a long day tomorrow, flying back to Managua and then on to Florida. Besides, I rationalized, suppose the tide pool wasn't as rich and wonderful as it was the night before? I wanted to keep that momentary illusion in my memory of the luminous octopus slipping over the sea urchins. That was perfection.

I distanced myself from the club. The night was dark. The distant green-and-red neon stripes around the bar had a thick eerie glow; there seemed be a fog, but the air wasn't wet. The "Club 8" was just about out of sight, and any minute I should be stumbling up to the hotel, I thought. But I soon ran out of beach. Before me stood a great black impassable mass, a great black wall that ran perpendicular to the water, and I couldn't place it.

In my fatigue and alcoholic haze, it looked like an old Spanish fort. I didn't remember there being a fort, or any large building, on the shore. But there it was, and the beach stopped at it. Anxiously I looked down the shore and felt suddenly lost. Feeling a degree of panic and disorientation, I wondered if I was losing my mind.

Wishing I had remembered to bring my flashlight, I did my best to visualize what the beach looked like in the daytime. I looked for landmarks or something familiar, like the fence at Florence Morgan's place where she had told me about the broken turtle rock. But there was only blackness and the shapes of houses against the night sky.

This can't be right, I thought. Trying to get my bearings, I turned and walked the other way, away from the puzzling dense dark wall that made no sense, back toward the lights of the bar. As I trotted through the darkness, I mulled over this situation. *What a farce*, I mused. *I lecture to my students and audiences about magnetite and animal orientation, yet I can't find my way out of the proverbial paper bag and never could.*

I thought of the Fairy Boy, another widespread and consistent myth along the Miskito Coast. Fairy Boy was a trickster, a mischievous and dangerous spirit that made people lose all track of their direction. He lured them into the forest and got them hopelessly lost; sometimes his victims perished.

I walked and walked and walked. There was an eerie heaviness in the air—an uneasiness, a feeling that something wasn't quite right. It had that tingling of voodoo about it that I'd experienced before, in Andros in the Bahamas, and in Haiti. It was like that business with the snake and the turtle meat; I had learned to pay attention to it. Yet another part of me said I was turning into a superstitious quivering bowl of jelly.

It's simple, I told myself, mustering my confidence. *I'll head down the beach toward the smaller pile of rocks, the Lundis' ruins where we saw all that marine life, and when I get there I'll know, without question, that I have gone in the wrong direction. It couldn't be more than a half mile. When I find it, I'll turn around and go back.*

I took off with a determined trot.

Down the beach, or up the beach, the music in the Club 8 was going strong again, boisterous and loud. I saw the crowd dancing again, but there were a number of people standing around outside. For a moment I envisioned asking Balford which way it was back to the hotel, and that felt even more stupid. Besides, he was so drunk it was doubtful he'd know.

Walking away from the glow of the lights and the beat of the band, I came upon a couple on the beach. A woman and a man, in the shadows. Had I interrupted something? Even though it was a public beach, inadvertently intruding on private affairs was always embarrassing. It wouldn't be the first time—I've been out chasing ghost crabs or looking for nesting turtles and stumbled over coupled couples. So I kept up my brisk, "mind your own business" pace.

Most of the time, when I met people on the beach, it was like ships passing in the night. Yet in that passing moment, I had the feeling that something was wrong. Their body language was all wrong. I noticed that their movements were anything but romantic. In the shadows, their silhouettes against the starlit sea, he grabbed her, or was holding her by the wrist. She seemed to be pulling away. The woman didn't cry out; she wasn't screaming or fighting. It didn't appear to be rape, or assault, or anything strong enough to make me want to run for help.

I continued on until I arrived at the rock pile, the wonderful rock pile, and sat and watched the waves rolling up on the dark rocks for a while. Mesmerized by white water rolling gently up on the beach, listening to the white noise of the sea, I dozed off and slept for while. I awoke with the stars above me and, finally satisfied that I had my bearings, I got up, wishing I had my flashlight so I could mess around the rocks.

Walking back, I came upon a man crouched down in the sea among the waves. It seemed odd that he was out here at two or three in the morning, far removed from everyone else, taking a swim. But I noticed that he was totally focused on something, bending over what looked like a dark shape among the waves, doing something. I've met lots of people doing lots of things on the beach at night over the years—fishing, playing Frisbee, making love—but this looked strange.

I stopped and stared at his head and shoulders in the starlit sea, trying to figure it out. It was puzzling. Maybe he was trying to raise a sunken boat, or land a large fish. If it were a fish, I thought, it was the size of a porpoise. That didn't make sense; no one ate porpoises here. I could put none of it into context.

As I drew near to the water's edge, he suddenly stood up and came forward, his dark, lanky form silhouetted against the sea. He was staring at me—I could feel his eyes. He was tall, thin, and muscular.

He emerged from the waves and shadows gripping something—a machete maybe, or a club. All his body movements were menacing. Suddenly all my instincts were aroused. Confused and warning feelings swept over my body. I didn't know what to think, but I felt terror in the pit of my stomach.

Watching him wade forward, I could feel him focusing on me hostilely. My heart really began to pound. Surely I was being paranoid, here in Nicaragua, a strange country, in a volatile community where life is cheap anyway. Darkness I was not afraid of; people I was.

I mumbled "*Buenos noches*" and walked past him.

I think he grunted or said something. I glanced over my shoulder and saw him coming in my direction, behind me, picking up speed. He was a shadow, but I sensed his growing presence taking long strides over the beach. Was he following me? I turned and saw his shadow against the sea. What did he want? Maybe he was just a harmless drunk trying to put a bite on a gringo. Maybe it was just to bum a cigarette. But maybe it was to rob me—or worse. How stupid it was to be on a beach all alone at two o'clock in the morning, unable to speak the language, down here in war-torn Nicaragua with God knows what or whom.

I felt panic rising in me, a real danger, and picked up my pace even more, ready to break into a run, ready to call on all those months of jogging I used to do through the wildlife refuge, to stretch my legs and make tracks toward the glowing lights and throbbing music of the bar.

If this man in the shadows was a real threat, I'd better keep moving. If not, and this was just a chance encounter, just a figment of my insecurity, still nothing would be lost by getting out of there quickly. Ahead lay the Club 8, the green-and-red lights in the distance. Alarms of fear, of panic, of uncertainty were ringing in my head. If I looked back and he was any closer, I was ready to start running to the focus point of the red-and-green glowing lights. The place you could go and get cold beer, where there were people, crowds. No one would try anything there. My friends from Corn Island were there, my students.

I glanced behind me—there was only darkness. I stopped, turned around, and saw only waves. The man was no longer following, if he ever was. Still I kept trotting until I arrived at the juke joint. Balford was out in front with a heavyset woman. He was leaning up against the wall, dead drunk. I didn't want to get involved with him; he'd want me to buy him more beer. Right now I wanted the hotel, grubby or not. I looked in the open doorway and saw people dancing; the students were still there, but I didn't want any part of it.

I still felt jittery, and I kept going, moving away down the beach toward the hotel. All I wanted now was to go to bed. Now that I had passed the Club 8, I had a feeling of relief, of being home free, of safety, although I was still confused. Safety from what? The real or imagined man in the shadows was far behind, and I had the beach to myself. I calmed down.

I found the hotel with no trouble. When I came to that "fort" that had blocked the beach, I remembered that it was a big rocky headland that jutted out into the sea. There was a house built on top of it and it stood between the bar and the hotel. Had the Fairy Boy grabbed me earlier, or was it just cumulative fatigue? I hiked back up the beach and easily found the hard pan road that led back to the hotel.

The morning sun woke me. Painfully I got up and walked down the shore, my head throbbing from the residual effects of last night's party and still feeling a shade unsettled from being lost on the beach and the inexplicable eerie feelings that had swept over me.

The sea was beautiful, and as I stepped out into the morning sun, its sparkling blueness soon made it all go away. I sat on the rocks and wrote in my journal until it was time to go. Suddenly I was very tired of the trip and the quest. I wanted to go home to normalcy, to Anne and the kids.

Suddenly I noticed a crowd gathering down the beach, staring solemnly at a prostrate form. A woman lay dead in the sea, the waves washing her corpse back and forth. Grotesquely her head rolled from side to side, over and over and over again. Her legs outstretched, she lay naked, her black pubic triangle dark against her bronze legs. A fragment of white cloth—once a blouse—that barely covered her breasts undulated back and forth with each wave.

It was bad business: murder, rape probably. A wide scrape of raw white meat showed on her forehead. The side of her face had been gruesomely hacked away—the obvious violent cause of death. Whoever did it must have been furiously strong to mutilate her so. Her half-flensed head lolled flaccidly in the surf. She was young, probably in her 20s.

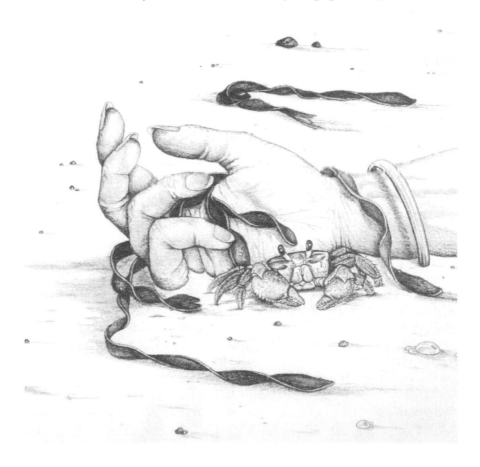

Her expression was one of tension, of fighting, of pain, of suffering, fixed in death. There was nothing peaceful in this death. And the waves wouldn't give her body final rest, just endless movement. The rolling sea pushed her up onto the beach, and then down. Her legs were rigid, her face and body blasted by sand and waves. She was so much detritus, like the rotting sea grass and algae she floated among.

Someone should drag her up and give her peace and a moment of quiet in death. But no one would touch her until the authorities arrived. Crowds arrived, to watch, to wait. Soon the beach became a mass of footprints.

The villagers came, had their fill of it, and moved on. Some drew near to gawk, as I did. Others stood back in groups and pointed down the beach in horror. Women moaned. Men stood around in grim silence. Children stared wide-eyed, watching human death and the ugliness of wasted passion.

The procession of onlookers continued. People walked past the dead body that had been washing around all night, taking in all they could stand, morbidly fascinated. Why do people gather around death, execution, and slaughter? The transition from a living person to a dead one was complete, despite the attention and the focus. A human life had been taken.

The music at the juke joint was still blaring out the loud rock-and-roll of last night. The generator puttered noisily in the background. The music brought back remembrances of the night before. Uncomfortable images began to re-form in my mind: my insomniac walk on the beach, the fear and horror I'd felt, a fleeting vague recollection of the man on the beach, the struggling woman trying to pull away. Pulling those shadows out of my mind now, I remembered the threatening man emerging from the sea and coming toward me, and my inexplicable terror.

What had I nearly been involved in? What if I had had my flashlight? Things might have taken a drastic turn for the worse, and I might have been floating beside her. I might have been the last one to see her before she died. But I couldn't identify either her or "him." Maybe the man emerging from the water with something in his hand an hour or two later had nothing to do with it whatsoever. It had all happened in shadows against a starlit sea.

Rumors abounded. Some said the dead girl was from Copra Hill, the military checkpoint we had passed through on our boat trip to Pearl Lagoon. Others thought she might be from El Bluff, the fishing settlement across from Bluefields. They said she and her boyfriend were at the bar last night. Drugs were blamed. Rumor said she ran away from her husband and ripped him off and he came after her. But no one really knew her. Later, the police (they said) arrested three men—her husband and two others. But I didn't see any others on the beach.

Suddenly I was afraid. This searching for Turtle Mother had its costs. It involved dealing with power and spirits, life and death, and death wasn't so easy to take. Death and life, yin and yang, the great wheel that spins through time. Maybe those Olmecs, Mayans, and Aztecs with their human sacrifices had come to grips with the reality of death. Maybe they knew there would always be murders and brutality, and simply organized it for society.

This lifelong quest to investigate Turtle Mother had led to confusion, disaster, and near death on numerous occasions. I remembered nearly walking into a revolution in Guatemala with Malmstrom, the Indian massacres, the rum bottles exploding at the bar in Tortuguero, the little girl drowning, nearly getting swept away in the currents at Chacocente. This sort of thing was not uncommon in shamanistic quests. Throughout mythology when one goes on a quest—obstacles, sometimes deadly ones—spring up. Scholars of mythology say it becomes a shamanistic duel, the classic battle between light and dark forces such as those Native Americans experience on vision quests. Power and understanding are not given freely; they must be wrestled from the spirit world, often with dangerous and sometimes fatal consequences. It was one thing to listen to anthropologists talk about it abstractly, another to have my heart pounding in my chest, icy with fear, running for my life down a Nicaraguan beach at three in the morning with a pursuer, real or imaginary, behind me.

Balford came by and stared silently for a minute. Then he said gravely, "Something very strange this side, Mr. Jack." We walked back to the hotel together and sat on the porch with the students, who had their gear loaded, ready to leave.

Soon a pick-up truck came by with the body in the back and people trotting behind it, as if they were going off to some event. No one seemed terribly upset about it now. That was the way it was in Nicaragua. Too many of the women in our class had lost husbands or fathers in the war, and all of them had lost friends.

By the time we loaded our gear onto a pick-up truck and caught a ride to the airport to fly back to Managua, the murder seemed to have been forgotten.

But I couldn't forget it. I had to either purge it from my mind or put this event into perspective if it meant going back to the beginning of time to find the origins of the myth. If Turtle Mother was a rock, even a magic one, then she was forged deep within the fiery guts of the earth. And part of reconstructing this puzzle was to get a look at her birthplace, the interior of the big turtle itself. Nicaragua is a land of volcanoes—political and geological. Back in the 1970s an earthquake had killed thousands in Managua and left the city in ruins. It was a country where the very breath and energy of the inner recesses of the earth reach up to the heavens, periodically venting fire.

I stopped off in Managua on the way home to visit Masaya Volcano National Park. Masaya was one of those "inactive" volcanoes—meaning that it hadn't blown up in the past ten years or so. In any other part of the world, it would have been considered dangerous. But here in Nicaragua, which has more active volcanoes than any place on earth, an active volcano is one that's in a state of eruption, belching out fire and spewing rocks and lava all over the countryside.

I drove up the steep drive to the park entrance, feeling the revitalizing wind blowing through the mountains. The grass swept before me in gusts like ocean waves. The mountain was resting uneasily. Its constant low-level rumblings were something of a tourist attraction; the government was busy building a visitor center. A few months after I left, they had to close it because it was too dangerous.

The great earth monster was sleeping now, but about 12 years ago it had blasted out tremendous amounts of ash that smothered the countryside, destroying houses and killing forests. The eruption was only a minor venting of gas. Two hundred and seventy years before that, the Masaya volcano blew. Lava smothered the countryside, and rocks the size and shape of the Turtle Mother rock were scattered everywhere. Wind had carried the ash across the countryside, and the ash had smothered the vegetation. Now there were still vast areas where no trees grew, only dwarfed vegetation that was slowly creeping back up. The immense, sweeping vista of treeless prairie vegetation was called El Cruceivo.

The highway to the Masaya volcano climbed into the clouds and ended in a parking lot full of buses and cars carrying tourists from Managua who had come to see the sights. A small hike over rough terrain, and suddenly I was looking at a great deep smoking hole, odious with sulphur, that went down, down, down into the very depths of the earth. I could hear the hacking coughs of visitors as periodic whiffs of the reeking sulfurous stench rose. The cool mountain breezes lifted the hot volcanic smoke in a vortex from deep in the crater and carried it up into the sky.

I gazed down into the immense panorama of one of the most spectacular vistas of geological activity on earth. In some places the burned red walls of the inner cone showed circular patterns like turtle scales thrown on top of large plates. There were swirls of molten red rock and earth, fractures flawed, abraded, and stratified, where the lava had erupted and splattered and seethed up with a vengeance, creating an imposing and chaotic lunar landscape. Clutching the railing, I leaned out to get a better look at the visible fissures and the lines of stratification, some curving and some straight, embedded in the rocks —fingerprints of the great earth monster; the fracture rings going up the facings, then radiating out on the lava flats; the frozen pumice with its porous pinholes and bubbles.

The vaporous mists rose in plumes and swirled around the center cavity, stinking of sulphur. The metallic odors stung my eyes. It smelled like your fingers smell after rubbing coins in your pocket, or like the harsh redolence of a blacksmith's forge. How thin this biological skin of the planet was; how much rock and fire there was far down beneath our feet compared to the life it sustained on the surface. Here was another edge, fire below and the sky above, and this thin skin of life and solid rock between.

Maybe the rocks, the sand grains, and the stones are themselves computers of life, I mused. Maybe they remember and keep track of all that come and go and fret and strut and are heard no more. Maybe they don't ignore us, but just record our passage into their crystalline structure. If we drop the bomb and wipe out life, leaving only cockroaches and jellyfishes, the rocks will bear witness to what was, and will be there ready to receive and give nourishment to the next wave of life.

Down below in the cone, amazing bright green parrots soared and fluttered through the acrid smoke, riding the vaporous updrafts, so far down into the cone of the volcano they looked like insects. How strange it was to look down on soaring birds. Above the uneasy rumble I could hear them crying the glory of the great monster below, their cacophony of raucous squawks almost drowning out the rumble of the volcano. Did they have lungs of iron? With their high metabolism, how could they tolerate the sulfuric acid in all that smoke? The tobacco companies and coal-burning power plants that blacken the skies with their smoke should make the parrots their corporate symbols. Medical laboratories should study them.

Turtle Mother works in geological time, which is absolutely inconceivable to us. A microsecond-length human life or a parrot's life flashing across a screen is hard for her to keep up with. If you're a rock, you may think vaguely back to yesteryear when the big scaly green things were slithering all over the swamps, or when the mountains pushed up, the earth sank, the continents drifted, and the woolly mammals appeared. Then those naked apes appeared, and now they're driving spaceships and killing each other.

Suddenly there was a tremendous rumble, a great sloshing, the sound of a huge wave. Lava splashed up and churned in the cauldron a thousand feet below, sounding like the waves thundering on the beach at Tortuguero, only a thousand times louder. So immense, so frightening, so overwhelming was it that I scurried away from the edge without knowing it. It was beyond frightening; there was no intellectualizing. The thing was alive, and I felt terrified and yet exhilarated.

I saw that the people behind me had taken to their heels and run back from the edge. Finding myself short of breath, my hands shaking, I went forward again and looked down and saw the parrots still circling around unperturbed. It's not a metaphor, I said to myself; the big thing down there is truly alive, with its sulphurous breath, and can bury us all with one mighty explosion. It just chooses not to; this was not an eruption, just a little cough.

We are but mosquitoes on the skin and shell of this big thing, making a wart here, a pimple there with our bulldozers and forestry and agriculture. This volcano was but a pore, an interface, between the fire below and the life on the surface membrane above. It was part of something so vast and powerful that it—she—could roll over and crush even her devout followers anytime without meaning to. And yet there was a tiny part of the "Big Thing" that seemed to arrange circumstance and fate, somehow guiding me along in my quest—something that kept me from drowning in Tortuguero and Chacocente, and from possibly being murdered on Corn Island. Somehow I was just another green parrot, flying around in the volcano, living on the edge, breathing brimstone, searching for Turtle Mother, and somehow it was okay.

16

TURTLE FATHER

F OR THREE YEARS THE SEARCH for the great Turtle Mother went no further. Then once again I found myself on an airplane, this time flying across the Pacific, 33,000 feet up, headed for Malaysia. The trip had that familiar bum's-rush, Turtle-Mother quality about it—a feeling I had come to recognize over the years of questing: a whole cadre of unlikely things had lined up and quickly fallen into place for me to make this 13- hour trans-Pacific migration.

I was back on the trail of the myth, this time with the sponsorship of a major *National Geographic* article on sea turtles. Six miles below the Air China jet, there were islands across the Pacific which had turtle rocks. Many also had petroglyphs of sea turtles, especially in Bora Bora, Tahiti, and Raiatea. Most of them were simple outlines etched in stone. But many of the petroglyphs had numerous concentric circles chiseled into the basaltic boulders. Archaeologists said they represented turtles, the sun, and the eye. These same symbols were found in Hawaii and throughout Polynesia, as well as on pre-Columbian vases in Panama and Costa Rica—more steppingstones across the Pacific; more possibilities of trans-Pacific migrations. The concentric circles, I speculated, could have also been turtle eggs, or a two-dimensional rendition of the great stone balls.

Traveling six hundred miles per hour across the globe chasing Father Sun across the western sky, I was hoping to finally meet Turtle

Mother on the east coast of Malaysia. I had it on good word that she was there.

Archie Carr had trained many students who continue the effort to protect sea turtles on beaches far from Tortuguero. One of them, Dr. Jeanne Mortimer, worked for the World Wildlife Fund. She was living in Malaysia, advising the government on how to better protect the declining populations of leatherback sea turtles that had become a major ecotourism attraction, and we wanted to cover the story for the magazine. Jeanne wrote me about another turtle rock in eastern Malaysia. The legend, she said, was the same as in Tortuguero; she had seen it and it was shaped like a turtle.

Several days later, Jeanne and I met for lunch in a hotel outside of Kuala Lumpur. A tall, thin woman with long blonde hair that came down below her shoulders, she was now in her 40s and had devoted her life to chasing around the globe working in turtle conservation. I remembered her as a young woman working in Costa Rica on the turtle beaches more than 20 years ago. Jeanne hadn't changed all that much, and she had warmth and an interest in life that few academics possessed. The press called her "The golden girl of Malaysia" because everyone liked her; she could talk to high officials as well as fishermen.

"The turtle rock is up on the hill right behind Rantu Abang," she told me cheerfully as we sat in a lavish restaurant, where Chinese and Malay people were eating. "It's a big rock, about twenty feet long. They call it 'Batu Penyu' which means turtle stone or rock. I don't think they use the word 'mother,' but I'm not sure. They say turtle rock. But then again turtles are 'ibu' in Malay, which means mother."

Two years ago, Jeanne and her roommate had been up to the top of the hill behind the beach at Rantu Abang. The hill was a backdrop to what was once one of the largest leatherback rookeries in the world. "The rock is disintegrating," she informed me, "breaking up, and that's the reason the local people say the turtles are declining."

"Can you take me up there?" I asked eagerly. "We'll cover all the expenses."

"I wish I could, but my schedule won't allow it," she said regretfully. "I'm finishing up work, my contract with the World Wildlife Fund is running out, and I have to leave the country in a couple of months. Besides, it would be better if you found a translator who could help you speak to some of the old-timers and get them to take you up there. The trouble is, not many people speak English in Rantu Abang. I might be able to get you some help at the Turtle Information Center, especially if I catch up with Taufiq Ahmad and Rahman Kassim, who are in charge of the hatchery and the beach protection program. They know something about the rock."

When I arrived at Rantu Abang on the east coast of Malaysia, I headed straight for the Turtle Information Center, hoping I would catch Jeanne's friend, Taufiq Ahmad, who might be able to point me toward the local Turtle Mother legend. I flew to Terengganu and took a taxi to a luxury hotel on the beach. I wasn't being decadent; I wanted to investigate ecotourism and its effects on sea turtles.

Malaysia had discovered that there was gold in those turtles—gold from the people who piled off the airplanes and stayed at hotels to see them. They were building a rash of hotels all over the country and had put up a lodge right in the middle of their green turtle rookeries in the Sandakaan Islands. I had seen their logo on billboards all over the country urging the people to be nice to tourists. It was a ridiculous cartoon of a goofy, fluffy-headed turtle sunbathing on the beach, wearing sunglasses, with a big relaxed grin on its face. It typified the lack of understanding of turtles.

The leatherback turtle populations had declined catastrophically over the last 20 years in Malaysia, from overharvesting of the eggs and from harassment. In Mexico, the Guianas, and elsewhere, the populations of leatherbacks were increasing in preserves, but in Malaysia the population graph went down, down, down.

Malaysia was no longer a major nesting area. In the late 1950s biologists estimated that two thousand female leatherbacks nested along the 15-mile stretch of beach at Rantu Abang. The state of Terengganu allowed harvest of the eggs, development and lighting on the beach, and shrimp trawling off the nesting beaches. Malaysia's famous leatherbacks declined. Now the population was scarcely a dozen. Crowds of tourists—sometimes a thousand at a time—surrounded the turtles, shining lights in their faces and riding them down to the beach. Chan Eng, a local college professor, publicized the plight of the turtles. Conservationists picked up the cause, and Malaysia was trying to improve things.

At the hotel I hired a driver to take me to the Turtle Information Center. Amin was in the tourism business, guiding affluent tourists from Japan, Australia, Europe, and the United States to all the local attractions. A tall young man with a short, trim little beard that followed the curvature of his chin, Amin was in business to meet the public. He dressed well and spoke good English; appearances were important in his line of work.

I got into his new air-conditioned minibus and we headed to the turtle station along pleasant, wooded roads. As we sped down the highway, I studied the terrain. Many of the low, rolling hills that had been covered with rain forest had recently been turned into rubber plantations; it was a bleak landscape, raw white from being freshly stripped.

The terraced hills, eroded and ugly in the desolation of monoculture, were planted with rubber seedlings.

"The government now owns the land, and they clear it off to put in the rubber trees," the guide explained. "It is to help the economy. There is a big demand for rubber gloves and rubbers for the AIDS virus," he said proudly, sounding like a booster for the chamber of commerce. Then, seeing my look of disgust, he added, "It will be green in a year."

"I see," I said sarcastically. "Destroy the rain forests and the plants and animals that might cure AIDS one day just to make rubbers. Makes a lot of sense!" Malaysia had a lousy international reputation for destroying its rain forests and indigenous peoples, as well as exploiting sea turtles. But I wasn't going to change that by arguing with the driver.

Instead, I lapsed into silence and looked to my right at the beaches and dunes, noticing the strange yellow sands that looked like the coquina sands along the beaches off the east coast of Florida, except that those were made of shells, and these of minerals. It was unlike any beach I had ever seen.

Amin had been pondering my remarks. "Many of the tourists feel the way you do about our forests," he said. "Perhaps the government should not be doing it."

We had to stop for a herd of cows, who made it clear that it was their highway and weren't about to move out of the way. Amin beeped his horn; they regarded him with faint contempt and annoyance, but finally moved out of the way. That made me feel better. Any place where cows were in control of the traffic situation had to be all right. Devil-ment, as one of my Chinese friends in Kuala Lumpur called it, hadn't totally taken over yet.

After a little more conversation, I felt the time was right. "Do you know anything about a turtle rock down here?" I inquired, as if it were just one more thing on an eco-tourist's agenda, after the waterfall, the bat cave, the Taoist temples, the reclining Buddha, and so on.

Amin turned and looked at me with wide-eyed surprise. "Yes, I know about it. The rock is the Mother of the Turtles. They say it calls the turtles in. There is supposed to be one up in the mountains here, not far away. But how do you know about it?"

"That's a long story," I returned, trying not to burst with excitement. I was amazed, thinking that only last night I was in the big urban city of Kuala Lumpur, expecting a long, difficult trip ahead to catch even a smattering of the legend.

"I have been studying the Turtle Mother rock for a long time. Have you seen it?" I asked, looking at him intently, no longer paying the slightest bit of attention to the mountains or the seashore.

The youth focused on the highway, deep in thought.

"No I've only heard about it," he admitted. "But they say that it is breaking up, falling apart. To know more you must see some old Malay man, some very old person."

"Do you think you could help me find someone who could take me to this rock and to translate?" I asked. "I will cover your time and expenses, and pay you a bonus if we find it." I had an uneasy feeling that if this were a spiritual pathway as well as a physical rock, I shouldn't use raw money to badger my way in. But ecotourism was Amin's livelihood.

"We can try," he replied vaguely. We drove on in silence for a while. I began to wonder if I hadn't shown too much enthusiasm.

Then Amin spoke again. "There are many such rocks here. They say there is another one in the river that looks like a turtle." The tone of his voice almost sounded like a chant, as if he were reciting some ancient bit of oral history. "They say that the turtles used to come into the river, swim around, and come to their mother, going around and around it in a circle before going back out to sea. They come ashore and lay their eggs. The old people say it has sunk down. Now they don't come there anymore."

Then he went on in the tone of a knowledgeable tourist guide imparting a cadre of information. "There is also a rock that has a turtle shape to it up near the waterfall where the tourists go. It is very pretty up there. I have a group going there next week; if you like you can sign up at the hotel. But I don't know any story about it."

That changed the scope of this trip. Now there wasn't just one turtle rock to discover, but two—possibly three. I had anticipated the usual slow, gradual work of trying to uncover the myth, unfolding the story bit by bit by talking to fishermen and getting a snatch of it here and there from old-timers. Such gains were supposed to take days of sleuthing and interviewing, just as they had in Central America, only it was supposed to be even more difficult in Malaysia because so few people spoke English and I had barely four days. But the rapidity of how things were unfolding here had all the earmarks of unseen forces paving the way.

We arrived at the Turtle Information Center. The Center was part of a tourist complex of shops and restaurants and a local grocery store that featured dried squid and fish hanging from a rack along with T-shirts and postcards of nesting leatherbacks. "You see. Turtle is very important here. Without turtle none of this would be here," Amin said proudly.

As the numbers of nesting leatherbacks began to plummet, and tourists began to complain of seeing only one or two turtles a night instead of 50, the government banned taking leatherback eggs for sale. They set up a program to rehabilitate the turtle, to increase their numbers by building a hatchery. If they could "scientifically" produce more turtles, they reasoned, it would keep the valuable tourists coming so the government would get more tourist dollars, which would keep building high rises in Kuala Lumpur and fuel the economy. And the hatchery itself would be a tourist attraction. But the turtles weren't cooperating.

The whole story was right in keeping with the legend I had first heard in Puerto Cabezas and Big Sandy Bay, Nicaragua, so long ago. Turtle Mother had lived there before she went to Tortuguero, but people came and played around the Turtle Mother rock, picnicking on it, and finally the Turtle Mother rock moved down to Tortuguero, taking her turtles with her.

Never had I seen anything so elaborate devoted entirely to turtles as the Turtle Information Center in Rantu Abang. It was practically an altar. It had two functions: it was a hatchery for leatherbacks and it educated people about the plight of sea turtles in general. Huge paintings of leatherbacks in graphics and photos showed their life cycles. There was a small auditorium for exhibits.

Unfortunately, only the workers were there—a couple of young men in blue uniformed shirts who knew nothing. The scientists and people in charge, Amin said, translating, wouldn't be back until late.

"You go look," Amin said enthusiastically. "I'll be over there." He pointed to a series of beach shops and rubbed his stomach. "I had no breakfast. I been to the airport this morning."

For a half hour I wandered around the exhibits of the turtle center, learning about their hatchery programs and how they were trying to restore the declining leatherback population. I went out to see the tanks where greens, hawksbills, and terrapins were kept. There was an empty tank that had once had a leatherback in it. It wasn't surprising to me that it was empty. Those big pelagic turtles that never cease their swimming are the most difficult of all turtles to keep in captivity because they eat only jellyfish. The exhibits were all science here; not a word about Turtle Mother.

I left Jeanne's contact a note introducing myself and asking him to call me, and went to the restaurant. Amin was sitting at a table with a big bowl of rice and beef topped with Malay hot sauce, drinking warm tea in a clear glass. "Mr. Jack, come have something to drink," he said.

Several men dressed in tattered old clothes seated nearby looked me over with mild curiosity. Sitting across from them were two attractive young women, well dressed in soft sarongs and headscarves. I wondered about these women. They didn't quite fit here. Certainly they weren't waitresses, and in Muslim lands women didn't hang out in coffee shops. Perhaps they were wives or daughters of the restaurant owners, but they didn't look like that either. They weren't in the least shy, and were having an animated conversation with the men. I gathered from their inflection and glances that they were talking about me.

Amin told me that they were discussing the rock. He translated for one of the girls, who was looking at me with great curiosity through her veil. Amin said, "They want to know why you are so interested in this rock. She says she has been to it years ago, and wants to know how you know about it from America."

Total honesty was needed—no holding back. I showed them my book which I had carried into the restaurant for just such a possibility. It showed an artist's conception of the turtle rock in Costa Rica. I explained the legend and how it was the same, adding the fact that the Turtle Mother was now "broken" in the most recent telling of the legend on Corn Island. I explained how Jeanne Mortimer had told me about the one here.

Amin leafed through the pages and saw my name. "You wrote this book?"

"Yes."

He told the rest, and they looked impressed as they passed it around and looked at the pictures, especially the artist's rendition of turtles coming to a big rock in the sea. Another man of about 50, with rough, hardened skin, who looked like a farmer, was sitting across at the next table. He joined in the conversation. "On the hill behind Rantu Abang there was a turtle big rock," Amin translated for him. "Now there are only pieces. It has deteriorated. The rock no longer has the form of the turtle. Only just the head is left now; no more body, no more flippers." The young tourist guide waited for the man to finish his next thought before going on. "When he first saw it thirty-five years ago, it was in one piece, but because the sand eroded and collapsed underneath it, it broke into pieces."

Through Amin I asked the people in the café all my usual questions about the type of rock and its color. One of the young women said that it was very soft, very sensitive, and crumbled easily, and the other two men agreed. But then again, many rocks were of soft limestone here.

"Would it be possible to find someone to take me up there?" I asked casually, when I thought the moment was right.

The farmer considered gravely for a few minutes. "This I do not know. It could be dangerous. The last five years ago, when tourists went to the spot, they get fever. Suddenly on the way back, they get a great sickness," he said ominously. It had the sound of taboo, just like the cave on Cerro Tortuguero, which was alleged to be full of poison gas, with a curse on it.

"Well, I'm willing to risk it. I would like to see it, and perhaps take some pictures."

"Some Europeans went up to take a picture of the rock," the other man said. He was dressed in a drab green shirt and worn pants. "All the negatives came out blank. There is some spirit of the rock. Not all the pictures are that way, I hear, but sometimes they are blank."

There also was a mythic story of disorientation that went with the turtle rock, about people knowing how to get up, but getting terribly lost—very similar to Nicaragua's myth of the Fairy Boy. Amin translated. "It was very difficult for the stranger to find the place because a spirit takes care of the place. The first time it is very difficult; you will find it only if you persist." The taboo had an eerie similarity to other stories I'd heard in Central America about seeking out mountains and caves, or bothering wildlife.

Madly I scribbled notes, and when I asked the farmer's name, he was suspicious and wanted to know why I was asking. I explained that I was writing an article, but he never did answer my question.

I kept the conversation going, asking more questions about the rock. The farmer recollected that the rock was about eight feet long, four feet wide, and about three feet high. It had been deteriorating steadily for a long time. "I was there thirty-five years ago and saw only the back part of one flipper that was falling down; the rest of it was intact."

"Is it far from here?" I asked when he finished.

"No. He said it is an hour to an hour-and-a-half walk from here," and pointed up to the hills.

"Would he be able to take me?" I asked my tourist guide. "I will be glad to pay."

There was much discussion, and Amin said it could be arranged. I was expecting to set up a later time, and for this whole adventure to drag out, which was fine with me because I could get some rest. But the man in the green shirt said he had time now, and that it was not far.

"How much does he want?" I asked with some trepidation, knowing that by now they figured I would mortgage my house to get up there. And they were probably right.

The old man thought about it a moment, then shrugged and said, "Whatever you think is fair."

This was another of Turtle Mother's surprises. I had stepped off the airplane less than two hours ago, caught a taxi from Terengganu to the hotel with no idea of where to start, and now suddenly an expedition was being cooked up to see the rock. Apparently Turtle Mother decided to throw open the gates and make it happen with the greatest of ease, in a rush and with a vengeance.

I thought of my long and wearisome quest through Central America: sitting around docks, at fish houses, on boats, talking to fishermen and to turtle biologists—20 years' worth, pulling out information little by little. Going back to Tortuguero, where everyone seemed to have amnesia on the subject of Turtle Mother. Getting laughed at. Looking at enigmatic carved stones and spheres, and hiking up jungle trails to gaze upon faded stelae where gods stood on the back of a turtle. Waiting in grueling lines to get a visa; waiting for buses, for trucks, for planes, for boats.

This was almost too easy. It had me worried. But when I thought about it, I realized that some of my greatest gains had always been made almost immediately. And it no longer surprised me, no more than it had when I arrived in Puerto Cabezas in 1975 asking about Turtle Mother and met up with a drunken fisherman on the beach named Monkeyleto; no more than it did in Guatemala with Malmstrom in 1978 when we drove to La Democracia and discovered that the Olmec Fat Boys had magnetic belly buttons.

"Let's go!" I said, getting up from my chair.

Amin insisted on paying for my breakfast. The man who offered to take me now introduced himself as "Ibrahim"; apparently I had gained some of his confidence. But I wondered why people were so reluctant to give their names.

We drove to Ibrahim's house, overlooking the East China Sea. It was a small shack, typical of third-world housing, sitting next to several workers' houses. All were unpainted and had bare yards of hard-packed, foot-worn clay and no grass. There were chickens wandering about, pecking at bugs. It was a far cry from the protected, tourist-pampering luxurious hotel up the road that I had just come from.

As soon as we pulled up, I saw a veiled woman duck inside; it is the Muslim custom for women not to be seen by men other than their husbands or male relatives. Ibrahim went inside and came out with another tall youth who had a mouthful of big teeth that desperately needed braces, but who spoke English, unlike his relative. He came out and shook hands with me. "So you come to see the turtle rock," he said. "Two years ago I take two girls up there before."

A little further questioning, and I found out that I had indeed struck bonanza. The women were Jeanne Mortimer and Jan, her roommate, so I was on the right track, and this was not a wild goose chase. Jeanne had told him about the other turtle rock in Costa Rica. It was getting popular. "Last year some tourists hear about it. A bus come and I take them. Also they have reporters who ask questions just like you."

So there it was: Turtle Mother was now a tourist attraction.

Maybe that's why it was breaking up, I thought ruefully. My mind went back the old woman on Corn Island who had told me about the rock being broken and had said, "some man wrote a book about it. . ."

I asked the youth his name, and he looked at me suspiciously. "Why you want to know that?"

I explained that I was doing an article, and he nodded understandingly, but didn't answer my question. Again I thought that odd, but dropped the subject. Perhaps I was violating some taboo. We took off in the huge gleaming, polished, air-conditioned van that read TANJUNG JARA HOTEL, down a one-lane dirt road—more a path than a road—heading west, away from the sea. I was surprised that Amin would take the van down this rutted road that was so heavily overgrown with bushes. Following the young man's directions, he stopped short of a fallen-down bridge and we proceeded on foot, stepping gingerly over the rotten boards until we met up with a narrow but well-traveled path. When I asked why the path was so foot-worn, Ibrahim replied seriously, "It is because most of the Malay people used to bring yellow rice to pray to the rock on full moon so that more turtles will come. But now they come up here and pray to the rock or spirit to give them special four-digit number—for the lottery."

I tried not to laugh as I fought through the brambles. We had to go through a small chili farm. The farm was overgrown with weeds and sensitive plant thickets that closed their leaflets and collapsed as we brushed by, pink flowers exploding from their thorny stems. They made wonderful scrub habitat for king and black cobras. "You watch for snakes . . . " my guides warned.

The path continued down into a dry, sunbaked bog of dense ferns, then began to ascend the mountain, winding through tall grass and scrub thickets. By no means was this a pristine rain forest; it had been cut long ago. But there were wild things moving about. The young man who led the way, carrying a club, glanced furtively at the walls of vegetation. He said he was afraid of tigers. As we climbed higher, the thick brush and brambles gave way to grasslands and trees.

We hiked on in the broiling morning heat, sweat pouring out of me, rising upward above the flat landscape, just as I had done so many times before, each time in search of the turtle rock. The vista reminded me of Tonalá, of Tortuguero, of any and all of them.

An uneventful hour later we found the rock perched on strangely barren white sand, surrounded by greenery, at the very top of the hill. The rock was raised up, as if it sat on some great altar. But the place looked like a disaster area, as if the rock had been blown apart by some great force. The shell and whatever was once thought to be flippers had broken into 12 or more large pieces.

Now they were fractions, being worked on by time, going back into the soil. The "head," which was about a meter long, did indeed look like a leatherback's head, with its pointed nose. But it was the only part that remained intact. "Now there is no more left," the brown-skinned man named Ibrahim said sadly.

Ibrahim pointed to the base beneath it, saying that was where the sand fell away and washed down, causing the main rock to crack and the pieces to crumble into disarray. Now I knew what Jeanne Mortimer meant when she said the rock was "disintegrating." Some pieces of limestone looked chipped and heat seared among the rubble of pebbles and stones. When I handled the big rock, chunks fell away in my grasp. To me it was very mysterious how there was grass growing a few yards away, but none around the base of the rocks, and only scorched earth and fine white sand.

"Why," I asked, "did this rock fall apart?"

The young man said it was because people took too many turtle eggs, and the turtles were not coming back. When the rock was still here unbroken, there were 40 to 50 nesting turtles every night. Now there are only one or two. "Taking the eggs does not hurt the turtle. The turtles do not come any more because the young people do not follow the old ways," the old farmer exclaimed. "Young people all use the computer, the TV. Today young people believe in science and don't believe the old ways, the old stories."

The younger man listened to the diatribe, controlling his irritation. Obviously he'd heard this speech before, and between the lines I thought that the old man, or perhaps his family, were involved in gathering eggs. In many ways it reminded me of the *hueveros* in Central America who couldn't see the connection between the overharvest of eggs and the decline of turtles.

The young man puffed on his cigarette and turned to me. "The turtles are less because they take the eggs, and because in the old days fishermen use hook and line to catch fish to eat and to sell in marketplace. Now they are too efficient. They use a very strong net, and turtle drowns. The people come down from Thailand and take the whole turtle away. Many are killed by the fishing boats. If Malay man catch a turtle and roll it up in the net, we set him free. But Thai people, Chinese people, they catch turtle in very big nets and take them to Singapore."

Curiously, Muslims were forbidden to eat turtle meat, yet the eggs were acceptable. I asked a lot of questions about how that was rationalized. Someone said it was because chickens laid eggs, and they ate them. But I was never able to figure that one out; it reminded me of the confused arguments I had had in Chacocente with my friend Eric, who wouldn't eat eggs, but wanted to try the meat.

A feeling of gravity came over me. The ancient ways that respected nature were disappearing all over the world. A century ago, the Seri Indians decorated the leatherback's shell in the Gulf of California and honored it before they ate it. And in Madagascar it was the same. Respect and gratitude for nature was inherent among so-called "primitive peoples." The decline came from our industrialized society, from our grasping the land and squeezing everything we could get out of the water. It happened when we stopped saying "Thank you" and started saying "mine!"

The old farmer in the faded tattered coveralls grew quite vexed and animated. It was not the egg harvest, he insisted. He jabbed his finger up toward the bare mountains to the south. Amin nodded with satisfaction and turned as if he could hardly wait to translate.

"You can see terraces all around from the rubber plantation. They burn the forests and create terraces all over the place and the fires make the rock fall down." Amin chuckled, remembering my sarcastic remark on our drive over about the destructive rubber plantation's practices.

I reeled at the symbolism. The crushing of the physical rain forest habitat resulted in the crumbling of the physical rock. Loss of spiritual awareness, greed, and ignorance of humanity caused the Turtle Mother spirit to withdraw her turtles and send them far out to sea, perhaps to another land. It was like Moses on the mountain smashing the stone tablets. The answer was crystal clear.

I looked out over the hazy ocean. The light was foggy, although the air was bone dry. There had been little bright sunshine since I came to Malaysia. The haze came from a volcano in the Philippines, which was blowing the ash high into the atmosphere and covering the sun. It was almost like a small nuclear winter; the days passed in a dreary half-light. It reminded me of that other volcano in Antigua, Guatemala, years ago, when we met Vince Malmstrom, right after the Indian massacre. The broken rock, the cleared forests, the terraced, scraped hills in the distance made me think about global warming and rising sea level. These were not cheery thoughts.

Standing before the rubble of the shattered remains, I thought of Humpty Dumpty and how all the king's horses and all the king's men couldn't put Humpty Dumpty together again. I felt very sad for the turtles and the people of the world, because the change seemed irreversible.

Faced with the impossibility of it all, I fell back on useless analysis and sample taking. The rock was white limestone, infused with red and brown streaks of rust. I looked at the craggy rock pile, wondering if there was something special about it, still clinging desperately to the hope that there was a simple answer. Maybe it had some special magnetic properties. Maybe it was made of kryptonite or yum-yum stone —or any other quick-fix alchemist's answer. Some of the red, white, and brown rock had crumbled and fallen down around the main turtle rocks and landed in what looked like tufts of wiregrass.

The young man with the buck teeth picked up a piece and showed me how it was "rusty" with streaks of red in it. "Different from other rock," he said knowingly, but I really couldn't see any difference. It had a rusty streak in it. He pointed to the worn, pitted, and eroded surface and said that it had been made by rain. Maybe by acid rain. Maybe it had happened when the rock was red hot after the fire and it started to rain. Who knew? Only a geologist could tell. And tell they would, with all sorts of strange mineral names, with scientific nomenclature describing weathering and change. And when he was done, all I would have would be a bunch of words.

"Are there other rocks around here like this?" I asked Ibrahim.

"The next rusty rock is two or three hills away, far from here," he said, pointing at the distant hill horizon to the west. "It is too far to go and there are tigers there." Looking over the cut-over terrain, I hoped with every fiber of my being that he was right; that a few tigers still survived. But it wasn't worth the trip to check it out, knowing that it couldn't be magnetic. I took a perfunctory compass reading, expecting nothing, and wasn't disappointed. It wasn't made of lodestone like the monolithic stone turtle head in Izapa. It was made of limestone, which is about as diamagnetic as the paper that this book is written on, meaning that not only will it not retain, but it will repel an electromagnetic field. Typically, calcareous sands from the dazzling white coral beaches where hawksbills and green turtles nest in Malaysia had readings of zero or minus three in Dr. Philip Callahan's magnetic susceptibility meter. Because the Malaysian Turtle Mother rock had streaks of iron ore in it, it was likely to be weakly paramagnetic. Indeed, several months later it gave a reading of 64 cgs, but it was weak in comparison to the wildly fluctuating, throbbing red rock from Cerro Tortuguero. The great stone ball chip I got from the Diquis Valley had a reading of 540 cfs. But what did it mean? Nothing! Everything! I was a fool on the mountain, confronting my ignorance and my frustrations while indulging my fantasies and mythologies; merely an intellectual pack rat, gathering rags, twigs, and plastic wrappers for its nest. The words of Shakespeare came into my mind: "It is a tale told by an idiot, full of sound and fury, signifying nothing!"

Trying to understand the nature of turtles and their relationships to rocks, and forces like the geomagnetic field that I could neither see, feel, nor touch, was like grinding down a computer chip and putting it into a mass spectrometer to see how it functioned. The only thing worse was putting it in print!

Off in the distance I could hear the highway. The mountain overlooked the ocean miles away in the hazy light. I gazed upon the distant river delta merging with the sea, remembering other mountains and other turtle rocks. It reminded me of Tonalá in Mexico, when we had climbed the mountain in the scorching heat and found the turtle altar. The ancients had taken great care to place these monoliths facing the estuaries, the mountains, and the stars connecting the heavens, the waters, and the earth.

Now I was on the other side, looking back. Vincent Malmstrom's words came back to me: "You'll never know what it means, and you'll probably never solve the Turtle Mother myth to your satisfaction. You may never put it all together, because most of the pieces are lost. But you'll probably keep on trying, just like I keep following the sun."

The men had a long discussion as I sat there looking at the vista, thinking of turtle rocks past. I waited for the talk to finish. The talk went on for quite a long while, with the participants pointing periodically to the blue ocean.

Finally Amin turned to me. "Out in the sea, or in the river, is another *batu penyu*. This rock on the hill is the man rock, and under the water is the woman rock. And when the turtles come in here, they swim round and round some big rock out in the ocean before coming here."

I had to chuckle. I don't know why, but it never occurred to me that there might be a "Turtle Father" rock. I was embarrassed at my reversed sexism. It seemed perfectly reasonable. Why shouldn't there be male *and* female turtle gods? Most religions, except the Judeo-Christian-Moslem tradition that originated in a human-created desert, have deities of both sexes. Hinduism certainly does. That statement helped put me back on track. I was chasing a myth, an allegory, not a geological specimen. Turtle Mother was just as much in the mind as it was a physical entity.

Ibrahim traced an outline of the shoreline in the burned yellow sand at the base of the Father Turtle rock, indicating a little bay where the river flowed out to sea, and positioned the rock in the center of it.

"There are many rocks in the sea," I countered. "Ask them why they think the mother rock calls the turtles, and why it is different from an ordinary rock?"

"Because it had the head, the flippers, and the body of a turtle," Ibrahim returned. "People would swim down and dive around the rock. It was to this rock that the leatherback turtles came and swam around their mother rock until it was time to nest."

"Do you have any idea how such a story got started?"

"The old people say that one time the mother turtle, the head turtle, swam into the river and swam round and round trying to get out," Ibrahim recounted through Amin. "She stayed a long time, and then, seeing that she could not get out, she changed into a rock. So when this turtle turned into the stone," he went on, "the family must come to visit this turtle once a year from then on."

Ibrahim paused for a minute, then looked into my eyes and went on. "People do not respect the turtle," the gray-bearded old man said. "Years ago the people made an altar for the rock. They take water buffalo and cut throat and spread the blood around."

"For the one in the river, or the one on the hill?" I asked.

"Both. In the river and up on the hill. But now they do not respect the turtle and they grow less, less," the older man said. "Years ago people not interested in turtle and there were many. But now they're very interested and the turtle grow less. The tourist now have the belief of old, old people." He went on. "Long years ago, they have a festival for the turtles coming in to lay their eggs. My grandfather tell me they welcomed the first turtle to come up and lay her eggs at the start of the season. He put offerings of flowers, many kinds, and takes nice-smelling water and pours it on the turtle, and people sing when she goes back to the sea. And when she goes back she tells the other turtles to come back. Then a man named Sajiaba take a lease on the beach for taking eggs, and the turtles don't come so much."

"I see. Are there stories about any other rocks, or animals that relate to rocks?"

The men conferred and Amin shook his head. There were no other rocks, and no other animals. There are no buffalo rocks, elephant or tiger rocks. Only turtle rock.

Don't spoil it, I said to myself. *Don't pick it apart like a boiled chicken. Don't analyze it to death. Take it for the miracle that it is.* Sure, I can pick these legends apart and find variations in the story. But suddenly the solemn thought hit me that here I was, clean across the world, ten thousand miles away from where I first heard the legend. And they were talking not just about a turtle spirit, as Native Americans did, or the Hindu or Chinese who depicted the world resting on the back of a turtle, but magical rocks that called the turtles to shore.

It wasn't important that I didn't have all the answers. What was important was that my search for Turtle Mother had been vindicated; that the inner voice that had driven me all these years trying to find the root of this turtle rock story was justified. I never wavered, never stopped listening to that voice within my head, because it was real and I knew it all along.

Turtle Mother wasn't an isolated myth or craziness, but what was it? A controller card in a computer, directing all the robotlike turtles to nest, even with hundreds of tourists standing on the beach and *hueveros* eating their eggs? Did Turtle Mother simply symbolize the magnetic orientation of turtles, as the work of Ken Lohmann had indicated?

The final answer was yet to come, if it would ever come. But right now, I was thinking of the turtle rock in the mountains and the one in the river or the ocean somewhere. The talk was finished. The men looked at me expectantly. It was time to go. I gave a final look at the rock before we started our descent.

Who broke the turtle rock? I wondered, as I braced myself, going down the steep incline back to the van. Was it the industrial revolution? Overpopulation, oil, wars, greed? Was it ignorance or the loss of innocence, being thrown out of the Garden of Eden? I believe that people buying and selling turtle meat and eggs broke it. Archie Carr broke it with his science, and when I wrote *Time of the Turtle* I shattered it with a sledgehammer. I remember the words of Bertie Downs, the old man who was murdered later in Tortuguero. "You get a little snatch of something like dat tor-tel rock, and you make a book about it, a movie, and it go round and round. Dat is money business!"

We all broke it—or no one broke it at all. Maybe, I thought, as I followed down the path, a new turtle rock would have to be forged in the guts of the volcano, or maybe the molten iron core in the center of the earth would bring forth a new one. But this one was made of sedimentary rock, laid down by mineralization of foraminfera over millions of years, built out of the sea itself. Like the turtles that nested on all different sands around the world, Turtle Mothers formed out of whatever minerals were available.

Amin said Turtle Mother was a miracle. So I asked the same question I had asked of Harold, the minister on Corn Island. How can you reconcile your religion with a magic turtle rock? They all agreed, "It is the gift of Allah."

So who knows, maybe when one goes to meet one's maker, there sitting beside the Creator is a great turtle rock that has a magnetic nose. Maybe the rock points you to heaven or hell. Since physicists speculate that the entire universe is a sphere, just like a cosmic turtle egg, maybe God is a great stone ball.

When we got back to the van, I gave them a gift of money (they never would say what they thought was fair, only accepting what I felt it was worth) and was about to say goodbye when the nameless young man shook my hand and said his name was "Azman." Only after we had seen the rock had he decided it was okay.

17

MOTHER TURTLE
IN MALAYSIA

I PUT MYTHOLOGY ON THE SHELF and went back to work as a journalist for *National Geographic*, writing about the natural history and conservation of sea turtles. At the Tanjung Jara Hotel at Kuala Terengganu, turtle watching is of prime importance, and I wanted to cover commercial turtle watching from an eco-tourist's point of view. If they're lucky, the guests get to see a leatherback crawl out and nest. Worldwide, turtle watching is becoming an organized enterprise. Guides patrol the beaches throughout the night. When a turtle is spotted, they radio in to the hotel.

The guests, who sign up for this adventure, are on call. Having spent the day lounging around the beach, the pool, the gardens and the restaurant, they await the telephone call, some with and others without enthusiasm, knowing that it can come anytime after dark and that it might be three or four o'clock in the morning. Hoping to learn why other people journeyed to Malaysia to watch, I had the $12 added to my bill for the turtle watch and went to bed.

I had arrived in the first few days of September, 1991, which was the end of nesting season, and it was questionable whether any turtles would be seen or not. Last year no turtles were found in September; however, one had emerged several nights ago, made a false crawl, and returned to the sea. I stayed awake until 1 A.M., hanging around the hotel lobby and bar, and typing up notes. Finally I said to hell with it and went to sleep—my clothes ready to jump into, and my notebooks and tiny flashlight ready to record the event. The next thing I knew it was morning and the telephone had not rung.

That morning, I saw Amin sitting in the hotel lobby. "Mr. Jack, I have good news. Last night, I find a man who say he know where the rock is. If you like, I take you to him."

Once again we drove down the highway and stopped at a tin-roofed hut. An old man wearing a turban ambled out the door and bowed a greeting. He was introduced as the Hajji, and he commanded great respect since he had traveled to the Holy Land. He got into the van, and we started down the highway with him pointing the way. We drove along the flatlands, past the lush vegetation that ran parallel to the coast and scrublands leading off into the mountains.

At last the Hajji pointed to a dirt path that intersected the highway, and told Amin to stop. We hiked down into the shelter of the dunes over hot yellow sand following a bone-dry ravine filled with low scrubby bushes and weedy shrubs. It was the dry season, and even though the river had a clay base, the sands had drunk up most of it. Although it didn't look it, the Rantu Abang River was one of the great arteries that drained the East Coast of Malaysia in the wet season.

We followed the dry riverbed that ran a mile or so parallel to the sea until it terminated in a low spot near the beach. There was a green spot and a flat stagnant hole filled with water, looking like an oasis in the midst of the dry yellow sands. The flat, low Spartina grass formed a great green carpet, save for the black, tannin-stained water that filled an occasional depression or pit. It was in these pockets, Amin explained, that they caught freshwater fish. Cows had been wading in the holes.

The barefoot old man hobbled along silently, threading his way over the worn path, engrossed in the landscape, looking for the right spot. Finally he spoke in a thin, high voice and my guide interpreted. "This man say sixty years ago he walked out into the water. He says he stood on the back of the rock and it was up to his chin. The water was very deep then; the rock was always under the water. He said he stepped off the rock and it was over his head, but he was small boy. The water was five or six feet deep."

I asked how he knew it was the Turtle Mother rock.

The old Hajji recalled how one of his friends dove down and felt its head, legs, and shell. "It was just like a turtle."

"Back then did everyone know where it was?" I asked, after scribbling down his last statement.

"It depend on the people. Maybe it something like moving.

Sometimes it's here and times it's there. Some people go and try to stand on it, and they cannot find. This man go and he find it. This man go and he not find it."

There it was again, the moving rock.

Finally he pointed to the deep puddle out in the middle, surrounded by uninviting wet mud, and gave a long discourse. As I waited for him to finish and the translation to follow, I felt really confused. This appeared to be our final destination, but this weed-choked mudhole couldn't possibly be the right place. He said it was.

"Ask him why he is so certain that this is the spot." There were no houses here, not even a remnant of one.

The old man pointed to one of the dwarfed trees that rose a few feet above the scrub, and with much certainty said it was the very same tree. And it was only a short distance from where he was born and grew up.

I sat there, listening to the cicadas whining in the flat hot afternoon light, wondering for the thousandth time what I was doing here, thinking for the thousandth time that none of this made sense. All I saw before me was a mudhole, some water surrounded by a flat carpet of low marsh. The landscape didn't begin to fit the legend.

"How could a whole bunch of big leatherback turtles come way up here, into this little river, and swim around the mother rock?" I asked, unable to hide my disbelief.

"It was long, long ago back in his grandfather's time when the river was much deeper, run much swifter, that the turtles came," Amin translated. "Much changed now." Looking at all the erosion from the rubber plantations on the gutted mountains that surrounded the area, it wasn't hard to figure out why. Or maybe the Turtle Mother legend was left over from the Pleistocene era, when sea level was much higher.

Or maybe this was a complete waste of time. Word of a crazy American doling out cash to look at rocks had probably spread through the village. There I was again, doubting. This should have been enough to explain the legend, but I still couldn't put it to rest. Rinzai, a Chinese Zen master who lived some 1,200 years ago once said, "If you know that fundamentally there is nothing to seek, you have settled your affairs. But because you have little faith, you run about agitatedly, seeking your head which you think you have lost."

I thought about wading out into that hot tepid soup and seeing if I could feel the mother rock with my feet, squashing mud and manure between my toes. At best I would be finding another chunk of limestone, or at worst the bumps of a crocodile's back. Enough already, go back to work! I'm here to cover the biology and conservation of turtles, I admonished myself, not mythology.

The next night the telephone chirped in my room at 2 A.M.. I was awake in a second, knowing what it meant. "There's a turtle," the heavily accented voice confirmed, "come quickly." Licensed guides patrolling the beaches had spotted a nesting leatherback and radioed the hotel.

A minivan in front of the hotel quickly filled with its sleepy, yawning tourists, who sat dazedly, or made sleepy talk as it bounced along the winding gravel roads and then onto a modern paved road. Minutes later we pulled up behind another large passenger van full of tourists from another hotel and parked on the road shoulder. Caravans of cars, vans, and buses were converging on the beaches as the hotels were notified and people who had signed up for the watches were being called. Before long it looked like the parking lot of a department store's grand opening.

The crowd was being worked by a couple of leaseholders, collecting admission fees. But as soon as everyone who did not have package deals from the hotels paid their three dollars, the procession of sleepy turtle watchers, among them families with numbed children fighting to keep their eyes open and reeking of insect repellent, tromped down a well-worn path, down a ravine, and up over the dunes. We were strangers in the darkness, moving single file one behind the other, crunching through soft sand, not knowing where we were going. At last we filed out on the open beach and met the gently rolling sea. The waves lapped softly on the shore, and off in the distance the lights of fishing boats burned in fiery orbs.

Ahead of us, down the beach, was a horde of people standing in a circle around what looked like a great black flat shape. In an almost surrealistic ritual, the onlookers stood in a hushed silence, gazing with amazement at the enormous black thing. Even though I had seen leatherbacks before on fishing vessels, and on the wild nesting beaches in Suriname, it came as a shock that anything so big, so alien, should be living in the ocean today.

Mesmerized by the mystery, the crowd kept a respectful distance as the behemoth threw sand about. Above the background murmur of voices—British, Japanese, European, and Malay—all blending softly together, came a periodic thunderous "slap, slap," as the great black flippers heaved sand over the nest cavity. The mother turtle emitted a cacophony of deep throaty sounds, gasps and loud hisses, as it laboriously went on with its work.

This was the mightiest of all turtles. With its gigantic streamlined body, it was the strangest and most alien of all reptiles, land or sea. Its plateless shell bore seven raised ridges, and one could see how the ancient Greeks believed that Mercury, the god of speed, used the leatherback's shell for a lyre. In a surrealistic scene, the tourists gazed down at the ten-foot-long, flattened shape. Save for an occasional giggle, or a little conversation, it was a subdued, hushed crowd, quiet almost to the point of reverence. Even as more newcomers trooped down the beach, creating an even bigger wheel around the big black thing in the middle, there was silence. "So huge . . . so huge . . . ," I heard a Japanese say in awe. All eyes were focused on the great flat thing that had crawled out of the sea and made a powerful clap of thunder with its flippers. So powerful are those paddles that they carry leatherbacks across the oceans and rocket them down to the great icy depths. Men have had their wrists broken by sitting too close. A squeal came from the crowd as the turtle turned and flung sand; someone had got sandblasted.

Over the next half hour the watchers continued to grow in number until the turtle was surrounded by a great ring of humanity. It was hard to see anything through the wall of people; small sleepy children, dragged out of their beds, were now wide awake, pushing between the legs of grown-ups to see. Some couples carried infants on their shoulders. There were several Malay women, wearing sarongs. There were Japanese with cameras, Germans carrying backpacks, and here and there fiery tips of burning cigarettes. An American mother explained to her two children loudly, "We have to stand back, so that everyone can see. . . ."

Only for the briefest of moments did the guard switch on his flashlight, giving a tantalizing glimpse of this great creature of the shadows, filling in form, substance, and detail. Trying to be helpful, now that the nesting was over, he shined his light, revealing two metal tags embedded in each of the rear flippers. They had been clipped on shortly after she started covering her eggs.

Suddenly a blinding flash went off.

"No flash, no flash," snapped an accented voice of authority, as an official approached the camera-wielding violator. Tourists had been warned at the hotels, and on the beaches, not to use strobes or flashes.

"Next time we take your camera away and throw it in the sea!" he said angrily, shaking his finger in the tourist's face.

Malaysia had been strongly criticized by the world conservation community for exploiting turtles. Crowds of five hundred to a thousand people standing around turtles with lightstorms of flashes were documented, and the Malaysian government was doing everything it could to control it while commercializing it. They closed off a large portion of the nesting beach to tourism and tried to regulate the rest.

Working with Jeanne Mortimer and the World Wildlife Fund, the government started training and licensing guides in conservation. They ordered all the food stands and houses off the beach and moved them back across the river. With a few exceptions, darkness returned. Sensitive to the complaints, the government started posting fishery officers on the beach to control the crowds, to stop the lightstorms of flash bulbs, and make to the tourists behave. The fisheries staff tried to educate the tourists, telling them how lights and harassment could make a turtle dump her eggs into the sea. They made them stand back ten feet. Sometimes it worked, and sometimes it didn't.

A guard once ripped the film out of a tourist's camera when he refuse to stop blasting it in the turtle's eyes. On another occasion a young woman from a volunteer conservation group, after shouting and screaming in vain for the tourists to give the turtle some room, butted them in the stomach and shoved them out of the way. Restrictions were placed on the numbers of tourists who could watch the turtles, all of which brought complaints from the hotels to the tourist board.

I counted about 70 people, standing in awe and fascination, with the turtle at the center of an ever-growing wheel. By the time the night was over the crowd had swelled to more than a hundred.

The watchers came as close as they could, with the guard shooing them away to keep people from stepping on her, their awed voices murmuring, the turtle gasping. Oblivious of the people and the occasional flashlight beam flicked on by the guards, she went on with her work, her great black flippers synchronously taking deep scoops of the beach and hurling it into the air to disguise her nest.

But before anyone arrived, her nest had been stripped of eggs; they were on their way back to the hatchery. But the turtle didn't know it. Pounding the sand like a pile driver, the great black mother turtle used her girth to pack the sand driven by her own internal ritual. Upon covering her empty nest, the great ponderous black mass began to move down the slope. Like a great cumbersome machine, she let out a growling throaty burble and heaved her eight hundred-odd pounds toward the sea. Her noise mixed with people coughing in the night air. Centuries ago, the Seri Indians in the Gulf of California once believed the earth was built upon the leatherback, and if the turtle ever collapsed, the world would end. Standing there with all those people, at that moment, I believed it too.

"Please open," one of the guards ordered the crowd in a loud voice of authority, as if he were herding cattle. Several beach keepers moved ahead of the turtle, clearing people out of the way, barking out orders, keeping the seaward side of the human circle open. Following along a step at a time, they formed a moving "U" around the turtle. The wall of humanity stopped every time the turtle did, waiting for her to gather her strength and go on, picking up speed as she moved down the slope an increment at a time, with the guard leading the stately procession.

Moving like a slow, shuffling dance, the congregation followed the great groaning black thing down to the sea. A small child reached out and touched the shell as it went by. But the general rule was followed: touching a turtle was taboo. Turtle watching at Rantu Abang had come a long way since there were a thousand people riding the turtle and stepping on their flippers as Dr. Chan Eng, a local conservationist and turtle biologist, had described to me. "People heard that the turtle won't stop nesting, so they used to torment it, trying to make it stop, stepping on its flippers or pulling on them, trying to get it to go into a circle. Before 1988 no one was stopping them. It's come a long way since then."

The people drew closer to the water's edge, knowing that the turtle was about to disappear, to enter the mysterious, inaccessible world of water. Feeling the sea, the mother turtle moved like an unstoppable bulldozer, her pace picking up, heaving forward a foot at a time with ever-diminishing increments of rest. She paused as the waves lapped around her, and then with an unexpected surge, she vanished into the starlit sea. A dark shape one instant, and then nothing.

In Malaysia leatherbacks have been tracked by satellite for a hundred kilometers between nesting periods, traveling far out to sea, then coming back to nest again—drawn back, I thought, by a controller father rock up in the hill, or the mother rock down under water, or both.

From the Pacific coast of Costa Rica, Dr. Frank Paladino of Purdue University tracked two leatherbacks with satellite transmitters on two separate occasions. Every time the turtles surfaced to breathe, the satellite beeped out their geographical coordinates. Almost as if they were following a flight path, both headed straight from Costa Rica to the Galapagos Islands, taking nearly identical routes, making a sharp turn at the Cocos Islands. One made it in 15 days, the other in 21 days, and they traveled within 50 kilometers of each other.

Paladino and his colleagues also tracked two leatherbacks off the Caribbean side of Costa Rica, and these two also followed identical paths. They headed directly from Martinus, Costa Rica, to the Cayman Islands, then went past southeast Cuba and into the Gulf of Mexico.

Neither the Atlantic nor the Pacific leatherbacks seemed to follow any particular magnetic vector. However, they stayed faithfully over undersea mountain ranges several miles deep, causing scientists to suspect that they were foraging. Paladino speculated that deep-sea currents hitting sea mounts and mountain ranges caused upwellings of cold, nutrient-rich water. Oceanographers know that wherever there are upwellings from the sea floor, mixing cold, nutrient-rich waters with sterile surface waters, productivity is increased, hence the turtles would find more food there.

However, I suspected there was a lot more to the story. Volcanic mountains rich in magnetite could also function as an antenna, emitting a signal to turtles and other marine life passing overhead. The earth's magnetic field is extremely weak, and magnetic anomalies on the sea floor or in iron mountains are hundreds of times stronger. Therefore it was possible that migrating leatherbacks were homing in on signals from rocks far below—in some cases ten or even 20 miles below—and using them as directional beacons. And these undersea mounts, symbolic perhaps of the Turtle Mother rock, were acting as way points. Perhaps the iron-rich rocks deep in the abyss caused the infinitesimally tiny crystals of lodestone in the turtle's body to torque, stimulating their nerves and sensory systems, telling them when and where to turn, and keeping them on track. Maybe, when the leatherbacks were hatchlings being swept long by ocean currents, following the sun and the earth's magnetic field, they felt those same rocks, and their magnetite chips "saved" the information in their brains, just like a computer saves data.

Leatherbacks are the most pelagic, the most hydrodynamically designed of all sea turtles. They are perpetual swimming machines. Their bodies are streamlined; the ridges on their shells and the tapered ends cause the water to flow easily over their backs. They dive to the bottom at the edge of the continental shelf, at frigid depths of a thousand meters, and also swim at the warm surface, perpetually on the move, stuffing themselves on jellyfish. They have to eat a tremendous amount to fill themselves up on their watery prey. Since some species of jellyfish are only one percent protein, a dab of mineral salts, and 98 percent water, how much nourishment can they get? A lot, apparently, because leatherbacks are the biggest turtles in the ocean, weighing up to two thousand pounds.

Below two thousand meters, submersibles find the world dark and cold, but it glitters and flashes with the bioluminescence of jellyfish and other creatures. They use the light to see, to communicate, to find a mate, to attract a meal. No one has ever seen a leatherback down in those depths, or tracked one with a transducer, but it's not hard to imagine them swimming through the darkness, swooping down on the flashes of light from gelatinous animals—mostly salps, jellyfish, and swarms of luminous copepods. One of the deep-sea comb jellies emits a bioluminescent ink that blazes in blue-green sparks like underwater fireworks as it swims away from the disturbance. Nesting females will follow a flashlight beam all over the place. You can lead them up and down the beach like a puppy dog and get them thoroughly disoriented, perhaps because their instincts draw them to flashes of light.

Leatherbacks, also called trunkbacks, are one of the few species that can easily move between these worlds—the warm tropical surface waters and the frigid depths. They stay warm because of their huge size and their great amounts of insulating body oil. Constantly on the move, they can swim up to a 50 kilometers a day. Scientists there showed that in Rantu Abang they dive to the bottom, but don't stay down there. They seem to go up and down eternally like a sine curve. They are unlike other sea turtles that sleep on the bottom. They may rest a bit, but there is some question as to whether they sleep at all. Satellite tracking shows that sometimes they float at the surface and hang motionless, then they resume swimming, perpetually on the move, perhaps feeling or being guided by the rocks so far below. And when it's time to nest, not even a thousand people on the beach will stop them from trying.

I stood there in Rantu Abang, watching the retreating tourists heading back to their buses on the road shoulder, thinking what a long way it was from the remote beaches of Suriname to Costa Rica, where I wandered over miles of open, undisturbed beach with mosquitoes whining, stumbling over logs, meeting strange creatures in the night. Ecotourism and too many people have made it a sanitized, controlled experience, where people sleeping in air-conditioned comfort, going to bed expecting a wake-up call, waiting to be told the precise moment of turtle emergence. The freedom to wander the beach at night by yourself with the waves and the stars has been taken away.

I spent several more days wandering around the countryside, taking notes, trying to find the "mother turtle rock" that was in the sea and getting nowhere.

Finally I caught up with Ahmad, the young biologist at the Turtle Information Center. We talked hard science and turtle biology for most of the day as he showed me the hatcheries where the handsome little leatherbacks lay buried in sand, awaiting release into the sea. Strange-looking little things they were, with black suits and white stripes on their ridges, scales that they would later lose. He explained how the Ministry of Fisheries had cordoned off sections of the nesting beaches where no tourists came, but the turtles didn't cooperate. Most were now nesting outside the delegated boundaries.

Ahmad was disgusted with the commercialization of the beaches, the fancy hotels, the tourist board, and the continued decline of turtles. He grew quite passionate. "I don't care who you are—the king or the rich or the poor people. If you take the picture, I smash the camera. We don't know what the turtle feels after meeting a mob of people; maybe she says, 'I'll never come back again!'"

"What kind of laws are on the books?" I asked.

He snorted. "If you disturb turtles in Terengganu you can be fined up to three thousand ringgits [approximately $12] and get six months in jail, but," he added contemptuously, "it is not enforced. The judge lets them off with a small fine, how you say, a wrist slap. It is not the policeman who can save the turtle, it must come from the politicians."

When I commented on how impressed I was with the grandiose Turtle Information Center, Ahmad laughed sardonically. "Malaysia is putting lots of government money into the turtle. They need a turtle museum because turtles are becoming extinct!" Then he repeated the grim statistics about the steady decline in nesting populations. And while the eggs of leatherbacks were being protected, the government issued licenses to cart away those of green turtles, olive ridleys, and hawksbills.

"Well, maybe we should go back to the old ways, and ask the Turtle Mother and Turtle Father rock to bring back the turtles," I said, testing. Until then our discussions had been strictly science and conservation-oriented. I had learned long ago that it wasn't wise to blunder into mythology with turtle biologists without being thought of as a raving kook. But I found his commitment and energy refreshing. "Everything else people has tried has failed. You been to the rock, and seen it?" the young man asked, looking at me skeptically with his brown eyes, yet with a feeling of concern.

"Yes, two days ago I went there. In the hills behind Rantu Abang. I went with Amin from the hotel, Ibrahim, and Azman. Unfortunately it was broken."

"I have lived here all my life," he said in a voice of wonder. "I know this rock is only five kilometers away, but I have never gone up there, not once. It's like ghosts and evil spirits that walk the beach at night here. You could not get me to go up there for a thousand dollars!"

"But the rock is good," I cried. "It is the Mother of the Turtles. In Central America, in Hawaii, throughout Polynesia, people talk about turtle rocks."

"And the rock is broken like they say?"

"Yes, it was. Shattered all to pieces. I too believe that is part of the reason the turtles have stopped coming. I believe that when people—all over the world, not just here—got greedy, the rock fell apart. Some people on the Miskito Coast of Central America are saying that the rock is broken there too."

Ahmad said nothing for a moment, pondering what I told him. "Well then, we must fix it," he cried, getting to his feet as if he were about to get started. "We must get up to that mountain with a bag of mortar and put the mother rock back together again. Then the turtles will come back!"

NICARAGUA—1993

18

TURTLE MOTHER
AT LAST

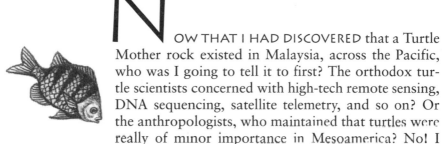

NOW THAT I HAD DISCOVERED that a Turtle Mother rock existed in Malaysia, across the Pacific, who was I going to tell it to first? The orthodox turtle scientists concerned with high-tech remote sensing, DNA sequencing, satellite telemetry, and so on? Or the anthropologists, who maintained that turtles were really of minor importance in Mesoamerica? No! I would break the news where it counted the most, on the Miskito Coast of Nicaragua where I first heard the story of Turtle Mother.

Months later I was back in Puerto Cabezas, Nicaragua, on a *National Geographic* expedition to write about the Miskito turtle culture with photographer Bill Curtsinger and his assistant Eric Heiner. We convinced the magazine to bring Dr. Bernard Neitchmann, who had written numerous books about the Miskito Coast, and his friend Modesto Watson, to handle the delicate politics and the difficult logistics of getting out to the Miskito Banks. I had met Modesto years before in San José, when I was hot on the trail of the great stone balls, and he had all sorts of insights into the Turtle Mother legend.

Before the war he ran a radio station in Puerto Cabezas, until he was forced to leave by the Sandinista government after criticizing them. During the peace accords held in San José, Barney told me, Modesto had become a strong political figure, serving as mediator and translating among Spanish, Indians, English, contras, and Sandinistas without missing a beat.

His family was from Puerto Cabezas and the Atlantic coast, and because of his radio programs, everyone knew him. He now lived in San José and ran an ecotourism guide service, taking people turtle watching in Tortuguera. This was the first time it had been safe for him to return home in years. One doesn't go skipping down to Nicaragua lightly. Even though the war was over, governments roll over like the destination signs on a city bus: "Today the government is . . ." There were many factions, lots of fighting and killing. When we stopped in Managua, Joe Ryan told me that the old guard in Chacocente, who had tried to protect the olive ridleys from the *hueveros*, had been found hacked to death by machetes. Both the Pacific and Atlantic coasts were in anarchy, with bandits holding up trucks at gunpoint and pirates in the Miskito Keys. And yet, for all its violence and strife, Nicaragua had laughter and good times, but they weren't shared with the outside world. As Modesto said, "We dance between the bullets."

We were preparing to leave for the Miskito Keys, a series of little islands where the turtlemen made their camps. Two chartered vessels were loaded with Bill's ten boxes of water-tight camera gear, lights, camping equipment, drums of gasoline, and food. Juan Francs, a teenaged boy whom everyone called "Negro" and who was somehow related to Bernard ("Barney") Neitchmann's wife, came along as our cook and back-up translator. Modesto came in looking upset—unusual for him, since he was always ready to laugh. He had bad news. He told us that he'd been talking to people in the village, who'd said the pirates were worse than ever. Two days ago lobster men had been held at gunpoint and robbed. Lots of money circulates out on the water among lobster buyers. The same banditos who held up trucks on the roads into Puerto Cabezas were starting to work out at sea. Everyone had guns. So we divested ourselves of our passports and cash. Leaving our valuables with Modesto's father, the parson, we headed for Morrison Keys, three emerald green islands 40 miles off the coast.

We sped over the bluest of blue waters and the shallow grassy sea bottoms that green turtles love so much. Barney, who taught geography at the University of California at Davis, was happy to be back. He'd been helping the fishermen and villagers set up the Miskito Coast Protected Area, which hopefully would stop the resource pirates from other areas from stripping out their seafood. "Tortuguero is the birthplace of the green turtle, but the Miskito Coast is their main address," he summarized grandly. "Here they forage in the grass by day and sleep in the rocks at night. And most everything comes from here: the lobster, shrimp, the turtle, and the fish. It's the food basket of the Caribbean coast, and everyone wants it."

Out here in the middle of nowhere, without a compass, loran, or radar, turtlemen set their nets on the reefs. At daylight, when the turtles came up for their first breath, many would get entangled. For six wet hours we pounded the waves in our noisy speedboat, which was built like a long wooden canoe, our gear stowed in watertight boxes. Crammed among the equipment, we watched the graceful catboats bucking the rolling seas before the wind, blown along with their sails puffed out, the orange sun gleaming down from among the clouds.

The *Sunshine Lady*, one of these graceful sailing sloops, was setting nets on Whippling Rock, famous among turtlemen because the green turtles mobilized there in the spring. We pulled up alongside for a talk at sea and saw they had a hull full of turtles. While Modesto chatted with them about their families, fishing, and politics, the *National Geographic* photographer took pictures. The Miskito dialect is a mixture of Arawak Indian, Creole, and Spanish. Now and then I heard a few words I could understand.

I wanted to know why they thought the green turtles came to Whippling Rock. When I first heard about it, I envisioned seeing some craggy black rock sitting up, emerging from the water, but it was 20 feet down, a dark, coral-encrusted shape on the bottom. After a long discourse in Miskito, Modesto translated Captain Pilar Lopez's words: "Before the turtle goes to the Bogue they come here. After they come back, they come here, and then go all through the Miskito Keys. If you drop a turtle in Honduras, it comes back to this rock."

"But why?" I persisted. "Why do they come here? Is there something special about the rock?"

Modesto conferred with the boat captain and his crew. "He says no. It is just another rock that the turtles like."

When I asked him how the turtles could find the rocks, he said with a great deal of respect, "Green turtles are very smart. The direction is in the head of the turtle. It has something like a compass and knows where to find the rocks."

From talking with the captain and crew, I gleaned new information about how Turtle Mother had something to do with wind and weather. Pilar said that when the mother rock was in Big Sandy Bay, it predicted the direction of the wind. The winds stirred the seas, and the turtles moved before the winds. Looking at the rock's head pointing to the south, it told the fishermen which way the wind would blow, just like a weather vane. Not only was the information critical for fishing and getting around in their sailing sloops, the rock could predict life-threatening storms. When the rock turned, everyone knew the winds would shift.

But one inconsistency remained, and I did my best to verify it. In all my travels and interviews over the Miskito Coast, I had never been able to verify Barney Neitchmann's statement that the Turtle Mother rock functioned as the intermediary between humanity and nature, as a control mechanism to prevent overfishing.

As Barney had written years ago, the money culture had taken root. The prohibitions against overtake that he described in *Caribbean Edge* were fading. The Turtle Mother, if it was thought about at all, was no longer a benign spirit that acted as an intermediary between humanity and the turtle. As long as the fishermen weren't greedy and didn't take too much, she would supply enough for their needs. But if they took too much, Barney wrote, the Turtle Mother would send her turtles far out to sea where the fishermen couldn't catch them.

The professor had learned about it back in the 1960s when he was living in Set Net, one of the Keys, while speaking with one of the elders in the village. But no one had ever repeated it to me. All I managed to get was that the Turtle Mother rock was a beacon, that drew the turtles to the shore or turned into the wind.

On this trip no one spoke about the rock being broken. Perhaps it was because the war was over and legal murder had stopped. I did pick up more variations on why the rock left the bluff at Puerto Cabezas back in great-grandfather's time and moved down to Tortuguero and hid in the cave. Women having their menstrual cycles sat on the rock making it unclean, fishermen recalled their parents saying, or people who had looked upon dead people messed with it and made it go away. And when the rock left, the beach eroded and turtles no longer nested in Nicaragua as they once had. It was a sort of "paradise lost" myth combined with long-standing taboos.

Apparently there was more than one Turtle Mother rock, just as there was more than one in Malaysia. There was one at Big Sandy Bay, one in Puerto Cabezas, and somewhere else on the coast near Bluefields, or least they were seen in different locations before the Turtle Mother vanished. Some of them were submerged like the "woman rock" in Malaysia.

I asked the turtlemen if Turtle Mother affected people, their fishing, or their actions, and they all said, "No. Only the turtles." This was contrary to what Barney had written 20 years ago. Maybe the beliefs had changed and humanity had turned further from nature, diminishing the linkage. The prohibition against overharvesting seemed to have faded away. In all my interviews, no one ever brought up that aspect of the myth.

"Turtle Mother is a rock," Pilar, the captain of the *Sunshine Lady*, explained through Modesto. "It is the god of the turtles. It protects the turtle, but it has nothing to do with man. It is made of earth, of rock." He went on to say that they were looking to the new ways, to have education for their children, electricity in their village one day, and laws that would protect Nicaragua's resources.

I looked at Barney, sitting in the stern with a big straw hat over his eyes. He shrugged. "Things change. It was different back then. They've just had ten years of war and murder."

Seeing I could get nothing further, I changed the subject. I wanted to know how the turtlemen could possibly manage to find this spot out in the middle of the ocean, with no landmarks in sight.

Pilar replied proudly, "We know the bottom and we look for rocks. We know when five o'clock in the evening comes, the turtle will come to these rocks to hide to get away from the shark that will bite him, so he can rest. So we hunt rocks." He thumped his chest. "I am a captain, from out here I know the direction to Bluefields, to Corn Island, to Puerto Cabezas, to the Keys. The waves come from the east. You see only water, but I know those rocks lay northeast. I can see a rock when I go by and I take it into my memory, and I will know right where that rock is. Another man who come by there sees rock and does not remember where it is."

Was that how turtles did it? I wondered. Did the magnetite crystals switch on when they picked up some low-energy emission from the rocks? Turtle biologists using radio telemetry and satellite tracking were just beginning to scientifically document what turtlemen knew all along, that turtles are attracted to rocks. Studies in Australia showed that greens and loggerheads not only hopped from patch reef to patch reef, but that certain individuals were faithful to specific rocks, returning year after year after year. When Barney Neitchmann was living in the Miskito Keys in the 1970s, he tagged hawksbills and saw they came back to the rocks like magnets, no matter how many times he tagged them and hauled them off. In Florida, loggerheads did the same. The fact that turtles come to rocks is more than adequately documented, but how they find them, and what draws them to the rocks, is not.

When we cast off, after an hour of baking in the open water, Barney was looking at me with a peculiar grin.

"What is it?" I asked.

"I've never seen anyone like you with this Turtle Mother," he said, laughing with amazement. "So determined, so one-tracked, you're like a bulldog, you don't let go. It's been twenty years now. I'm impressed."

"I can't help it," I said defensively. "My wife calls it monomania. I'm not especially proud of it; it's a detriment to a normal life, but that's the way it is."

"No, it's good. I've been watching you."

That made me feel better. It was getting to the point where Bill Curtsinger would yawn loudly and moan with great exaggeration,

"This is BOR-ING!" Then he would slump over in the cramped boat and pretend to snore loudly. I couldn't blame him. Over the past year he'd heard about Turtle Mother while we were traveling through Costa Rica, Nicaragua, the Bahamas, Antigua, Mexico, and finally on this assignment. It was good-natured teasing, and I did the same to him every time he stopped and made us jump through hoops, circling boats, stopping, backing, and making us get out of the picture so he could get his spectacular and inspired photographs.

As the afternoon sunlight turned gold, we headed over to Whippling Island, a series of sand bars covered with mangrove islands surrounded by flats of turtle grass. "Whippling Island is where the people sleep," Modesto explained. "Whippling Rock is where the turtles sleep." There was a series of shacks built on platforms, perched on stilts. Some had thatched roofs, others were just open. Over the years, hurricanes blew them down, and Indians built them back up.

After setting their nets on the rocky reefs, the fishermen took shelter there for the night. The A-frame dwellings made a hub in the ocean. Some had floors, but most didn't. All were oriented east–west, with pangas (small skiffs) and catboats moored to them. We looked for a place to spend the night. People used the huts on a first-come, first-served basis. But that day all the shacks were occupied, and for a while it looked as if we would have to sleep in the boats.

We motored up to one with an open-front porch, and beneath the palm-thatched roof, men were sitting, eating fish and rice, relaxing, waiting, a fire going in a cut-off metal drum. Beside them on the cramped wooden deck was an enormous hawksbill—the biggest one I had ever seen, easily weighing over two hundred pounds—awaiting butchering. Of all the sea turtles in the world, hawksbills are probably the most endangered, hunted relentlessly for their shells, which are made into jewelry.

International conservation agreements had just made it illegal for nations, particularly the Japanese, to buy and sell "tortoiseshell," but obviously the trade was still going on. Seeing this beautiful creature with its imbricated shell, its yellow-and-black leopard skin, I wanted to buy it from them to set it free. We talked it over. Bill Curtsinger was opposed. "We shouldn't interfere, it's not our role." Besides, it wouldn't be a good idea to come out waving cash around.

"I'm a little confused," I said to Barney. "How does it protect turtles to have your Miskito people slaughtering them."

"It's a case of use it or lose it," he said emphatically. "The Miskito people have lived here long before the Spanish arrived, eating turtle. If they get pushed out by the government in Managua, and it all becomes condo development and a haven for the rich and famous, you can kiss

the habitat, the people, and the turtles good-bye. They're all tied together."
Modesto nodded in emphatic agreement.

Finally we came to an empty structure, with some of its thatch
missing, and Barney pronounced it "Home, Sweet Home." The shacks
seemed to belong to everyone. Fishermen stored their turtles inside to
keep them out of the sun so they could fish for weeks before hauling
their catches off to the villages. From our point of view on the water,
the hut seemed to have a good floor for spreading out sleeping bags and
equipment, but when we climbed up we found four sea turtles. Their
flippers were tied, and they were lying on their backs with their belly
shells up.

"This place is occupied. We'd better clear out," I said worriedly,
remembering all the warnings about pirates, robbers, and guns. But
Modesto laughed. "It's not a problem here," he said. "If the owners
come in the night and they want us to leave, we'll leave."

The only other alternative was to sleep sitting up in the boats,
since there was no room to stretch out. So we hauled up our gear,
spread our sleeping bags among the turtles, raised a tarp over the roof,
hung a lantern from the ceiling, and made camp, while Negro started a
pot of beans and rice cooking on a gas stove. There wasn't much room
to move in the tiny hut; I had to use one of the turtle's bellies for a writing table. The turtles didn't seem to notice, but seeing me madly scribbling my impressions in my notebook, Barney said, "Isn't that a bit sacrilegious?"

"They make wonderful tables," I replied. But I squirmed my way
between the shells, put the notebook in my lap, and continued writing.
He was right; animals about to be sacrificed certainly needed respect.

The big greens lay on their backs, not moving, totally quiet, bringing to mind how perfect a turtle is. If they fought, struggled, and tried to bite, they couldn't be so easily carried and handled. What other creature could be taken from the sea, brought out into this world of air, and be kept alive for weeks—even months? No fish, no marine mammal had such resilience, not even a seal. But a turtle is a rock with innards. Out of water, on its back, all digestion stops. No wonder the Mayans thought these great shelled reptiles were sacred. So un-reptilian these reptiles. No wonder Chinese, American Indians, and Hindu cultures once believed the world was built on the back of a turtle! The New World was settled by Spanish and British sailing ships loaded with green turtles, which they kept alive and ate during the long sea voyage back home. Turtles were the perfect food.

Barney pulled out his compass, as all geographers do sooner or later—it's in their blood. "Look, this building was built exactly on ninety degrees, east–west alignment. Every one of these buildings faces the wind. It keeps it cool and keeps the mosquitoes out. But how do they do it? There isn't a compass or loran in the place, and yet the people know. They can head straight across the ocean, go forty miles, and arrive exactly on a speck of underwater rock, and it's all in their heads."

Bill and Eric were busy cleaning their camera equipment, inventorying film, and keeping notes for captions, while the rest of us talked about the mysteries of magnetic orientation. Barney spoke about the raftsmen who floated thousands of miles across the Pacific, riding the waves, swells, and currents, arriving at tiny islands while following the stars. Was this, I wondered aloud, the way the Turtle Mother legend came across from Malaysia and the far east? Or maybe it was the other way around.

"Oh no," Bill Curtsinger wailed, "not Turtle Mother again!"

Everyone laughed, but we kept on the subject. Out here, lying next to turtles, in the thick of turtle habitat, we all wanted to talk about it. And I felt a particular need to summarize and discuss my findings over the years with the man who had first written about Turtle Mother. Sitting here, among the bound-up turtles in the hut, overlooking the sea, with Negro, our young cook, taking in every word, it seemed to be more like a tribunal, a rite of passage, than a dissertation defense. It was a gathering of wise men, a culmination to my quest where the secrets were being unfolded. Modesto Watson, who grew up in the Miskito Keys, had known about the turtle rock all his life.

Modesto came from a very religious family. His father was a parson in Puerto Cabezas, and for years Modesto had considered becoming a minister himself. "You see, the Turtle Mother is a gift from God," he explained, after I had told him about finding the rock in Malaysia.

"The Christians say it here, and the Muslims say it there. So it must be true."

This warm-hearted, personable man was, in a sense, a turtle hunter, only a modern version. Instead of using the harpoon or the net, he would take groups of tourists out from Limon in his canopied 24-foot boat down the Tortuguero river, show them howler monkeys, parrots, and other wildlife, and then lead them to the turtle beaches. He had a genius for pointing out the tree sloths, the herons, the crocodiles, the needle palms, and the bromeliads. He also pointed out the clear-cutting and bulldozing, and the banana plantations which he abhorred.

Several months earlier, Modesto had taken us down to Tortuguero. And after much hunting in the village, he found a young man named Johnny Artavia who could actually show us where the cave was, although he said the entrance had been buried by an earthquake years ago. Johnny seemed to be a responsible, hard-working young man. He headed the Tortuguero Development Committee and was a fishing guide with a good reputation, so we hired him to take us to the cave entrance. As we headed up the lagoon, Cerro once again loomed up as the great, green, jungle-covered enigma. My wife Anne, Modesto, and his wife Fran sat in Johnny's wooden boat listening to his recollections of the mountain while Modesto translated. "The first time I was at the cave was in 1953 when I was ten years old and went with my father and it was totally open. It was very dark, a lot of bats, and everything was in steps going down."

"Steps?" Anne said. "That's interesting. What kind of steps?"

Johnny replied through Modesto, "They were made by primitive people. But I don't know when. They were made of stones and rock. It was too well fitted to be made by nature. They were three meters long and about twenty centimeters high. They weren't made like an engineer would do, but they all had the same dimensions.

"We only went down three stairs," he went on, "as far as the daylight went in; after that we don't go further. When we considered the amount of snakes and bats, we changed our minds. But my father and I had the feeling that it was a drop-off. We yell in the dark and we hear the sound, an echo going all the way down."

Leaving the boat at the base of the mountain, we hiked along the overgrown but distinctive path that led around to the back of the mountain that rose from the jungle like the wall of a skyscraper, until Johnny stopped and announced that we had reached the entranceway. But it was blocked. He pointed to an earthen mound forming a lump beside the earthen wall that looked as if it had been sheared away by a giant butcher knife. "The cave was down here," he said, "on the ground, just at the swamp level. But the top of the hill has fallen down to the ground and sealed off the entrance. It may have been an earthquake, or maybe a landslide from the rain, and loose volcanic particles covered it. Something made the top of the mountain fall, but we don't know what."

We all stared at the mound in disbelief and looked up as our guide pointed to an indentation in the rock facing about ten feet up, speculating that it had resulted when the cave's roof fell in.

It did look like an entranceway. Our eyes followed the great red wall of solid rock up above the treetops, to the vegetation perched on top of the mountain. "Before, you could just walk right into the entrance of the cave," Johnny went on. "It was wide and high, but it is now so deep it would take a tractor to dig it out. It's too much to dig out with a shovel!"

We stood there in dumbfounded silence, aware of the hopelessness of penetrating the interior of the mountain. When Turtle Mother retreated, she had slammed the door permanently shut behind her. Johnny said he could find the entrance to a smaller cave on the eastern side, which be believed fed into the interior of the mountain. He theorized the interior had been hollowed out by pre-Columbian people who built a temple to the turtles inside.

We hiked back around the base through the dense green foliage, until we came to another facing of granitelike solid rock, smooth, black, and very dense, totally unlike the rest of the old relic porous volcano.

"It doesn't look like volcanic rock at all," said Modesto, running his hands over the great slab of smooth dark rock that ran up the mountain's face. "It is not porous, it is very solid. No wonder they call it 'the rock,'" he concluded in awe. "It is one!"

"It's certainly a complex place that needs a geologist badly," Anne agreed.

Suddenly Johnny called out that he'd found the back entrance to the big cave. Palm forests and brush hung down covering a black hole not more than three feet wide at the entrance. I looked in dubiously. It was like a vault inside, full of spiderwebs and bat droppings. The sour smell of decay and mold was overpowering. Seeing my reluctance, Anne called out, a shade gleefully, "All right, Jack, you're on. You've waited twenty years for this; now go for it!"

Anne had gamely put up with all my absences from home. After being repeatedly left as a single parent raising two small children, she wasn't at all amused about some of my misadventures in Central America, nor with my monomania with rocks. Even on this trip, and all during our travels on this *National Geographic* assignment, when we worked together, she had to help lug our suitcases filled with stones and bags of sand. And when she was off covering a story while I stayed home, she had to bring back samples for me.

As I crawled on my hands and knees into the dark entrance, shining my flashlight, an explosion of bats suddenly bolted out in a great panic, flying into my face, squeaking. I couldn't control my revulsion as the hairy little mammals battered me. I jumped back, banging my head and swearing. That caused Modesto to start rushing to my aid, thinking I was snakebit, and I had to yell back that I was okay.

Overcoming my total repugnance to go forward, fearing I'd put my hands on a snake, I crawled on my belly deep into the black hole, shining my light before me, squishing my knees through the moist layers of bat droppings that had built up on the floor. The Mayans believed that caves were the entrance to the underworld, the place where the parallel lines of the spirit and corporeal worlds crossed. But this cave only went in about ten feet before it got narrower and narrower, until I could go no further. I lay on my belly, shining the light into a crevice that seemed to continue deep into the mountain. I saw one unhappy bat, shivering, hanging there upside down. Unable to proceed any further, I backed out and abandoned my quest. It didn't feel right anyway; I was intruding.

We took Johnny's boat and puttered around the backside of the mountain until we came to a series of fallen trees and a gouged-out hole left by a construction crew which was mining the mountain for gravel to pave an airport in the town of Colorado, 20 miles up the coast. A gaping hole had been cut in the red earth, and a dozen huge rain forest trees were pushed over before the operation was stopped by the villagers.

Johnny said that when the Tortuguero Development Committee found out about it, the miners had been digging out gravel for two or three days and caused a lot of damage. They had no permit. The local policeman came and fined them heavily for each bag of fill. The construction company then loaded up their barge and left.

All this happened around the time of the Earth Day earthquake on April 22, 1991, which killed approximately a hundred people and destroyed the nearby village of Matina, where egg poaching and the slaughter of nesting leatherbacks for their eggs had been rampant. The earthquake raised up the entire canal from Limon to Tortuguero, leaving the riverbed dry, draining out the water, and creating a giant mudhole. It caused severe economic loss and inconvenience to the village of Tortuguero. Johnny said that after the earthquake, smoke was seen coming from Cerro.

But if anyone related this to the assault on the sacred mountain, nothing was learned from the experience. Plans were also underway by the Ministry of Transportation and local developers who owned the Tortuga Lodge to dig out 1,500 cubic yards of aggregates to resurface the airstrip in front of Casa Verde, the turtle station.

No longer was Tortuguero the tiny remote village it once had been. It was on its way to looking like a South Florida waterfront, with houses, hotels, power lines stretched across the river that lit up the village at night, fiberglass speedboats with big outboard motors zooming up and down, and pontoon boats full of tourists reeking of suntan oil. Only the freight boats still give it a Central American flavor.

Modesto said, and Johnny agreed, that unless there was strong protection enacted immediately, bag by bag the mountain would be hauled away. The village government was making money out of it, selling that rare, highly paramagnetic volcanic gravel to developers who mixed it with cement and gravel to build homes and businesses.

Naturally, local boosters and chamber-of-commerce types maintained that Cerro really had nothing to do with the turtles coming to Tortuguero, and that it was mere superstition.

But now, sitting in the crowded shed overlooking the Miskito Coast with its mangrove island, beside green turtles that were probably hatched out on the black beach beneath the mountain, Modesto and I knew they were wrong.

I told them about how scientists like Jim Spotilla of Drexel University were starting to verify that there was indeed something special about the Turtle Mountain of Costa Rica. The Drexel University professor, who normally studied the physiology and deep body temperatures of leatherbacks and other turtles, surveyed the beach at Tortuguero with a magnetometer from five miles north of the river all the way down to Parismino 20 miles south. He discovered a big magnetic anomaly at the mouth of the Tortuguero River, right in the Bogue and on the mountain itself—a big spike in the magnetic field. The field was far stronger near the mountain than when he went further south or further north. "Spotilla thinks there's enough of a magnetic signal on that beach that it could give a location position to the turtles." I concluded.

"But I seem to recall that green turtle nesting is heavier south of the mountain," Barney countered, "and practically nonexistent north of it."

"True," I said, caught up with my own enthusiasm. "The bulk of the nesting is in the south, about eleven miles down. But the field may be too strong at the mountain, and the turtles home-in on a weaker gradient. Joe Kirschvinc did a paper showing that loggerheads migrated along the Atlantic coast, following the magnetic minima between the stronger magnetic anomalies. Whales do the same thing! In a few years, they'll be able to prove that the magnetite crystals in these animals are influenced by the earth's magnetic field, and then we'll have it cracked."

Modesto laughed delightedly. "So the scientists are just now discovering what the Miskito people have known since the beginning of time—that the mountain was magic. The old Indians were in tune with nature. They could feel the power of rocks and the earth because they didn't live in a world of asphalt, buildings, and television. If everyone lived like this"—his arm swept across the vista of mangrove islands and seagrass beds glowing in the setting sun— "we could all feel it just like the turtles do. But the mountain is so strong that whenever anyone sees it they want to go up there. It calls to them; it has some kind of draw."

"I do not understand," said Negro, who had been quiet all during the discussion. "What does the Turtle Mother rock have to do with the mountain?" He had been busy putting rice and beans and fish on tin plates and passing them around. All the while he'd been cooking over the camp stove on the front porch, listening with rapt attention. He too had heard about the mountain all his life, but had never been there.

"People also call the mountain 'the rock,'" Modesto explained. "It gets confused. Some people say the whole mountain turns. But when Jack and his wife Anne went up there with me back in January, we saw that parts of it really are solid rock, especially around the cave. But I think the Turtle Mother rock was put there to tell people when it was time to take turtle eggs and meat, when they needed it, and when it was time to quit. All through the season the rock pointed toward the sea. And people could take what they needed and the turtle was bountiful enough to meet their needs and not be depleted. Then the rock turned and that told people not to bother the turtles anymore. The eggs could hatch, leaving turtles for the future."

Barney joked that if the mountain was going to be used as a doormat for ecotourism, the developers would be required, in some sort of sick mitigation, to put up a giant electromagnet on a giant revolving turntable, so it beamed out an electromagnetic forcefield to draw the turtles to shore. We all laughed.

"But I still believe the real magic comes from the mountain," Modesto declared while picking through the bones of a deliciously spiced mangrove snapper that Negro had served. "I can't help thinking there's a pyramid under that red earth. Look at the way you go up to it, in steps almost. It rises in layers, and look how steep the sides are along the river. The front side looks like a ramp, just like a pyramid.

And you heard Johnnie Artavia tell us that when the cave was open, there were steps leading down inside of it. Nowhere in all of Tortuguero is there any red clay or rock except for on the mountain. It's sticky red clay, and the only other place you can find that is in Barra Colorado, twenty miles to the north."

After a minute of silence, Barney said thoughtfully, "You're both right about that mountain, Cerro Tortuguero. Even when you see it from miles out at sea," he said in a slightly hushed voice, "it has a strange draw. I guess it's the magnetic attraction. I've felt it myself."

"Tell me about it," I said, sucking the bones of some of the tastiest fish I'd ever eaten anywhere. Getting Negro as our cook had been a good choice.

Barney's normal jovial manner ceased. He was somber, with a faraway look. "In 1984," he began, "some of my friends from the Miskito Coast called me up in Berkeley and said, 'Mr. Barney, please come down, we're having a bad time of it. And someone must see.'

"That was right after the revolution, Somoza had been overthrown, and the Sandinistas had started a "relocation" of the Miskito.

"So I went down, and I saw the abysmal conditions, the persecution, the beatings, and the murders. They had people in camps—concentration camps. I had cameras and tape recorders, and the underground took me around the coast. Modesto was with me in Puerto Cabezas, and we filmed what we could. Many of the people I knew from past years had been killed, or had died of disease and malnutrition.

"When the Sandinistas got wind of what we were doing, they started searching for us. So we decided to make a run for it, to head to the Costa Rican border. All the land was blocked off, there were checkpoints on all the roads, and they had military gunboats stationed up and down the coast. If they caught us with all our paraphernalia, there was no question what would happen. We were spies. For four days, we hid out on the Keys, running at night, working our way down south trying to make Costa Rica, cramped in that little boat."

Bill and Eric had stopped working with their cameras and sat there eating and listening, taking it all in. It was dark now, and the moon shone upon the waters off the turtle hut. Mullet splashed off the mangroves, and charcoal fires burned on the sailing sloops as the turtlemen cooked dinner on their boats.

"When we approached the border, where their gunboats patrolled, we headed straight out to sea; we had no choice. Rolling around in that cramped, leaky dugout, we were so far from land we must have been on the edge of the Gulf Stream. There were five of us, running all night in this narrow dugout boat, with a decrepit outboard motor that kept breaking down—me and four Miskito Indians, one of them shot in the leg, half delirious from loss of blood, with gangrene setting in, and no food. The motor broke down, and here we were in one of those long tipsy canoes rolling around in ten-foot seas, swamping, bailing constantly to keep afloat. But those guys are amazing: they had to overhaul the carburetor in the dark, but they can make anything run."

As he spoke, I recalled being in Tortuguero at that time, a hundred miles to the south of where he was. It struck me as an interesting coincidence that I had been down there that same year, looking for Turtle Mother, while the man who first wrote about it was out at sea. At the time the village of Tortuguero was bursting with near-starving Miskito refugees, escaping the war. Most had fled the country to keep from being drafted by one army or another.

"By the time dawn came," Barney continued to his captivated audience, "we could have been anywhere off the coast of Cuba for all we knew. We were afraid the northbound equatorial current could have carried us back up the Miskito coast right into the hands of the Sandinistas. A boatload of freedom fighters. We would have all been shot.

"And then we saw it. The mountain, Cerro Tortuguero, this big lump just sitting there on the horizon. It looked like a big turtle. I can't tell you how good it looked to me. I thought I was going to die, I really did. But when we saw it, we knew we were safe, we had passed the border."

Barney took a deep breath, shaken at the memory of the experience. "But it wasn't just that. I had this eerie feeling—it's hard to explain—but there was a draw, something magnetic about it. That's when I thought about you."

"Me?" I jolted up in surprise. I was lost in his adventure, thinking how tame my experience down there had been in comparison. "It had been nearly ten years since we were last in touch!"

"Yes, but I did. You and the turtles, and the mountain. You, Jack Rudloe, just sort of flashed into my mind. All along you were right about that mountain. There is something powerful; it defies words. I can't explain it. But I could feel it, that incredible draw."

An eerie sensation swept through me. Something was going on. At the time I had had only an inkling of the picture—the climb up the mountain, the broken bottles, the dead child. All the while, when I was not out pulling nets, or trying to keep fish alive, I lay on the cot in my little room in the Green Turtle Lodge reading Barney Neitchmann's *Caribbean Edge*.

I read every word, thinking Barney was someplace in California, or the Torry Straights by then, never knowing that he was out there in a boat, fleeing the Sandinistas with a boatload of refugees lying in the bottom of the canoe, with the waves nearly breaking over it, frightened, exhausted, without food or water, fighting their way to the shore.

Vividly I recalled standing on the top of Cerro, overlooking the angry Caribbean, the interminable wilderness of rain forest coastline, and thinking of all the trouble to the north. Then coming down, breaking off the rock in the pounding surf, feeling so triumphant at having survived the sea, then all those horrible experiences of going to the bar in the village, with whisky bottles flying off the shelf and exploding all over the place, cutting up the proprietor, and then the little girl drowning. This was a shamanistic quest; something powerful was going on.

"You said it was in 1984? What month?" I asked Barney.

"January."

A strange and electrifying feeling went through me.

"What day?" I demanded, wracking my brain, trying to remember the dates of my trip down there.

"It was mid-January, around the 14th."

I bolted upright. "All this was going on when I was climbing the mountain. I was there, in mid-January, around the fourteenth!" I cried. "Turtle Mother . . ." I couldn't form any words. I sat there in stunned silence.

Barney shrugged it off, and finished his tale. "We went on to Limon and I was able to catch a plane to Los Angeles. But I'll never forget that mountain."

We talked into the night, lying beside the turtles in the shack on stilts. Finally we scraped our plates into the sea, shut off the lantern, and went to sleep: Bill, Eric, Modesto, Barney, Negro, and me, lying side by side, all cramped together in the little hut. It was quite a cacophony of snores and turtle gasps. It was hard to tell who snored worse, the turtles or the members of our expedition. We were sharing the space with two doomed greens and two hawksbills, each of which made occasional loud gasps and hisses like someone blowing through a straw. I lay awake listening to the noise and chuckling until I dropped off.

Around midnight, the owners of the turtles and the lodge returned, stepping among the derelicts and their outstretched legs that had taken over their cabin. There were muffled voices, someone turned on a flashlight, and I heard Modesto's voice talking with them. I tried to wake up, worried that we were in for trouble.

The Miskito men started dragging the turtles out, carrying them by the black ropes that bound them, sliding them down into the canoes moored out the front door. I heard Modesto speaking to them in Miskito and then they left. After they left, he told us what they said when he asked if we could stay there. "He became philosophical about it," Modesto said, chuckling. "He said, 'The only time there has ever been a problem for anyone staying there was when the Sandinistas had it. Now Nicaraguans are free to stay here, and we're free to be here.' Besides they were all clearing out, it is the Holy Week, just before Easter."

The next morning, we followed the catboats back over to Whippling Rock and watched the crews hauling up their nets. They toss out a gaff anchor, an oblong lead weight with three hooks on one end and the rope on the other. The weighted ball shoots high into the air, like a baseball with a rope tail, sailing through the air until it splashes into the sea next to the net. It lands in the meshes of the net and they pull their way up to it against the webbing.

The seas rose and fell. The turtlemen held the mesh up, knowing that it was empty. No turtle. They rowed, bucking the sea, going from one net to the next. "You see how hard is the work we must do," Pilar laughed. "We never get tired. This is our work!"

In the middle of the next net, the grayish, flat dome of a turtle broke the surface. The head popped up—the flippers were entangled. Another turtle to give up its life to feed the Miskito Coast peoples. Its chief downfall is that it is fat and delicious to eat, and therefore in jeopardy.

Bill and Eric were in the water, getting shots of the turtle being hauled up into the boat. Struggling, the fishermen got it up on the gunwale, and it hung there while Bill snapped pictures. Half out of the water, its serrated birdlike mouth was agape, biting and chewing a strand of webbing. When he was finished, the turtlemen began hauling the huge creature up to the cat rail with all their might, straining against the three hundred pounds. Suddenly there was a loud snap that sounded like a gunshot. The beak cut through and a strand of webbing snapped like a violin string. A crewman yelped like he'd been hit with a whip, but he held on.

All hands were on the net as the turtle emerged from the water. They whooped and hollered, in a good mood. The three-hundred-pound green looked bewildered and distressed, opening its mouth and gasping. Holding it by its scaly brown flippers, strong callused hands were at work, pulling it out of the webbing, freeing it, breaking it loose and stashing it below.

They paddled to the next net, which had another turtle in it. The hooks zoomed out again, snaring the webbing. Other catboats were working other rocks and patch reefs, hauling in tangled turtles totally snared in their bags of webbing. I was caught up in the adventure. It reminded me of how we went net fishing for Kemp's ridleys in the Gulf of Mexico to tag and release. But these greens faced a much gloomier future.

We followed the flotilla of catboats to the village of LeDuke on the mainland and spent the night camped out on the front porch of one of the fishermen's huts. Dawn came. The sun crept up into the cloudy sky, silhouetting the palm trees. A gentle breeze rolled in from the marsh. Clothes flopped on the clothesline, and the chickens cooed and strutted among the turtles that lay on their backs, flippers tied together, their white belly shells gleaming like pearls in the morning light. A dog scratched fleas, and men and women woke up and headed down to the beach.

The green turtle's plastron swelled with air. It gasped and opened its mouth, as if waiting for the end to arrive. This creature of resistance, which has survived so long on its back with its flippers bound, this totally compact creature is a living can of meat just waiting for a can opener.

The butcher stood by waiting while several men dragged the big green down to the water and splashed water over the carapace to clean off any dirt. Without fanfare, without emotion, with the normalcy of an act that is done over and over again, an arm, attached to the sharpened machete raised and hung in the air for a moment, then slapped down hard. Blood splashed. The turtle pulled his head back, the gaping gash across its throat.

Then started the dance of men, stepping around, swiping with their razor-sharp machetes and knives. Flippers were coming off, the turtle splashed with water. Again an arm raised up and slapped down again, slicing through leather, flesh and bone. It seemed so easy, so quick.

The knife went relentlessly to work dismembering this turtle, severing flesh, hacking through bone like so much sugarcane, the sawing, the separation. It was a scene that could have taken place anytime in the past million years, only instead of sharpened flint or obsidian knives, they used steel. The metallic clank, the chop of meat, a great flowing mass of blood turned the upturned carapace into a punchbowl of blood. But nothing was wasted. Every organ, even intestines, liver, stomach, and fat—every piece of flesh was hauled away by the villagers in their baskets and bags.

The smallest boy, not over five years old, bailed the last bit of blood out of the inverted carapace into a cooking pot with a yellow plastic cup and carried the pot home to one of the thatched huts, careful not to spill a drop of the precious liquid. It was to be made into blood pudding, which Barney and Modesto said was delicious. Bill hopped around taking pictures from all angles, the motor drive whirling and the shutter snapping. I could see the pained expression in his eyes, but he stayed focused, getting the type of shots that had made him famous.

Only three or four turtles are butchered to feed the village. The rest are hauled down to Puerto Cabezas, down the coast. There a giant wharf reaches out from the shore, crammed with fishing boats, and the bustle of people wearing T-shirts, bright against dark skin—yellow, green, red. Sailing sloops and catboats come in with green turtles, their flippers bound front to back. They lie in the shade beneath the dock, deathly still, heads lying back—meat, soon to be butchered. The Indian, the Negro, the Creole are there. Spanish, English, and Miskito are all spoken. All eat turtle that forages on the sea grass. Pigs and dogs sleep next to each other on the wharf as the sun sets.

Modesto felt compelled to say, "We have seen the beginning of the turtle, from the little ones hatching off the beach, to the feeding grounds where it grew up. And now we have seen where it dies. And there is nothing wrong with this because we shall eat the turtle, and we are part of the good ourselves."

Barney and Modesto had agreed to stay only a week with us. Barney had classes to get back to, and Modesto had his ecotourism business. They took one of the boats back to Puerto Cabezas and caught a plane out the next day, and we stayed with the turtlemen until Holy Week started. When Bill and Eric had taken all the pictures they wanted, and my notebook was full, we came back to Puerto Cabezas and hung around for several days, trying to get a plane out.

But not a speck of time was wasted for me. Negro had taken a great interest in finding out more about the Turtle Mother legend. As we worked the marketplace, he translated for us. At night, he slipped away to see his relatives and fishermen neighbors, returning in the morning to report his findings to me. He was a good-hearted boy, always anxious to please, a very serious student, 17 years old. He had taken off from school to be with us and had his books with him, studying every chance he could get.

Finally, on our last day, we went down to the giant dock to say our final farewell to the Miskito Coast. Somehow I felt that the Turtle Mother quest really had begun on this enormous dock for me. It was here that the first major pieces of the puzzle began to be put together. When I first came to Tortuguero, Archie Carr had told me about the legendary rock that turned; he knew nothing of some vague entity or force called "Turtle Mother." But it was here that a drunken fisherman, named Monkeyleto, staggering down the beach, told me that Turtle

Mother and the rock were one and the same. I had learned much, traveled widely, found the deteriorating leatherback rock in Malaysia, and still something was lacking. Something was incomplete.

Wandering out among the crowd, looking down on the beach, I saw three men with ropes dragging green turtles off the shore. The unusual sight of turtles right-side-up, being pulled through the water with ropes around their foreflippers, caught our attention. As soon as the big greens had their flippers cut loose from the thongs that bound them, and started churning their flippers in the muddy water, the fishermen dragged them back into the boats.

I asked Negro, who now served as translator, to ask them what they were doing. The market was glutted, we were told; the fishermen were taking the turtles back to their village because they could not sell them in Puerto Cabezas. The fleet of turtles had mobilized, getting ready to migrate down to Tortuguero, and the boats were there to meet them. Everyone had turtles to sell, and after the early boats had unloaded, the ones that came to the dock late had no market.

Suddenly I felt a great urge to blow all my expense money by buying turtles left and right. I had already bought two hawksbills out on the Keys and turned them loose. Negro asked the price for me. They'd sell them for a hundred cordobas apiece. I asked Bill Curtsinger if he'd chip in and emphatically he said, "No, I'm opposed to it. Really, I don't think we should interfere. It bothers me just as much as it bothers you, but I didn't think you should have bought those hawksbills. But that's up to you entirely."

I wrestled with the ethics. I also looked in my pocket and saw that I had only a 50- and three 20-cordoba notes. Was he right? By buying a turtle's life and freedom, was I interfering? Hadn't we already interfered, by just being there?

If I bought the turtle I would not be taking food out of anybody's mouth. Turtles were stashed under houses, in canoes, everywhere, and the turtlemen complained that the meat was "cheap, cheap."

If a big town like Puerto Cabezas couldn't take them, they had to distribute them to the Keys. The old captain of the sailing sloop was going to take his turtles to Corn Island, a long, long sail through a vast void of blue water, a straight 24 hours of sailing. Food was usually scarce and expensive there, with multitudes of people crammed together, but at this time of year, with turtles everywhere, they were suffering glut there too. And then the fishermen would have to buy provisions to go back, and everything was tremendously expensive on Corn Island. In other words, there was no great gain for all that trouble.

"How much for a turtle?" I asked, gesturing to the creatures being dragged to the boat and the other ones lying on their backs, belly shells up, with their flippers bound.

The boatman, not the captain, looked me over appraisingly and said two hundred cordobas.

I shook my head, said "No," and acted as if he could take his turtles and sail on, for all I cared. I knew turtles were going for 100 cordobas apiece. Haggling was part of the process here. I made a counter offer.

The captain, sitting on the wharf near me and looking down at his workers towing turtles, spoke to Negro for a minute. I gathered that he was going to accept my offer. The captain was a tough, wiry old man. Gray-haired, he was all muscle and toughness, no fat. Weathered, aged with his sea-lined face, he was a grim man, a man of decisions, responsibility, and no nonsense.

"Don't interfere, that's my view," Bill pleaded. "It's their world, and you're integrating yourself into it. It's not right, but you do what you think is right."

Hadn't this Miskito coast integrated itself into my life during the past 20 years of chasing the rock? From the first time I stumbled into Tortuguero, then Bluefields, Puerto Cabezas, and Corn Island, I was hopelessly sucked into it. Seeing that I was going to do it anyway, he walked off.

I pulled out my 100-cordoba note. Suddenly everyone was watching us. "Eighty cordobas for a big turtle," I said in my best fishmonger tone, and then pointed to a young green turtle that was too small and shouldn't have been taken anyway. "And ten for the little one."

The captain nodded, studying me, and said nothing.

Now it was a question of which big turtle to take, which life to spare. What a dilemma for me. Which one to choose? Which one to spare, knowing that sooner or later the rest would have their heads chopped off.

I looked at the female, and then at the big male with his long tail. I could have either one. Surely the male should be sacrificed, since the female, after all, bore the eggs, the next generation. "Women and children first . . ." It's the macho thing to do. It's a survival instinct, right? Motherhood was precious. And there were plenty of replaceable males out there, ready to mount her. All the protection, fisheries management, and population modeling proved that. There were tons of papers at the Marine Turtle Conference saying it. That was the way it should go, wasn't it?

No, it isn't, I thought angrily. *Life is metered out to both sexes. Why must men always be strong, the aggressors, ready to shed their seed and die in war?* Everyone was watching us. "I want to see a male," I said.

Negro translated to the young crewman who stood in the catboat below us. The captain said something to him, and he began throwing a bunch of nets out of the stern, moving things and turtles around, digging down deep into the belly of the oversized canoe. I saw the yellow belly shell from up there—it was a monster. The crewman tried to drag the turtle out, but it was too big for one man. He looked up and shrugged. "He's too big, I can't move him."

It was obvious they wanted to lighten their load. We looked down at the great turtle and the sea was pounding; the catboat was jerking against its moorings. Negro started to climb down, but another crewman on the boat scrabbled down ahead of him. It was dangerous. But he moved with great, catlike agility, this dark, lithe muscular figure.

They crouched over the creature in the boat, working in the cramped space. The two men gave a great heave, and they hauled the turtle up to the cat rail. And there they held it, balancing it for my inspection. It was a big male, with a long tail, that weighed a good 350 or even 400 pounds.

Its front and rear flippers were bound by thongs. I looked down at the blinking behemoth, wondering how this imprisonment, this binding of front to rear flippers was going to affect its chances of survival. But it didn't matter. After all that work to raise it, I really had no choice but to buy it even if I wanted another. I nodded approval.

Knowing that white-skinned gringos just don't come strolling down the dock, speaking English and buying whole sea turtles, someone asked what I was going to do with it. It was obvious that I had no truck, no butcher standing by, and that I was staying at the hotel. It didn't make sense.

I told Negro to explain to him that I was going to turn the turtles loose, right here and now.

He looked me over for a moment, studying me, looking deep into my eye, and again nodded his assent. Everyone on the wharf was looking at me, thirty or forty people, to see if I was really going to pay this man to throw his turtles back into the sea. It was a spectacle: here I was once again drawing attention to myself. The moment hung in time. The money for the turtle. I had the bill in my hand. The air hung tensely. The captain looked down at his crew, who watched the transaction. The two turtles—the little one had also been produced and was placed on the cat rail—were poised to pitch.

The moment of truth arrived. "I want it to go free," I said with a little trepidation, knowing that very statement, that action, was a condemnation of their killing the turtles. I anticipated their anger, but it didn't happen. There was a hushed silence on the dock. All eyes looked at me with amazement, disbelief and astonishment. In a moment word got out: this crazy man said he was going to pay to release the turtle. Would he do it, or was it some kind of trick? I saw suspicion in their eyes.

I handed the bill to the captain who, was sitting on the edge of the dock. He looked at it, put it in his pocket, and nodded to the men below. He never smiled, or said thank-you. But he nodded a slow, reserved assent, and then looked at me appraisingly. I knew I was being judged right then and there. Was I a fool, a mad man, or something else?

Out came the lethal machete—one that had sliced turtle throats and carved the meat out of countless shells. The crewman slashed his machete down just as if he were butchering this turtle, too. It looked as if the turtle were done for. But he cut the thongs, and the flippers suddenly unfolded and stretched out, moving freely.

Again the men on the dock looked at me, their eyes full of surprise and disbelief that I was really going to go through with it. They were my turtles now. One of the young men called up, "If we catch this turtle again, he's our turtle, yes?"

I laughed aloud, "Of course he's your turtle, if you catch him. How would I know you caught him? I have no pins here to mark them, and even if I did, the turtle would still be yours."

On the face of things the boatman's question seemed preposterous, but I could feel their fear that the gringos were going to control things. As Curtsinger had taken pictures for the magazine, and I recorded their stories and asked questions, several captains had worried aloud and said angrily that we were really there to take their turtles away. We could do it with our money, our education and superior technologies, all in the name of conserving endangered species.

Earlier, sailing along with them beneath the starry skies, alone in the vast Caribbean, there had been a few tense moments. The Miskito were a fierce people who defeated the Spanish back in the 1500s. Even though they spilled lots of blood, they had also driven out the Sandinistas. It was their coast now, and they looked upon us with some suspicion, perhaps rightfully.

We saw a satellite hurtling through space amidst the gleaming stars and they wanted to know if there were monkeys and dogs flying it, as they had heard. Negro translated my reply that most likely it was instruments that did it all. That brought on speeches: how they needed education for their children so that they could join the twentieth century.

One turtleman asked me, "Does the United States own the moon?"

"No," I replied, "it belongs to Miskito people," and got a big laugh.

So standing on the dock at Puerto Cabezas, listening to the fisherman worrying about which turtle belonged to whom seemed preposterous, but then again, all that white man has done seemed preposterous, and in the end so devastating.

In great bewilderment they looked at the captain of the turtleboat for his final orders. He gave a short stiff nod, and then they looked to me, and I gestured for them to push the turtles overboard. Laughing, shaking their heads with utter disbelief, they pushed. There was a great splash as the big turtle toppled overboard. It sank like a boulder, out of sight, then sprang to life, and the flippers churned into motion. Popping up, it took off, heading north, throwing a great wake. From up there, everyone could see its shape. The head popped up, breathing, expelling air, its legs stretched out. The flippers grasped the water and it sped away from the dock. Free to swim, free to take its chances again. Then they pitched the little one.

Everyone watched them go. Two old men were sitting on the pier and watching me, and when I walked by, the two old turtlemen nodded with approval. "So you buy de turtle and let de turtle go. Why, mon?" one asked.

"For Turtle Mother," I said seriously, and they looked at each other with amazement, and a big grin came to their faces. An old woman asked Negro why I did that, and he said I was just that way. And she nodded with approval and said I was a good man.

And then something very strange, mystical, and wonderful happened. All of a sudden birds seemed to darken the sky. Sea birds, hundreds of them, white spirit forms rising, circling, drifting like confetti in the air, circling, gliding, undulating up and down, swarms of white and black birds, moving as a whole, rising up, dipping down, rising up again. They seemed to come from nowhere and everywhere all at once. They were riding the wind, blowing in the breeze, circling immediately above the patch of water where the turtles were speeding away into the bluest of blue waters, filling the air with their cries.

We stood there, mouths agape, hearing their screeches, their calls. There were maybe five hundred, maybe a thousand. They all had materialized so quickly, going round and round in a giant spiral, an avian cloud that swarmed above the dock, calling, their cries ringing through air. It was the stuff legends and myths are made of. They appeared just as the turtles were swimming away, not a moment sooner or a moment later.

The birds winged out wider and farther, and then took off. Black sea birds moving in synchrony, screaming their long, pitched calls. Laughing gulls, black-headed terns, they spiraled up, dominated the sky for a few minutes, and then disbursed.

The moment was caught with magic. Something hung in the air. Once again belief and disbelief all rolled into one.

I heard Negro beside me. "Look at the birds. It is a sign. Never have I seen them like this. They are telling us there is something between man and turtle—some connection—it must be the Turtle Mother."

I gazed at the open water, swept up in the moment, feeling the synchronicity of humanity, nature, and the unseen forces. With deep emotion, I turned to go home, feeling complete, putting science to rest—maybe believing in Turtle Mother for the first time.